Organizational Change Sourcebook I:

Cases in Organization Development

Edited by

Bernard Lubin

Leonard D. Goodstein

Alice W. Lubin

University Associates, Inc.
8517 Production Avenue
P.O. Box 26240
San Diego, California 92126

Copyright © 1979 by International Authors, B.V.

ISBN: 0-88390-150-1

Library of Congress Catalog Card Number 79-63006

Printed in the United States of America

Contents

Introduction to
Cases in Organization Development

The case study has a long and honorable tradition in many professional disciplines but, with a few exceptions such as Festinger, Reicken, and Schacter (1964) and Keckhoff and Back (1968), social and behavioral scientists have avoided case studies. Because case studies are not rigorous enough, involve an N of 1, and use no control group, and because it is difficult to apply statistical and methodological manipulations to them, behavioral scientists have concentrated on the experiment, which permits rigor, large N's, control groups, and statistical manipulations. Unfortunately, no sense of what actually transpires emerges from most research reports, and the psychology of the individuals involved is simply overlooked. Although the laboratory apparatus and the instructions to the subject are painstakingly and faithfully reported, the experience of the person (depersonalized as a "subject") is never considered. The subjects' spontaneous remarks and other observations, which may have been important, rarely are reported. We are not suggesting that formal scientific research is not meritorious, but the preoccupation of behavioral scientists with appearing "scientific" has led to a rejection of the case study as a legitimate, alternative way of understanding our world.

VALUE OF THE CASE STUDY

The unique value of the case study for the behavioral sciences is illustrated by the studies that have become part of our traditional literature. Detailed studies of social phenomena, especially those provided by trained participant/observers, enable us to gain an in-depth understanding of the events as they unfold. For example, Festinger, Schacter, & Reicken (1964) chronicled the behavior of a "Doomsday group" as they awaited the end of the world on a certain date and what happened when that time arrived and passed. Their book provided an early test for the cognitive dissonance hypothesis and a blend of a case study and field research.

1

In planned-change strategies of organization development and conflict management the case study is especially useful. The technology involved is new and relatively untested, and complete case studies can provide valuable insight. In these rapidly evolving fields, such developments as team-building workshops, third-party intervention in conflict management, transition-easing interventions, etc., are too ill-defined for much more than a case-by-case analysis. Theory verification is still in the future.

In a way, the detailed case study reported by a participant/observer is like an instant replay of a Monday-night football game narrated by one of the quarterbacks involved. Even allowing for his bias, his explanation of events will be different from that provided by a more neutral and objective observer. The quarterback can explain what was intended by a particular play and why it succeeded or failed; the observer can only guess at an explanation. Of course, in the best of worlds, we would hear from *both* quarterbacks and the defensive team captains as well.

Walton (1972) noted that the case study serves two unique purposes: (1) it facilitates the inductive development of new theory, and (2) it facilitates the refinement and further specification of existing theory. Detailed case studies also can provide the beginnings of a theory of planned social change. As Bennis (1968) observed, Freud built the outlines of his comprehensive theory of psychoanalysis from only five individual case studies. It is thus possible to use case studies to build theory and to develop hypotheses that then can be tested experimentally.

But a very special kind of case study is required to understand the process of planned change, not to mention developing a theory. Rigor is necessary to distinguish pertinent facts from trivial detail. All too often case studies give a detailed description of the time schedule of the intervention, but such critical issues as how the contract was negotiated, what counter forces were at work to undermine the intervention, what alternative strategies were considered, and so on, simply are not mentioned. Furthermore, the proportion of analysis to description is very important. Description alone leaves too much interpretation to the reader. Analysis alone leaves the reader too much at the mercy of the author(s)' judgment and interpretative skills. Case reports have room for each, but each must be carefully labeled for the reader's benefit. Although probably not a single case study ever published meets all of these criteria, they do need to be considered when evaluating the potential usefulness of a case study for understanding the change process and for developing a theory of change.

It is sometimes difficult for those involved to differentiate between description and analysis and between fact and opinion in order to write an objective report. But, as we noted earlier, an objective report loses the immediacy a participant may give — the confusion, uncertainty, and anguish of the change process as it impacts those involved. In our judgment, an insider's view is a necessity, although we recognize the dangers and limitations imposed by such reports. It would be best if not only the consultants but the clients told their side. Ideally, the story should come from the consultants and from representatives of each of the sides in a conflict-management controversy. But in reality, although occasional reports are written by clients, the bulk of the professional literature on planned change is written by practitioners.

To use case studies for maximum benefit, the reader must be aware of the special limitations of case studies written from this perspective. The consultant's report may contain protective and ego-inflating devices and, at least to some extent, narcissistic and exhibitionistic needs are involved in the preparation of any published report, which no doubt account for the fact that most cases have a "happy ending." Indeed, the publish-or-perish quandary of the academic world hardly leads one to write about one's failures nor will the report of failures do much for one's consulting practice.

Because most case studies are written by participant/observers with a strong investment in putting their best foot forward, a reader may have some trouble distinguishing opinions from facts, assumptions from data, and inferences from behavior. However, Freud himself was a participant/observer in precisely this context, and his studies are not simply dismissed. Neither should we dismiss the modern case study but rather realize its biases and limitations.

THE PRESENT VOLUME

This volume presents nine case studies of planned change on the organizational or community level. Each is an in-depth analysis prepared by the consultants who were actively engaged in the change activity. We believe that the cases we chose for this volume meet most of the criteria for a useful case study.

All the cases were first published two to eight years ago. Recognizing that writing time and publication lag added another two or three years to the age of these studies, we asked each of the authors to prepare an update on his or her case. We asked them (1) to report what had transpired within the client system since they wrote the case report; (2) to consider, with 20/20 hindsight, what they might have done differently; and (3) to judge what the experience of reviewing the case taught them about the case or about themselves.

We set fairly stringent word limits on the updates (our negotiations with the authors around these limits would provide an interesting case study), and there is a great deal of variability in the degree to which our three concerns have been addressed. The authors have had different levels of exposure to the original client systems in the intervening years. In some cases, the authors were able to give detailed reports on what has happened since the study was done; in others, the focus is by necessity more personal.

Without exception, the authors experienced some degree of pleasure or satisfaction at being asked to participate and in rereading their case studies. Most had let the memory of their involvement fade. Indeed, the publication of a case study may be one way to obtain a sense of closure, allowing one to turn to other matters. The authors seemed genuinely excited by the opportunity to rethink the case and its impact on their lives.

The updates bear witness that in every case the intervention affected the intervener as well as the system. Who would have expected the wide-spread ripple effect reported by Berlew, LeClere, and Pineda? Or the short-lived effects noted by Beer? Even less likely to be foreseen was the impact the cases had on the writers. Each consultant has in some way been changed by the experience. Sam Culbert is especially eloquent on this point, although it is possible that such an impact is not an ordinary effect of organization development, but occurs only in special cases that so affect the consultants initially that they need to write up the case study to obtain closure. That such cases still have an impact years later is no surprise. But perhaps even the most routine consultation does affect the consultants involved more than has been understood previously, and published cases are the tip of an iceberg.

The consultants also were concerned about the adequacy of their own diagnostic formulations. Looking backward, with the help of additional experience, personal development, and the knowledge of how their interventions affected the systems, many of the authors questioned how well they had understood the dynamics of the client systems. It seems clear to us that most of the authors have moved from reliance on a love-trust model for working organizational issues to concern with issues of clarification of purpose, structure, and power. Especially noteworthy is the decline of the T-group as an intervention strategy. Once the "foremost social invention of the Twentieth Century" (Rogers, 1968), the T-group apparently no longer is used as the primary intervention on the organizational level. But the alternative interventions — technostructural changes, action research, and problem-solving workshops — require a more thorough diagnostic ability and careful, thoughtful attention to specific design features. This issue is implicit in many of the authors' updates.

POTENTIAL USES OF THIS VOLUME

Consultants and other behavioral scientists who wish to gain a better understanding of the process of planned change will be especially interested in these nine detailed case studies in a variety of settings and with a variety of outcomes. The targets included business and industrial organizations, schools, and rather amorphous communities. The strategies ranged from T-groups to action research to technostructural change — the entire range of behavioral-science-based interventions. Those unfamiliar with such technology will find this volume an action-based primer.

The book can also be used as a teaching-learning tool, both in formal educational settings and in workshops and seminars. One potential use in a class or workshop would involve the teacher or leader previewing a case as the focus of the day's activity and identifying times at which a consultant must take an action step. For example, in the Berlew and LeClere case, such a point is after the description of the background of Curacao. The workshop participants would not read the case before the seminar session but would bring their case books to the workshop and read the section on *Intervention*. Then, a number of questions could be discussed, i.e.: What is the nature of the client's social system? With whom is your contract? What data do you have? What data do you wish you had? What alternative intervention strategies could be considered? What strategy would you implement? Each of the students or participants could be asked to spend ten to fifteen minutes attempting to answer these questions alone, jotting down notes. Then the participants could be divided into groups of three to six persons and asked to agree on some answers to the questions, which could then be listed on a large sheet of newsprint. One member of each subgroup could be prepared to answer questions from other participants. There are no "right" answers, and the purpose of the activity would not be to guess what the authors actually did but to learn about one's own intervention strategies. Typically, one would think of looking for the entry conditions, the diagnostic issues, the intervention plan, and the outcome, including evaluation. The role of the leader or teacher would be to facilitate discussion about these issues, highlighting concerns about values, theories of intervention, data bases, intervention techniques, and evaluation procedures. Our experience has been that these are highly engaging activities and that the better part of a day can be spent by even a group of inexperienced participants.

REFERENCES

Bennis, W. G. The case study I. Introduction. *Journal of Applied Behavioral Science*, 1968, *4*, 227-231.

Festinger, L., Reicker, H. W., & Schacter, S. *When prophesy fails: A social and psychological study of a modern group that predicted the destruction of the world*. New York: Harper & Row, 1964.

Henderson, L. J. From introductory lectures: Sociology 23. *Journal of Applied Behavioral Science*, 1968, *4*, 236-240.

Keckhoff, A. C., & Back, C. W. *The June bug*. New York: Appleton-Century-Crofts, 1968.

Kurland, P. B., & Casper, G. (Eds.). *Landmark briefs and arguments of the Supreme Court of the United States: Constitutional Law, 1977 Term Supplement*, Vol. 100. Washington, D. C.: University Publications of America, Inc., 1978.

Rogers, C. R. Interpersonal relationships: Year 2000. *Journal of Applied Behavioral Science*, 1968, *4*, 265-280.

Walton, R. E. Advantages and attributes of the case study. *Journal of Applied Behavioral Science*, 1972, *8*, 73-78.

Organizational Development for Thornlea: A Communication Package and Some Results

John C. Croft

The author introduces his facilitative role in organizational development at Thornlea School[1] with the following two statements: "Most organizations have a structure that was designed to solve problems that no longer exist" but "I am less interested in inducing any particular change than I am in fostering and nourishing the conditions under which constructive change may occur." In one sense the author's work at Thornlea could be classed as in-service training, but as the case developed the training was found to be of a very different kind from that which school people are accustomed to or acquainted with. This case study begins with the assumptions and objectives of organizational development (OD) in general; proceeds to some background of a school which recently participated in a very brief taste of OD; presents some essential features of the communication package itself and some of the results; and concludes, of course, with some implications.

ORGANIZATIONAL DEVELOPMENT

Think of an organization as a unit or system which has parts and which exists in an environment. If the system is organic, that is, if the parts are

The author wishes to acknowledge the help of Arnold Falusi and Ken Cluley—two schoolmen and organizational development enthusiasts who read earlier versions and contributed substantially to the positive features of this case study.

[1] A new nongraded Canadian secondary school dedicated to the learner's personal growth.

interrelated and interdependent, then the system is taking inputs from its environment and processing them in certain ways to produce outputs. The more its parts are interrelated and interdependent the better it is in its internal processing and in its external relatedness. In other words it is a better or an improved problem-solving climate. Like other systems, schools as organizations require maintenance and renewal. Unlike most kinds of organizations, however, schools have people *both* as input and as output, as process *and* product. All the personal attributes and characteristics brought to the school as well as the relationships that occur within the school make it a very rich and complex social milieu. Under these circumstances a fully organic, interdependent state is no accident—it must be worked at and perhaps is never completely achieved.

How can we work toward this kind of organizational development? How can a school organization be helped to improve its self-renewing capacity? The solutions to these questions are not all in; they are being created by behavioral science practitioners in the expanding field of organizational development.[2] The best prototypes seem to be in some industries which ironically find it easier and more practical to *actively* consider the human side of their enterprise than do most schools which are more comfortable thinking about it or setting some remote goals or "philosophies" of education vaguely expressed as "learner-centered" or "self-directed" curricula.

When asked to describe briefly organizational development, I have found it useful to make an analogy to the human body as one kind of system in relation to an environment. No one can guarantee anyone else a hazardless physical (or mental) existence. And knowledge of itself about the functioning of a particular human body or about human beings in general is not much help. Applications of this knowledge by way of specially designed, individually understandable, and relevant repetitive actions or behaviors are needed to help keep the human body in top organic condition. Some obvious examples are the regulation of diet and physical exercise. Although broad general rules can be followed in these examples, in the specific details subtle nuances and differences between particular bodies emerge.

---

[2]For some beginnings within an educational context, *see*, for example, Goodwin Watson (Ed.), *Concepts for social change* and *Change in school systems*. Cooperative Project for Educational Development. Washington, D.C.: NTL Institute for Applied Behavioral Science, NEA, 1967; and William C. Schutz, *Joy*. New York: Grove Press, 1967. *See also*, *Living and Learning: The report*. Ontario Provincial Committee on Aims and Objectives of Education in the Schools of Ontario. Toronto, Canada: Newton Publishing Company, 1968.

Looking now at the school as a social system or organization, organizational development is directed toward developing the capabilities of an organization in such a manner that the organization can attain and sustain an optimum level of performance; it is a problem-solving process, and it is undertaken on a collaborative basis by a combination of the members of an organization and behavioral science practitioners. It reflects the belief that even in organizations which are operating satisfactorily there is room for improvement. In keeping with my analogy to the human body as a system, I would classify my organizational development work under the general term *exercise*. Effective organizational development work would be the systematic induction of appropriate exercise. And exercise, as I am using the term, means systematic repetitive activity designed to keep the school organization in a more adaptive state.

This "exercise" approach is quite different from the use of written rules, personal guidelines, advice-giving, or special organizational arrangements which are derived from personal experiences, or extrapolated from research findings or theoretical treatises which I sometimes label a "cookbook" approach. I shudder when I use either term, however, because "cookbook" seems to carry with it negative connotations and "exercise" is sometimes understood as only doing and never thinking—neither of which pejorative interpretation is intended here. A person would be inviting difficulties if he did exercise without also taking some gross measures of his physical and emotional states, e.g., without *thinking* about it. Exercise, therefore, as used in OD does not refer to vicarious or accidental activities unless such spontaneity seems to speak to some particular purpose or need of the organization. This would rule out, of course, calling such unplanned activities "exercise" if the justification for using them were based only on the following arguments: "School A does it! . . ." "Teacher B runs his class this way." "At the university. . . ."

OD in a School Setting

Considering the school as an organizational system, one can make some assumptions about its people-processing and growth-facilitating qualities which are fairly well supported in the behavioral science literature.[3]

---

[3]Noted in *NTL Institute News and Reports*, June 1968, 2 (3), which is available from the NTL Institute for Applied Behavioral Science, P.O. Box 9155, Rosslyn Station, Arlington, VA 22209.

- Work which is organized to meet people's needs as well as to achieve organizational requirements tends to produce the highest productivity rate and a superior quality of production.
- Individuals whose basic needs are taken care of do not seek a soft and secure environment. They are interested in work, challenge, and responsibility. They expect recognition and satisfying interpersonal relationships.
- People have a drive toward growth and self-realization.
- Persons in groups which go through a managed process of increasing openness about both positive and negative feelings develop a strong identification with the goals of the group and its other members. The group becomes increasingly capable of dealing constructively with potentially disruptive issues.
- Personal growth is facilitated by a relationship which is honest, caring, and nonmanipulative.
- Positive change flows naturally from groups whose members feel a common identification and an ability to influence their environment.

From these assumptions, then, an organizational development program introduced in a school setting would have the following *general objectives:*

1. To create an open, problem-solving climate throughout the organization.

2. To supplement the authority associated with role or status with the authority of knowledge and competence.

3. To locate decision-making and problem-solving responsibilities as close to the information sources as possible.

4. To build trust among individuals and groups throughout the organization.

5. To make competition more relevant to work goals and to maximize collaborative efforts.

6. To develop a reward system which recognizes both the achievement of the organization's mission (profits or service) and organization development (growth of people).

7. To increase the sense of "ownership" of organization objectives throughout the work force.

8. To help managers to manage according to relevant objectives rather than according to "past practices" or according to objectives which do not make sense for one's area of responsibility.

9. To increase self-control and self-direction for people within the organization.

THE THORNLEA IDEA

> *I know that good will and materials as resources will always be available to the teachers at Thornlea. If the school will be strong in the use of group processes, easy and free in communication, interested in professional growth, and able to combine a high level of personal security with challenging insecurity in problems—the success, the real success, will manifest itself in young Canadians who will be graduated from there. These will be our reward.[4]*

This statement of the philosophy of the Thornlea Study Committee which worked tirelessly to develop and nurture the Thornlea idea was paraphrased and echoed many times by various persons to whom I talked in the school district. The school seemed to be a natural place for an organizational development project, especially when one considers the following key points which capture the essence of Thornlea.

- *The school should be library-centered* both physically and in function.
- *There should be provision for discussion areas and individual work areas* for longer projects by individual students.
- *There should be maximum professional involvement.* Teachers worked on the Thornlea Study Committee which developed the major directions and recommendations for the school. The program offerings were created by the principal and the teachers who had been appointed to Thornlea. During the two weeks prior to opening the entire staff was involved in preservice programs and other organizational matters.

Administrators were well aware of the degree in which the "medium is the message" and attempted to build into job descriptions some role flexibility so that no person does only one thing. Thus the principal teaches as well as serving as administrator; the second-line administrators, called "Directors," teach some classes; and many teachers take other responsibilities such as chairmanships, memberships on policy committees, and so on.[5]

- *The educational program should be learner-centered, nongraded, and based, therefore, on continuous progress.* Learning was seen as dynamic.

---

[4]Stephen Bacsalmasi, "The report of the Thornlea study committee," in Proceedings of the Ninth Annual Study Conference of the Ontario Educational Research Council, December 8-9, 1967, p. 209.

[5]Further elaboration of the rationale for the organization of this school is available in an article by the superintendent of the district. See S. L. G. Chapman, Some observations on the opening of a new school. *Bull. Ontario sec. school Teachers Fed.*, March 1968, 73-76.

These few points convinced me that the educators who nurtured the Thornlea idea and the persons who by and large selected themselves to work in the school were thinking very different thoughts about how schools should operate and about how they should work in *this* innovative school. The value commitment, the essentially uncharted directions, the highly visible situation, all these combined to mandate that the staff members *must* creatively collaborate in their work in this school if it is to be successful. Or put another way, they must be in touch with one another, must be committed to one another as they work on the myriad problems which do and will confront them in the forging of a new tradition.

The problem for me as presenter and facilitator was how to approach this school staff about the possibility of organizational development work—how to get across all the ideas behind such a project. Previous discussions with schoolmen led me to believe that words were not enough and that some demonstration was needed. Thus, Arnold Falusi and I proceeded to develop a "communication package"—roughly a week of activities specially tailored from all our resources to the needs of Thornlea—to describe and demonstrate the potential of a full-scale organizational development project set in motion at this school. We realized that we were attempting the improbable in talking about and demonstrating to the Thornlea staff for such a brief period of time what organizational development is all about.

As things turned out, even though the communication package was a very *brief* intervention into the ongoing life of the school, it seems to have had some impressive "soft" results which should be revealed even though numbers cannot be assigned to them. The next section describes our activities and some of the difficulties and results.

THE COMMUNICATION PACKAGE: OD FOR THORNLEA

The set of activities which I have referred to earlier as a "communication package" was conducted at specially scheduled staff meetings about three weeks after Thornlea School opened. These meetings involved three hours on a Saturday; one and one-half hours on Monday, Tuesday, Wednesday, and Thursday; and three hours on Friday. Since the package was specially tailored to Thornlea, details are not presented. However, some essential features and resulting difficulties will be of interest.

Essential Features

Doing and thinking were pervasive throughout all the activities. The staff members had both to engage in as well as discuss and think about what was happening to them during the exercise.

Attempts at constructive *feedback* at three levels—personal, interpersonal, and organizational—were designed and hopefully enhanced the activities. Expressions of feelings about behaviors of individuals, groupings of individuals, and organizational problems were facilitated where possible.

Some time was devoted to *skill building* at the personal, interpersonal, and organizational levels. That is, staff participants engaged in practice sessions around problems which were real to them and in methods of helping with these problems at the three aforementioned levels.

While directing these sessions, Mr. Falusi and I (herein referred to as the "facilitators") attempted to *model* appropriate and helpful behavior. Realizing that imitation is a strong form of learning, we remained as open and nondefensive as possible in our interactions with the staff.

The problem of *breaking in*, that is, of becoming accepted as a truly interested helper and setting norms for behavior, was dealt with in the following way. The facilitators realized that in the opening sessions they would be the most influential "tone-setters." Accordingly, at the start of the opening session the facilitators spoke briefly about their background and the objectives of this package and then asked the participants to write some answers to the question "Who am I?" which would then be shared with other staff members in a "milling-around" exercise. We hoped to legitimize any openness which might occur as well as to respect a person's separateness in responding to this in any way he might wish—including not responding at all.

Some Difficulties

Difficulties were encountered around five major clusters. To begin with, there was much *suspicion* and *mistrust* of the facilitators and their motives for conducting the program. Some of these suspicions were built up before the "package" began and before the facilitators had arrived, through some very important and impressionable circumstances. In a discussion with the principal some months before the activities with the staff, I insisted that the staff themselves should have an important say in whether (and what kind of) a full-scale organizational development program would be implemented in the Thornlea School. This was the reason for preparing the communication package, and our understanding was that the teachers would then decide whether to continue with organizational development without feeling that such a program had been imposed by the principal. In arranging with the staff the times for the communication package, the principal mentioned to them that I was a "sensitivity trainer" (which I am)[6] and that each person might want to send a brief autobiography telling something about himself so that the facilitators could "know" him via this little introduction before beginning the package. And the results of this exercise evidenced some very interesting distortions about the coming events as well as the mistrust and suspicion mentioned above. In fact, the package was publicized on a calendar in the faculty room as a "sensitivity workshop" (obviously a misnomer).

These fears and misconceptions were somewhat allayed, though not completely I think, through various written handouts about the objectives of OD (as outlined earlier in this paper) and by insisting repeatedly during the communication package that no person was under obligation to continue beyond the week's activities and that the participant's decision could be made after the package was over. Even so, personal suspicions were so high at one point that the facilitators improvised and played a recording of the Bob Dylan song "All I Wanna Do" to convey their relationship to the staff. Still members concentrated more on the teaching methods of the facilitators than upon what was happening to them and between each other.

Another difficulty encountered was *psychological absence*. Staff members often did not listen to one another, did not "hear" one another or the facilitators, and seemed by and large to ignore the readings, though few in number and germane to the activities and to organizational development in general.

Pupil control concerns also clouded the learning.[7] Members could not rest easy knowing that some 500 students were "loose" in the halls, and unsupervised. Of the difficulties actually occurring during the entire package, I am aware of only two. On the third day paper was strewn on a washroom floor, and on the final day mischievous youths set off a fire alarm, effectively closing the last session.

The *physical absence* of some members from some of the sessions prevented an optimum continuity of learning. While this was to be

---

[6]I am becoming less and less enthusiastic about conducting T Groups with strangers or with "cousins," a term for people of like occupations or roles in different work settings. My intuitive hunches about the nontransferability of skills out of such "cocoon" settings, which are well supported by the comprehensive review listed below, excite me about working with *living systems* such as I am discussing in this case. But the techniques for approaching and working with these systems need to be developed and clarified—what this paper is all about. For the review mentioned above, *see* J. P. Campbell & M. D. Dunnette, Effectiveness of t-group experiences in managerial training and development. *Psychol. Bull.*, August 1968, 70 (2), 73-104.

[7]Pupil control is a concern in many schools. See, for example, D. J. Willower, T. L. Eidell, & W. K. Hoy, *The school and pupil ideology*. The Penn State Studies Monograph No. 24. University Park, Pa.: Pennsylvania State University, 1967.

expected, it made it difficult to update new members about what had happened and also made it impossible to backtrack on skill-building activities. Like all exercise, these sessions had to be appropriately paced and could not be "made up" like a missed lesson. Related to this was the problem of *fluid membership*. The same teachers were not always present.

Thus the Thornlea communication package contained the essential features of (a) including *doing and thinking* in all the activities, (b) providing for knowledge of results, or *feedback*, about how the exercises were affecting each person, (c) allotting some time for *skill building*, (d) *modeling* appropriate behavior by the facilitators, and (e) designing some *break-in* activities to legitimize norms of openness. We encountered the difficulties of (a) *suspicion* and *mistrust* of the practitioners, (b) the *psychological absence* of some members, (c) *pupil control concerns*, (d) *physical absence*, and (e) *fluid membership*.[8]

RESULTS

On an evaluation sheet which was filled out by each member at the close of the last session a mixture of feelings and opinions ranging from confusion to excitement was apparent. Many of the difficulties alluded to above were identified on this form, and some of the staff reacted to the timing of the total package. Yet another significant element was the personal style of the facilitators. In addition, some other occurrences were noted later either by the facilitators or by other observers in the system as being caused by this communication package. These two types I have separated for convenience into results observed during the package and results occurring after the package.

During the Package

For one member of the staff this communication package represented his introduction to the school. The communication package itself provided a most unusual and fortunate way for this person to be introduced fully to the rest of the staff. Here was one unplanned beneficial and side payment resulting from the activities.

Quite early in the package many of the staff realized that in focusing on the behaviors and methods of the facilitators they were throwing up "smoke screens" to avoid looking at and understanding

---

[8]These difficulties were anticipated by the facilitators, but this fact does not make them any less difficult. Similar difficulties in research designs have been noted by C. Argyris, Some unintended consequences of rigorous research. *Psychol. Bull.*, 1968, 70 (3), 185-197.

their own behaviors and improving their organizational functioning. This was a slightly different perception from the ethos of excitement that existed in that school staff before this time. From certainty that they were getting along quite well before the package, some progressed to uncertainty by the end of the package.

Later in the sessions staff members became willing to confront one another concerning value differences related to rating the principal of the school. Even though everyone liked the principal, some felt strongly that they should rate the principal while others felt that they should not.

In working through some paper-and-pencil responses about social norms operating in the school staff, it became apparent to many that they had a "public image" which was not their real feeling about what should be done in the school. This provided many data for further inquiry on their part.

After the Package

More interesting, however, are some results attributed to the communication package from observing events which have transpired since the package. Three events have been independently identified by several observers in the school system. The first has to do with a staff meeting at which the superintendent was in attendance not long after the communication package was completed. At that meeting much openness was apparent, and many confrontations around interpersonal functioning occurred. This event was reported to me in separate conversations with several persons on the staff; apparently, staff meetings have never been the same since the communication package.

Another important result relates to the behavior of one of the staff members at a conference outside the school. This staff member was willing to confront the superintendent on an important value difference between them. The difference in behavior was noted favorably by the superintendent and was also described by some other observers outside the school but in the school system, who attributed this to the communication package and the activities in which the staff member had participated.

More recently the staff has felt the pressure of external constraints. It is one thing to say that Thornlea will be a non-graded school but quite another to have the internal strength and capability to meet the pressure to present evidence of student achievement of a type which would enable comparison with other students in other schools. Value differences around this topic as well as many previously unconscious or hidden or unshared expectations and assumptions about the operation of the school are beginning to be explored. A recent staff meeting exhibiting confrontation between some of the members seems to have "bothered" some, excited others, and interested all in attendance. Three of the staff independently attributed the open communication in this meeting to the communication package.

IMPLICATIONS

At the outset of this paper I said that most organizations have structure that was designed to solve problems which no longer exist. In this specific organization a more appropriate statement is that new problems have arisen. The Thornlea idea is an exciting one indeed—educators have never been short on utopian visions.

The problem with such ultimate goals is that we know little about comprehensive implementations toward these goals. It is one thing to *say* that we will trust students or even one another and quite another thing to *do* it, but with certain conditions or reservations. The Thornlea staff knows full well that the curricular architecture is not the total answer, although it helps. We must also consider the social or inter-personal resilience or "muscle state"—the social architecture of the school as an organization.

In describing the features of the school to close friends, and perhaps to you as well, I fear I may have presented it superficially—like every other school built around a new vision. Indeed, it has a house plan, phases of courses, which are groupings of students into classes according to their level of readiness, and considerably more student option in choice of courses, and so forth. More important, however, is the fact that there are people (both teachers and students) in this school who have previously only *talked* about a different kind of education and now have as much opportunity as possible to *effect* a personal-growth-centered education. Such action possibility inten-sifies value differences and increases the probability of confrontation concerning them. The question is, What will happen when con-frontations occur?

The staff of Thornlea is a committed staff.[9] My experience so far convinces me that clearer role prescriptions, job descriptions, or attri-bute preparation à la revised teacher selection and training programs are not enough. We must create ongoing organizational arrangements and mechanisms whereby stronger relationships can be built and such individual strengths enhanced. How can a school be any "differ-ent" if educators bring with them their previous backgrounds and unclarified expectations with no continuing program to support them

---

[9] My work with this committed group of people has been most rewarding, and I hope it will continue.

in thinking in an innovative way about school and about teaching and learning as well as about one another! And even if different thoughts are occurring, how can we encourage the divergent attitudes and deviant perspectives needed to foster and nourish such tradition-breaking attempts?

We in education need to pay a little less attention to the *setting* of utopian goals and the designing of ways to evaluate whether we are attaining these goals and to *deal more creatively* with what is available and to build the strong relationships and organizational health necessary to creating a strong enough internal state or stamina for such an organization to flourish and grow.

Regarding methods of implementation, I stated at the outset that the solutions are not all in. I have tried to describe a possible way and to demonstrate its importance to the Thornlea staff in the communication package presented. One thing is certain: Industries are more advanced on this score than are educational organizations.[10] Thus, when *people* are the sole products of these latter organizations, can we afford to ignore, and not to experiment with and adapt, successful prototypes from business enterprises where people are also a strong concern? We have a long way to go in education, and we had better hurry!

---

[10]In a recent series of lectures at the University of Toronto, and entitled "Organizational illness: An analysis and possible cures" (October 15-16, 1968), Chris Argyris noted that his experiences with all kinds of organizations incline him to place industry in the lead regarding concern with personnel problems, education in second place, and church organizations in third place.

THORNLEA TEN YEARS LATER

John C. Croft

Everyone I have interviewed who has worked at Thornlea Secondary School agrees that the school today is strong, healthy, and fun to visit. This is also the opinion of many who are now related to Thornlea through membership in a larger administrative unit that was created at the end of the school year following my work with the faculty.

Because my only organization-development involvement with the school was the week-long laboratory set up to assist the newly selected faculty in opening and starting the school (Croft, 1970), I can take no credit for Thornlea's currently abundant adaptive capabilities. As I stated in the case-study report, my work was a demonstration; but Thornlea then became an example for the rest of the school system, and many events have occurred in the larger system.

SOME IMPORTANT CHRONOLOGY

Thornlea is one of about fourteen secondary schools in the York County Board of Education. The OD Laboratory at Thornlea took place during the last week of August, 1968, and it attracted the attention of others in the school system. In response to that attention and to the interest of many in knowing more, I prepared a case description for the Ontario Educational Research Conference in December, 1968. Warren Bennis, to whom the description was sent for comments, asked that it be published in the *JABS* case-study section, and it subsequently was published in the Winter, 1970, issue.

During the fall of 1968 the minister of education for the Province of Ontario decreed that all small school systems would be reorganized into much larger administrative units, usually incorporating entire counties. The new school board was to be elected by January 1, 1969; the chief school executive was to be selected by February 1, 1969; and the entire reorganization was to be operational by July 1, 1969. (OD researchers and consultants could learn much by scrutinizing the short- and long-range effects of "change-by-decree" strategies, which are common in parliamentary political systems and largely obscured by a North American "consultative" bias.)

The new organization was created rapidly. Results observed in Thornlea and further consultation between me and the new director of education (the chief school administrator) and the school trustees led to the establishment of a three-person, full-time, OD unit. I recruited the members, who began their employment in July, 1969.

SOME RESULTS

The OD unit used a "top-down" perspective. Top priority was given to facilitating the functioning of the administrative cabinet, which was composed of ten people, including the director, the associate director, the business administrator, and the central office and area superintendents. Significant development and functioning within this task group that occurred over the 1969-70 school year can be attributed to the interventions of the OD unit (Croft & Falusi, 1973).

Next in priority was an OD intervention with the management system of the larger organization. A four-day meeting with all superintendents and principals and some school board members was held in August, 1970 (Croft & Barker, 1973). As a follow-up, the OD unit collaborated with Robert B. Morton in conducting the Morton OD Laboratory for the administrative committee in February, 1971, and then for some forty principals and assistant principals in 1971-72. The OD unit remained "on call," as required by board policy, and was perceived by all clients as very helpful. Some effects of the interventions with the management system have been described by the OD unit (Duffin, Falusi, & Lawrence, 1972; Duffin, Falusi, Lawrence, & Morton, 1973).

SOME UNANTICIPATED INFLUENCES

During 1972 the province-wide teacher's federation, comprised of all secondary teachers, acquired considerable political strength and capabilities, perhaps due to the sudden increase in size of administrative units throughout the Province of Ontario. The federation's province-wide capability, coupled with the strongly participative, problem-solving, and consultative ethics of the administration in York County, encouraged an extensive period of intensive professional and personal soul searching for both teachers and administrators.

When forced to choose, administrators in York County opted to be representatives of management and of the board of education rather than of the federation, although most were members of the latter. Over time, a "cold-war" situation came about in which administrators and teachers felt compelled to be "against" whatever the others were "for." One three-month strike led to immediate financial gains for teachers and what was probably a long-range, extensive loss for everyone. One of the many effects of the strike was a drastic reorganization of the school system, which eventually resulted in the disbanding of the OD unit and the absorption of the three members in other positions.

THORNLEA

In spite of the changes in both the organization and the community, Thornlea seems to be thriving as intended. Students and faculty do *choose* to attend, work, and learn at the school. The Thornlea idea describes the school today very well. The commitment of all people in the school is to personal and professional growth, to individualized and involving education, and to development for all. The school presents an option for students and faculty who prefer an innovative and problem-solving environment to "back-to-basics" educational programs, authoritarian teaching methods, and controlling management systems. Of course, the latter options are also available.

Few of the original staff members are still working at Thornlea, but the original OD work encouraged the already self-selected faculty members, who have worked with others who came to the school later.

I was criticized by one reviewer of the case study for a loose use of the term "exercise" and for many confused analogies between organic functioning in human bodies and in organizations. However, the exercise analogy still seems useful for summarizing my observations and my second thoughts about my work. Compared to the other secondary school staffs during the three-month strike, the Thornlea staff was the most creative in finding solutions and the most supportive of each other under considerable tension. Thornlea was clearly in "better shape" to meet the problems that came up, and the school remains in good shape although many faculty and students have come and gone. The success of the school has meant a great deal to both participants and observers. Although my input ,was not necessary after the week I worked with the staff, I would have been pleased to be associated directly with the many milestones of the school's development.

REFERENCES

Croft, J. C. Organizational development for Thornlea: A communication package and some results. *Journal of Applied Behavioral Science*, 1970, 6, 93-106.

Croft, J. C., & Barker, C. The organizational inventory meeting: Gaining and integrating administrative commitment. *Journal of Educational Administration*, 1973, *11*, 254-271.

Croft, J. C., & Falusi, A. J. Organization development interventions: Effects upon feelings, confrontations, and double messages. *Education and Urban Society*, 1973, 465-485.

Duffin, R., Falusi, A., & Lawrence, P. Organization development: What's it all about? *School Progress*, 1972, *41*, 34-36, 62-64.

Duffin, R., Falusi, A., Lawrence, P., & Morton, R. B. Increasing organizational effectiveness. *Training and Development Journal*, 1973, 37-46.

A Laboratory-Consultation Model for Organization Change

William G. Dyer

Robert F. Maddocks

J. Weldon Moffitt

William J. Underwood

Behavioral change agents engaged in management and organization development efforts recognize as crucial, solutions to the recurring problems of entry and transfer. The major feature of the project reported here and still under way is the attempt to optimize both entry methods and transfer activities by a single developmental approach which includes the unique feature of using laboratory training to build a consulting relationship between internal consultants and their operating managers in an industrial organization.

The essential elements of the total design included: (a) laboratory training as an initiating vehicle, (b) the use of internal Trainer-Consultants, (c) the use of data collection and feedback, and (d) a single management and organizational conceptual framework. A single framework was used to overlay prelaboratory, laboratory, and post-laboratory activity. Data about each of the 25 participating managers were collected from peers and subordinates prior to the laboratory. The laboratory allowed each manager to receive data from other participants, to receive data from back-home work peers and subordinates, to establish a working consulting relationship with internal consultants, and, with them, to begin to formulate a plan of action for back-home application.

Initial results from back-home application within the organization indicate that these design features have reduced the entry and transfer *problems experienced in utilizing laboratory learnings in organization development. However, certain problems still exist in transfer of learning, namely: uneven skill on the part of the managers to implement laboratory learnings, some lack of skill on the part of the Trainer-Consultants to intervene effectively, and the existence of certain organization conditions that do not support change.*

With the increasing number of organizations turning to management and organization development as avenues for increased effectiveness, two difficult problems have arisen as a real challenge to those engaged in such endeavors.

The first problem is mainly the result of organizations which place management and organization development in staff functions and hence confront the staff manager with the task of entry into the line organization. This problem of appropriate entry and responsibility is a recurring one for behavioral change agents.

The second and broader problem is that of the transfer of laboratory learnings to organizational improvement. Most of the attempts to do so can be subsumed under three models.

1. *The Training Model.* Managers can be sent to training programs geared to develop a motivation and conception for organizational improvement. Popular examples are Grid seminars, NTL Institute laboratories, and company-sponsored programs.

2. *The Survey-Feedback Model.* Data can be collected about the organization and fed back to management as a basis for initiating problem solving. Examples are Beckhard's (1966) or Blake's (Blake, Mouton, & Sloma, 1965) confrontation designs and much of the survey action-research work of The University of Michigan (Mann, 1957).

3. *The Process-Consultation Model.* A consultant can engage directly with a management group and use their ongoing business activities as a vehicle. Much of the development work at Esso R & E and Union Carbide Corporation serves as examples.

THE ORGANIZATIONAL SETTING PRIOR TO THE CHANGE PROGRAM

Recently, a method of combining desirable features from all three models into a single approach for initiating an organizational improvement project was completed by the Radio Corporation of America (RCA) training group in conjunction with two external consultants. The enthusiastic response of management and the training group suggests its usefulness to those working in the organization field as well as to those more specifically concerned with the issue of transfer of training.

RCA is a large international organization of some 120,000 employees engaged in manufacturing a variety of products and providing services primarily in the field of electronics. The organization has a highly successful business image in terms of growth and financial return.

In the company there are two organization development persons at the corporate staff level, and out in the divisions are six experienced staff persons and five others who are less experienced. This makes a total staff of 13 persons available for OD work in the company, but only eight staff members considered experienced in OD.

There was no sense of urgency in the company on the part of management or the OD staff for beginning immediately an organization change program. Certain conditions were identified as pushing for change, but the desire was to build an OD model carefully with thoughts toward long-range results rather than some immediate transformations.

Previous Work of the OD Staff

Prior to the beginning of the organization change program, most of the internal OD staff were thought of as trainers (i.e., persons who diagnose management and organization needs, design a training program for certain personnel, and then conduct the program). The strategy for change was the hope that such training programs would lead to a change in management performance and perhaps in some organization change. It was felt by the staff that the training programs they were conducting were not producing adequate transfer into the organization, and that a different model of change was necessary— including a different way for the OD staff to work with managers. Although the staff felt competent in training and felt comfortable with their knowledge of new methods of OD, they lacked experience in carrying out new OD programs, e.g., consulting, team building, intergroup building. The image that the managers saw in the OD staff was a trainer image—these were people who conducted training programs but did not work regularly and consistently in the organization with the manager. It was felt necessary to change this image.

FEATURES OF THE CHANGE PROGRAM

For this project, laboratory training was chosen as an initiating vehicle. However, the problems of entry for the internal training group and connecting the laboratory learnings with the organization were critical design issues. Recognizing the continuing problem of transfer of training, the authors knew that some organizations provide internal consultants to serve as an application resource to their managers who attend residential laboratories, while others use the "family" concept of composing the training group of managers who have ongoing working relationships.

It was within these experiences that the authors designed the RCA project and attempted to optimize both entry and transfer by a single approach. The essential elements of the design included: (a) the use of internal Trainer-Consultants, (b) the use of a single management and organization conceptual framework, and (c) the use of data collection and feedback.

Internal Trainer-Consultants

The key factor in the total design was the utilization of a corps of full-time internal Trainer-Consultants (presenting the trainer image mentioned above). The individuals used were RCA division training staff who carried the training responsibility for managers in their organizations. This group was to be the major link between the training laboratory and back-home organizational application. The Trainer-Consultants (hereafter called T-Cs) had been attempting to establish a working consulting role with management as a supplement to their normal training activities; however, at the time this project was conceived, the consultant-manager relationship had not been fully developed. It was decided that this project would be used to build such a relationship and that this relationship would be the instrument for back-home application. The T-Cs would be expected to follow their managers back into their organizational units and to continue to find ways of transferring laboratory learnings into the organizational setting.

It was decided, therefore, that the laboratory would be restricted to only those managers who would be willing to come to the program with their respective internal T-C and who would commit themselves to working with him prior to, during, the following the laboratory experience. A description of the proposed development project was discussed with a select group of managers who, in the past, had indicated a desire to initiate development activity within their organizational units. All 25 managers who were invited agreed to participate in the project.

It was necessary to build a set of conditions within the laboratory which would enable the consultant-manager relationship to be established. One requirement, therefore, was to bring the T-Cs and managers into contact during the laboratory in such a way as to establish an open and trustful relationship similar to the one which often develops between laboratory trainers and participants.

The design must also allow the T-Cs and managers to share the learnings of the laboratory, thereby cementing the consultant-manager relationship and avoiding the blocks that often appear when two people have to work together on issues which have not been shared in a common experience. This is particularly important since an effective consultant-manager relationship can be blocked by forces in the organization.

Since establishing a working relationship would also require that the T-Cs be seen by their managers from the beginning as being an integral part of the laboratory, the design of the project called for the internal T-Cs to do the following:

1. Collect data prior to the laboratory about each of their managers from his subordinates and peers.

2. Consult with their managers during the laboratory regarding the experiences the latter were having in the laboratory itself and on the back-home data which were given to the managers at a precise time during the laboratory.

3. Develop the kind of relationship with their managers which would carry over to the organization.

4. Continue to work with their managers within their organizational units after the laboratory to design and implement a plan of action to move the laboratory learnings toward organization application.

Unifying Conceptual Framework

A second major design feature was the decision to provide a single unifying framework to the total project which would provide a cognitive map for the learning taking place in the laboratory and for relating laboratory learnings to the organizations of each of the participating managers.

The idea of a cognitive framework is not new. "We should always be sure in designing learning experiences that they have both confrontation and a support for current orientations built into them. Cognitive models have particular value in the analysis of problems of transfer of learning" (Harrison, 1965).

The idea of using a single framework to overlay prelaboratory, laboratory, and postlaboratory activity *is* new. We wanted to avoid the fairly typical response to laboratory learning, "I think I learned a lot, but I really can't say what it is or how it applies"; or the condition stated as, "Laboratory values are so different from the values of most organizations that if the individuals learned well while at the laboratory, they would probably tend to conclude that they should *not* use their new learning back home except where they have power and influence" (Argyris, 1966). The choice of a single framework for simplicity and understanding but which was broad enough to avoid oversimplification was seen as critical. Likert's (1961) system of organizational characteristics, which arranges several behavioral categories into a matrix with four general styles, was chosen as an appropriate vehicle.

Data Collection and Feedback

Another important project element was the use of three separate data-collecting instruments. While each was geared to a different purpose, all three were designed under the Likert conceptual framework. The instruments measured behavior along the following dimensions: leadership, motivation, communication, interaction-influence, decision making, goals, and control. Measurements of each dimension were differentiated across four broad management styles ranging from autocratic to participative.

One instrument was built to focus on the individual behavior of the manager in his organizational role. Each manager had subordinates and peers fill out this instrument just prior to the laboratory. Data were received, profiled by T-Cs, and held to be fed back to the manager at a certain point in the laboratory.

Another instrument was constructed for the dual purpose of assessing the processes of a T Group and for assessing individual T-Group member behavior. The latter purpose provided the manager with systematized feedback on his behavior from his fellow T-Group members in the same conceptual framework used for the data gathered from his organizational subordinates and peers.

The third instrument designed for the project was cast at the organization level and built specifically to assess the processes of an organizational simulation exercise used in the laboratory.

The use of this instrumentation was expected to meet several objectives, the most important of which was to aid learning transfer. The instruments appeared to be an effective method of illustrating the operational value of the management and organizational conceptual framework. Data collected under a common framework were expected to be useful in helping the manager relate his laboratory behavior to his organizational behavior. In addition to their transfer value, the instruments were expected to aid the laboratory learning process and to illustrate for the managers the feasibility and value of collecting quantitative data about human behavior and relationship processes.

These three key elements—internal consulting resources, a single conceptual framework, and data collection—were viewed as bringing together for this project successful approaches from prior experience in the fields of training and organizational improvement.

PREPARING THE INTERNAL CONSULTANTS

Prior to the beginning of the laboratory, the seven internal T-Cs were brought together to prepare them for the laboratory experience and for their follow-up work with their managers in the back-home organizational application. During the two and one-half days thus spent, part of the time was used for giving the T-Cs an opportunity to contribute to the general design elements of the laboratory since its preliminary design had been done by the outside consultants and two internal trainers. The design work completed to this point called for the internal T-Cs to have a major decision role in locating and prescribing the timing and nature of consultations which would take place between them and their managers.

The major role of T-Cs during the laboratory experience was to act as ongoing consultants to their managers. They were to observe their managers in all aspects of the laboratory—T Groups, exercises, and theory sessions. They were to interact with their managers in a consulting capacity which would help them to function more effectively during the total laboratory experience. The week was to be used to practice their consultation skills and to build the type of consultant-manager relationship which would be functional when they went back to their organizations.

The T-Cs were also briefed on the use of data. They were responsible for feeding instrumented data back to their managers. Time was spent in helping the T-Cs interpret data and in examining ways data could be fed back in usable form so that the managers could identify those characteristics in the Likert system relating to their managerial performance which required planning for improvement.

Time was also spent in talking about and role-playing the building of the consultant role. A model of the consulting process was presented which examined the various dimensions of control. The T-Cs looked at the types of requests which could be made of them by the managers during the laboratory and the ways in which varying response to these requests would result in the T-Cs' either exercising control over the managers or allowing the managers more autonomy. The T-C saw that his function with his manager was to help the manager increase his awareness of the processes going on around him, recognize the feedback given in the T Group, and to begin to plan more effective behaviors for himself without relying on the T-C for direction.

THE LABORATORY PHASES

By way of overview, the major phases of the laboratory design were as follows:

Overview

Phase I — 2 days. Concentrated T Grouping focused on general personal and interpersonal issues. A day-long marathon was used on the first full day.

Phase II — 2 days. T Grouping was combined with organizational exercises and theory sessions. The learning focus was shifted to group and organizational issues.

Phase III — 1 day. The collection, feedback, and analysis of data. Managers were supplied with data from both their organizational colleagues and their laboratory colleagues. The learning focus was the manager's impact on others along managerial and organizational dimensions.

Phase IV — 1 day. Participants were assigned to use this period in whatever way they considered to be important. They chose concentrated T Grouping both to process their instrumented data with others and to resolve remaining issues developed in the T Group.

Because these phases were intersected by the key elements previously described, the laboratory will now be described to illustrate the use of each feature.

Phase I

During the concentrated T Grouping in Phase I, the T-Cs took three roles. First, they acted as observers watching the behaviors of their managers as they interacted with others. Second, they met with their managers in three private consultations interspersed throughout this period. The initial consultation was used to clarify the purpose of the several consultation periods scheduled in the laboratory agenda. Generally, this was described as helping the manager obtain maximum value from the laboratory events. The remaining consultation periods in this phase were used to help the manager focus more deeply on his experiences in the T Group. The third role taken by the T-C was to collect, tabulate, and feed back data. During the marathon on the first day, managers completed a group questionnaire designed around the Likert format. The results, in profile form, revealed to the managers that nearly all perceived their T Groups to be operating somewhat autocratically but that each perceived himself to be operating more participatively. This brought into the design the features of the conceptual framework and data collection as well as opening up data for analysis in the T Group.

Phase II

During the focused exercises on group decision making and organizational processes in Phase II, three more private consultations were scheduled. Each of these was located immediately following either an exercise or a theory session and in turn was immediately followed by a T-Group session. This scheduling gave the T-C an opportunity to help the manager assess his behavior in structured task work and to relate it to his behavior in the T Group. These consultations tended to open for the manager new dimensions of concern which he could then test out in the T Group.

Also during the second phase, a Likert-type questionnaire assessing organizational processes was used during the organizational exercise. For the second time the managers were exposed to the use of quantitative data by a replication of the conceptual framework, but applied to a different context.

Phase III

Phase III was used entirely to collect, feed back, and analyze data. First, each manager completed a questionnaire on every other manager in his T Group. The questionnaire was designed within the Likert framework but geared to assess individual behavior in a T Group. After each manager had received the results from his T-Group peers, he met with the T-C for help in analyzing the data. A T-Group session following this analysis was used for processing concerns raised by the data.

The final event in this phase was particularly significant to the entire design. It consisted of the T-C's making available to the manager the profiled results of data collected prior to the laboratory from the manager's organizational subordinates and peers.

Thus, at this point the manager had available comprehensive data which included: (a) systematized perceptions of his management behavior in his organization; (b) feedback he had obtained from the T Group and exercise sessions of the laboratory, and the analysis of this in previous consultations; (c) systematized perceptions of his T-Group behavior; and (d) the resources of a T-C.

The hazard of data overload was reduced by the single conceptual organization of most of the data and by allowing a considerable amount of time for processing in private consultation. The substantial impact of this event derived from the direct relatability of laboratory data to organizational data by the single framework. Plainly, the manager had considerable data about himself in relevant roles—and in what to him was management language. The T-C helped the manager relate the various pieces of data and make his own personal assessments.

Phase IV

In Phase IV the managers were requested to decide for themselves what activities would be most useful. They chose continuous T Grouping. There were, therefore, no further consultations or data collections.

APPLICATION TO THE ORGANIZATION

The first laboratory took place in May 1968. Since that time two more laboratory programs have been conducted which utilized the same design. Approximately 90 managers have gone through the change programs. After the first group, the next groups included the subordinates of those managers who had attended the first session, with the plan in mind of building a pool of persons with a common experience with whom the consultant could continue to work in the organization.

Initially, the T-Cs had no specific design for working with the participants back in the plant, except for a general notion of continuing the consulting started at the laboratory. However, it was discovered that practically all the managers felt a strong desire to reveal to their subordinates something about their laboratory experiences, including data and analysis of the questionnaire ratings which the subordinates had given them. It became the role of the T-C to help the managers plan and carry out such a communication process. Sometimes the T-C agreed to present the Likert framework in order to give the subordinates background and introduction to the data analysis.

Results of these meetings with subordinates have varied widely. Some managers presented the data, had a limited discussion, but did little follow-through for reasons to be discussed. Others used this as a base for continuing a set of problem-solving meetings to work on the issues raised by the data. As might be predicted, the meetings of a manager with his staff were characterized by the following processes:

1. *Initial Threat*. This was a unique experience for almost all of the persons involved. By and large the culture of the company did not have norms that supported such openness of discussion. People were often embarrassed and uncertain about what to say and do.

2. *Reluctance to Respond and Flight*. After the manager and/or T-C had reported the laboratory experience and data, subordinates

were asked to respond. This invitation was met by reluctance and often by elements of flight behavior.

3. *Provisional Resolution.* If the units were able to deal with the first two conditions, an attempt to work out resolutions to problems raised followed. The units which decided to continue generally set up procedures and times to work on the issues raised in the early meetings. It was noted that the units that did not continue could not make decisions to work on their own staff problems. The continuing groups have gone in different directions: Some have initiated direct family T Groups; some have used data collection-feedback sessions; others have stayed with the discussion of the original laboratory-generated data.

Continued OD Efforts

Results of the program have been determined by reports coming directly from the T-Cs working with the managers; systematic research designs have not been used. The direct reporting and anecdotal data indicate that about 25 per cent of the managers who have participated in the three laboratories over a one-and-one-half-year period have *not* continued in any detectable OD efforts beyond the first meetings. Another 50 per cent are continuing to make an effort toward OD, but the results are not considered totally effective by the T-Cs who are working with them. The remaining 25 per cent have accomplished and are continuing to work on organizational change efforts that are considered significant improvements.

One manager who has been seen as particularly effective was perceived in the prelaboratory data as being very stiff and formal with his men; and since he was younger in age than most of his subordinates, some real barriers were created in working effectively with them. His organization, a staff service to a production operation, was, up to that time, widely judged to be mediocre in effectiveness. As a result of the laboratory experience, the manager and his T-C began a series of team-building meetings which reduced the level of formality, rigid role differentiation, intellectualization, and one-way influence. As this manager's staff team changed, the effect spread to the other parts of the organization because of the renewed energy exhibited by his staff. Organization improvement in terms of hard data began to emerge. As the case continues, recently this manager was given an unusually substantial promotion. He was placed in charge of a sizable plant whose business is critical and which has experienced considerable difficulty. His superior acknowledged that a year before this manager would not have been considered for the new position, but the fact that he was able to change and was able to bring about an improvement in his organization gave them some confidence that perhaps he had learned how to bring about change in another problem situation.

Characteristics of Abortive OD Efforts

Where managers have not continued to develop an improvement program, it has been felt that one or a combination of negative factors has been present in the following organizational components:

1. *The Manager.* Some managers have not seemed to benefit from the laboratory experience either for certain personal reasons or because their own anxiety about engaging in an open, leveling process with subordinates has been so high as to make further action difficult.

2. *The Organization.* It has become painfully evident that certain parts of the organization culture do not support continuing OD efforts. Sometimes the manager who went through the laboratory was faced with a boss who would not support new behaviors. Others found that work pressures requiring frequent travel, heavy overtime, and urgent time deadlines prevented the manager from moving ahead with the development meetings he would have liked holding.

3. *The T-C.* It must be admitted that this is no "game" for a novice. Inappropriate interviewing or mistimed or inadequately handled interventions by the T-C have undoubtedly had negative effects. This issue is so sensitive that a single fault by a T-C has in some instances permanently blocked further OD efforts for some units.

Four models are now being used to engage the participating managers in development activity. These are: (a) private consulting with the participating manager, (b) process interventions in regular business meetings, (c) direct and instrumented examination of staff teamwork in meetings established especially for this purpose both on and off plant premises, and (d) data collection and feedback from subordinates and other organizational members using a Likert conceptual framework to assess interpersonal data and as a data source for staff group action. (No T-C is engaged in private consulting with his participating manager as an exclusive process. Private consulting when used is being done in combination with one or more of the other processes.)

CRITIQUE

In reviewing the approach thus far, several weak and strong points can be identified. Two problems emerged during the laboratory, and another became visible during the application period.

Weaknesses

One problem concerns the number of managers worked with by the T-Cs. One T-C brought nine managers to the laboratory while another brought only one. The remaining ratios fell between these. Therefore, while in the 1-to-1 ratio team the T-C could spend a given time period in individual consultation, team ratios of more than one manager required the T-C either to reduce the individual time or work in sub-groups. Although the design was timed to provide as much balance as possible, the consensus among the training staff was that more consulting time was available than the low-ratio teams could productively use and not enough time was available for the high-ratio teams. The optimum ratio for this design seemed to be about three managers per T-C.

Another problem concerned the use of one of the questionnaires. It was anticipated that collecting and feeding back group process information via the Likert framework during the first-day marathon would aid group development as well as introduce the framework and the use of quantitative methods. In fact, the managers displayed very little interest in these data, and it was not observable that the method had any effect, positive or negative. It is probable that such quantitative data were too "cold" to fit the context of the personal involvement of a marathon in a T Group.

Another problem has become visible during organizational application attempts. A few of the managers, while highly motivated to apply, have defined change goals more in terms of others than of themselves.

Strengths

The entire project to date has yielded several results which are considered highly valuable. It is clear that a successful relationship has been built between the T-C and his managers. From all observations of the T-Cs, their managers see them as useful resources, understand the nature of their role, and are desirous of utilizing them as adjuncts in the manager's back-home application efforts.

As indicated, a majority of the managers have either initiated application activity or have voiced intentions of doing so. This is interpreted as a clear indication that the project has produced an intention to apply laboratory learnings. At this point, there is every reason to believe that training will be transferred to the job in significant ways.

With respect to the laboratory features which can be judged as helpful, the following appear salient:

First-Day Marathon. This "up-front" period of continuous and intensive T Grouping was judged by the staff as moving the groups to a point approximating the third day of a standard laboratory design.

Single Conceptual Framework. The staff considered the use of a single overall framework to be quite useful. During the laboratory it provided a consistent set of dimensions which were inclusive enough to refer and relate most of the laboratory phenomena as well as organizational phenomena. This framework has continued to be highly useful as an organizing system for considering application goals and approaches.

Relating Laboratory and Organizational Data. It was apparent to all the staff that having an opportunity to compare laboratory-produced data with data from their organizational realities was highly valuable for the managers. It provided a means of cross-validation and of relating similar concepts. It seemed a sufficient method for combating the typical tendency to compartmentalize laboratory experiences.

Cross-Feed Between Consultations and Other Laboratory Activities. The T Group and focused exercises provided the data source for consultations; on the other hand, the consultations had a visible effect on managerial behavior in the T Groups and focused exercises. Many a T-C observed his manager's explicit attempts in the T Groups to explore dimensions which the consultations had previously exposed and dealt with. It is difficult to assess, but the staff impression was that private consultations produced a beneficial effect on the more traditional laboratory experiences.

Application Problems

In terms of organization application it seems that the Likert framework has given an expectation for and a focus on changing an entire organization. The managers have worked at the level of their own staff—a small-group orientation. They are impatient with the length of time which is seemingly required to change a total organization. We feel it important that the laboratory give the small-group element a greater emphasis and that it help managers to see that the place to begin to influence the total organization is to improve group process within their own staff.

More attention needs to be given to careful selection of participants for the program. It seems that there are some types of managers

located in certain kinds of situations for whom the laboratory experience can result only in minimal change efforts. If these can be identified, perhaps managers can be selected in whom greater possibilities
for change are present.

It is our belief also that the laboratory should focus more attention
on change strategies in addition to self-insight, interpersonal, and
group and organization learnings. Managers who plan to engage in
change efforts need to learn more skills, e.g., how to conduct confrontation meetings, data collection and feedback sessions, process
analysis of meetings, team-building meetings, and so on.

CONCLUSION

The field of behavioral science interventions has developed a number
of approaches to planned organizational change. The one reported
here has been a systematic attempt to utilize workable features from a
variety of methods. It has been shown to be possible to build a laboratory design which incorporates internal T-Cs, quantitative data collection and feedback, and a single general conceptual framework into
the more traditional laboratory experiences of T Group, exercises, and
theory input. The total approach, which has been evaluated as successfully facilitating entry into the organization and transfer of laboratory learnings into the back-home setting, hinges tightly on the
continued use of an internal resource person.

REFERENCES

Argyris, C. Explorations and issues in laboratory education. *Explorations in
    human relations Training and Research*, 1966, 3, 15.
Beckhard, R. An organizational improvement program in a decentralized
    organization. *Journal of Applied Behavioral Science*, 1966, 2(1), 3-25.
Blake, R. R., Mouton, J. S., & Sloma, R. L. The union-management intergroup
    laboratory. *Journal of Applied Behavioral Science*, 1965, 1(1), 25-57.
Harrison, R. Cognitive models for interpersonal and group behavior: A theo-
    retical framework for research. *Explorations in human relations Training
    and Research*, 1965, 2, 109-110.
Likert, R. *New patterns of management*. New York: McGraw-Hill, 1961.
Mann, F. C. Studying and creating change: A means to understanding social
    organizations. In C. M. Arensberg, S. Barkin, W. E. Chalmers, H. L.
    Wilensky, J. C. Worthy, & B. D. Dennis (Eds.), *Research in industrial
    human relations*. New York: Harper & Row, 1957.

RE-EXAMINING THE RCA EXPERIENCE

William G. Dyer

It is an interesting experience to review and analyze an article written about a program that you conducted nearly ten years earlier. My first reactions were of surprise and pleasure. I thought, "That's really a pretty good design—I'm still proud of what we did."

As I look more closely at the program we designed for RCA, I feel that there are some things that I would do differently given the same conditions; I would push for some changes now that may not be possible even now.

In the original program we tried to involve internal training people more in internal consulting and to increase management's acceptance of this new role. I still think the program was good for this purpose. All of the internal trainer-consultants (T-Cs) did interact with some managers—with varied results. If we were to do the program again, I would want to be explicit about the follow-up agreement between a T-C and a manager. I would want each manager to develop a detailed plan about his or her program for change, including the role of the T-C. This was rather loose and ambiguous in the original format. A better plan would have been for the manager and T-C to agree on the specific action steps, time frame, and method for evaluating results and to agree on a schedule for working together over the next six to twelve months.

I would also want to alter some of the training given to the T-Cs, because I think we know more about consulting theory, method, and technology than we did at that time. We trained the T-Cs for only two days prior to the management laboratory. I would push now to bring them together two or three times over several months to review what they were doing and to give them additional coaching and training to deal with the specific situations they were facing. The whole follow-up activity was weak in the original program, although this is generally true of most change efforts.

It would have been helpful if levels of management had been linked so that each manager could set his or her change plans in connection with a boss, supported by the internal T-C. The change plan would include meetings with one's boss, who would provide a formal review of what was being done.

I also would like to have seen more evaluation done in connection with change plans. If each manager in the change program could have better feedback about what was happening as a result of his efforts, this would be a great stimulus to continue. If data were gathered prior to the training program on such factors as output, profits, costs, morale, turnover, accuracy, etc., and the same data were gathered later, we would have a better idea of the impact of a manager's performance in certain key areas. It would also be useful to gather data again from each manager's subordinates and peers three and four months after the original program to see if any improvements were made in any way connected with the manager. I also would gather data from superiors and have the manager fill out a self-perception instrument. We are now capable of handling this type of information by a detailed computer print-out that pinpoints strengths and weaknesses and identifies goals for change.

In the original design, the management-training program was basically a T-group with some management activities, during which time the T-C observed and consulted with the managers. The back-home data were reported at the *end* of the training week. If I could repeat the study, I would reverse the process. I would give the back-home data on beginning a program of change to the manager, then have the manager try to implement some of his or her change goals during the week. The T-C could consult with the manager on how well he or she was working on the improvement plan. Then the focus would be on areas identified as needing improvement.

In the original article we mentioned that there should have been a better method for selection of participants. Selection is especially important because all of the data on change indicate that people do not change unless there is a felt need—a sense of "hurt." I would try to select only those managers who identified some real, specific reason to have the training. This would eliminate those who participate because they want some time away, or because it's "their turn," or because someone else thinks it would be useful.

Through the years I have become increasingly pessimistic about management-training programs that are the domain of staff training people who are separate from management functions. I would like to see a group of high-level managers be responsible for the development of management within their system. If I could repeat this study, I would like to have the managers be involved in the design, help in the training process, evaluate the results, and devise ways to ensure the continued impact of the results on the management process. They would be responsible for finding ways to support new ways of doing performance appraisals and giving promotions and raises. Orientation programs could be planned to emphasize the new philosophy and specify the style of management that was expected. Then it might be possible for the laboratory-consultation approach that we originally created to have some real impact on the organization.

A Systems Approach
to Organization Development

Michael Beer

Edgar F. Huse

Organization development (OD) efforts are often exclusively oriented to one method, one set of theoretical concepts, or one organizational variable. An input-process-output model of an organization was used as a framework for planned change.[1] The program dealt with many organizational dimensions and used several intervention strategies and OD technologies. The effort resulted in substantial changes in organizational inputs, processes, and outputs. A number of findings about organization development have emerged from this OD experience and include the following: (1) OD efforts must not always start at the top; (2) the organization itself is the best laboratory for learning; (3) structural and interpersonal changes must complement and reinforce each other; (4) adult learning starts with behavioral change rather than cognitive change; and (5) the selection of change leaders as initial targets for the change program is a useful OD strategy.

Although the plant has since grown considerably, at the beginning of the change effort there were approximately 35 hourly employees, mostly women; some 15 weekly salaried technical and clerical

Based on a paper presented as part of a symposium entitled "Organizational Change," at the American Psychological Association Convention, Washington, D.C., September 3, 1969.

[1]The authors would like to acknowledge the innovative and farsighted approaches to management implemented by the managers and supervisors of the organization described. Particular thanks are due to J. G. Sabin, C. F. Wheatley, and J. Johnson. Many others were and are involved, and we thank them also.

personnel; and approximately eight professional and managerial personnel, who were paid monthly.

Some particulars about this plant which need to be considered in generalizing the results obtained in this study to other organizations follow: (1) the products are complex; (2) the operation is primarily assembly, as opposed to fabrication; (3) a majority of factory workers are women; (4) the organization is nonunion; and (5) the organization is relatively small. In other words, approaches which might work with female assembly workers in a nonunion plant might not have the same impact with male union workers in a plant utilizing a different technology.

Because the organization was relatively new when this organization development effort started, it did not have a well-established historical culture and set of norms. It was in its formative stages, and crucial decisions were in the making concerning the technology in the plant (means of production), methods of setting production standards and controls, personnel practices and policies, managerial practices and philosophy, and the like. For example, at the time of our entry this was one of the relatively few nonunionized plants in an organization having about 50 geographically separate plants. Thus, an opportunity existed to do work in a plant which had not yet completely internalized the practices and traditions of older plants and of the corporation as a whole.

INTRODUCTION AND HISTORICAL PERSPECTIVE

> Since I've been working here, my husband is a much better supervisor in *his* plant. I tell him what he should do to make his people more interested in what they are doing—based on what *our* supervisors do here. (*Assembly Worker*)

> I hate to say it, but I think that I could be off the manufacturing floor for a month and my girls would still make the manufacturing schedule. (*First-Line Supervisor*)

The comments above were gathered in one plant of a large company which, for several years, has been the focus of a successful systems approach to organizational development (OD) at all levels. It is important to point out at the outset that no single OD approach was used with this plant. Rather, in the systems approach, a wide variety of behavioral science concepts concerning organizational change and effective management were operationalized.

This article is written to provide the reader with an understanding of the systems organizational model that guided our efforts as change agents; to describe the varied approaches used for organizational change; and to describe the results and what we have learned about the process of change and its prospects in large, complex organizations. Rather than consigning the conclusions to the end, we shall underscore our major findings as we proceed through the sections of the case study.

The organizational development program took place in a plant designing and manufacturing complex instruments for medical and laboratory use.

Through the efforts of the personnel supervisor, enough interest existed initially for our holding a series of seminars which contrasted traditional approaches with newer approaches based on behavioral research findings and theory. Although these seminars never succeeded in getting an explicit decision on the pattern of management that would prevail in the plant (indeed, as will be discussed later, there was considerable resistance to "theory"), they did start to unfreeze the managerial group (which was steeped in the tradition of the parent organization) sufficiently to commit themselves to "trying" some new approaches on a very limited basis. This constituted much less than commitment to a new pattern of management, but it did open the door to experimentation and examination.

Overworked Theories

A number of practitioners of OD stress the importance of top management commitment to OD if such a program is to be successful. As one author puts it, "Without such support, we have found no program of this kind can ever succeed. . . . First, we worked with top managers to help them fully understand. . . . This proved vital, not only in helping their understanding of the concepts but also in earning their commitment to the program" (Roche & MacKinnon, 1970). In the same vein, Beckhard (1969) and Blake and Mouton (1969) stress that OD must be planned and managed from the top down.

Certainly no one would dispute the proposition that top management commitment to OD is highly valuable and helpful. However, our experience in this study [Finding 1] indicates that a clear-cut commitment at the top of the organizational unit to a particular OD approach is not necessary for a development program to succeed. Indeed, an attempt to obtain too strong a commitment from top management in the early stages may be threatening enough to cause the withdrawal of any commitment to planned change, especially since the concept of OD and its technologies (e.g., Theory Y, job enrichment, sensitivity training, and the like) are foreign and threatening to the established beliefs of many managers.

Moreover, we found [Finding 2] that total top management understanding of where the OD process will lead and the state of the *organization at the end is not necessary for successful programs to take place.* Indeed, given the current state of the art, the OD practitioner himself may not have a clear view of the road ahead, except in very general terms.

What *is* necessary is that someone in a strategic position feel the need for change and improvement. In our plant, that person was the personnel supervisor. Although the plant manager was mildly interested in the initial stages, he was mainly submitting to pressures from the personnel man. Throughout his tenure in the plant, the plant manager's commitment and interest mildly increased, but he was never a strong proponent nor the most skilled manager in some of the new approaches. Furthermore, the plant manager's "boss" never fully knew what was going on in the plant nor did he ever commit himself in any way to the OD program. We now believe that it is possible to change a relatively autonomous unit of a larger organization without the total commitment or understanding of top management in that unit and, in larger and more complex organizations, even without their knowledge.

Initial Commitment to New Approaches

In addition to felt need, the second essential condition is that there be, somewhere in the organization, some initial commitment to experimentation, application, and evaluation of new approaches to present problems. A case study report by the second author (Huse, 1965) describes a successful OD program that took place because a middle manager in a large organization felt the need for change and requested help. He could not have cared less about specific OD principles. He simply wanted help in improving his organization. Davis (1967) points out, in his now classic case study, that top management was not really involved at the beginning and that a majority of the effort was expended in "on-the-job situations, working out real problems with the people who are involved with them."

Of course, it is obvious that top management support of both theory and practice makes it easier for the change agent; conversely, the lack of such support increases the risk involved for consultants and managers, and causes other systems problems, as we shall discuss later in this article. Furthermore, the conditions of a felt need, a strong and self-sufficient commitment to change, and relative unit autonomy are needed. What we are saying is that the commonly heard dicta that one must start at the top and that top management must be committed to a set of normative principles are overworked. *Change can and does begin at lower levels in an organization* [Finding 3].

A CONCEPTUAL MODEL

If the client system and its management in this case did not (need to) have specific OD concepts in mind, who did? The change agents did.

It is important that the change agent have in mind an organizational model and a flexible set of normative concepts about management with a systems orientation. The organizational model should be general and reflect the complex *interactive* nature of systems variables. The concepts must be updated and changed as new research findings become available and as more is learned about the functioning of the client system, the environment in which the client system operates, and the effects of changes made in the client system. This is, of course, an iterative procedure.

Figure 1 represents the model of organizational change which guided our efforts. This model has some basic characteristics which must be understood if we are to see how it can shape the planning of a change effort. It represents an organization as an open system engaged in a conversion process. Employee needs, expectations, and abilities are among the raw materials (inputs) with which a manager must work to achieve his objectives.

Organizations have many processes. Figure 1 includes only the more important ones in general terms, and these exist at both the structural and interpersonal levels. Leadership and communication, for example, are two of the interpersonal dimensions which serve to pull together, integrate, and shape the behavior of organizational members. They convert into effort and attitudes the potential brought to the organization in the form of needs and abilities of individuals. The structure or formalized dimensions of the organization obviously cannot exist independently of the interpersonal variables, but they are different from the interpersonal variables in terms of their susceptibility to managerial control, the means by which they might be changed, and the timing of their change. Previous literature on organizational change has emphasized interpersonal variables; more recent literature (Lawrence & Lorsch, 1969) has emphasized structural variables. It is our opinion, based upon experience, that both interpersonal and structural variables are crucial to effective organizational change. The effects of organizational design or managerial control systems on employees have been researched and documented but are still insufficiently understood. For example, we are convinced that an operant conditioning model can be used to understand the behavior of managers with respect to controls. "Beating" goals and looking good on standard measures are like food pellets to the manager.

In the output column, we have listed multiple outcomes. These are not completely independent, but they are conceptually distinctive

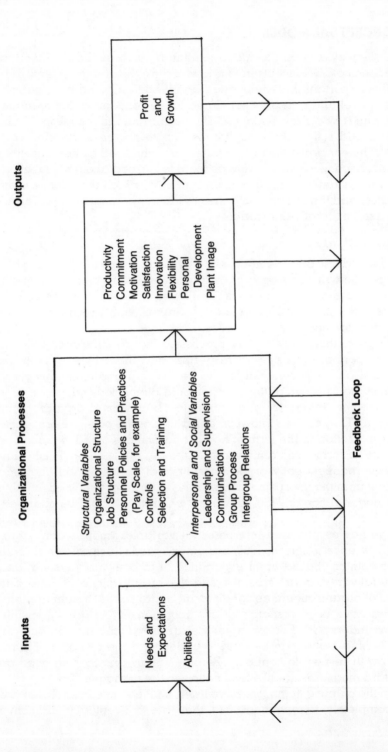

Figure 1. Systems Model of an Organization

enough in their relationship to the organizational process variables that it is useful to think of them individually. It is the optimization of the organizational outputs that leads to long-term profitability and growth for employees and the organization. Other final outcomes could be listed if we were discussing organizations with different objectives.

Inherent in this model are several basic notions: An organization is an open system which, from the human point of view, converts individual needs and expectations into outputs. Organizational outputs can be increased by improving the quality of the input. An example of this would be the selection of people with higher levels of ability and needs. However, because there are costs associated with selecting personnel of higher quality, we might say that efficiency has not increased. The organization may improve its performance, but this gain has been obtained only because the input, i.e., the quality of personnel has improved, not because there has been a change in the manner in which the organization *utilizes* its human resources.

Since organizations are open systems, organizational performance can also improve by unleashing more of the potential inherent in the human resources. If you will, outputs will increase because we have made the conversion process more efficient. This can be done, for example, by designing organizational processes which better fit the organization's environment or by changing organizational processes so that human resources can be fully unleashed and brought to bear on the task and objectives of the organization. The adjustment of organizational processes to reflect more accurately the needs of the environment and of the persons in it is one of the key objectives of our organizational development program.

Figure 1[2] does not cover some of the more traditional but vitally important concepts of an organization as a total system. For example, capital budgets, the R & D thrust of an organization, overhead or indirect budgets, and the marketing direction of an organization are extremely important aspects which need to be considered. Blake and Mouton (1969) have developed the Corporate Excellence Rubric as a means of assessing the health of the organization through a traditional functional framework. Furthermore, current research (Lawrence & Lorsch, 1969) points up the fact that the differentiation of functional units has a tremendous influence upon the effectiveness of an organization. However, for purposes of brevity, these aspects are not covered in this article.

---

[2] Cf. The traditional aspects included in the conceptual model developed by Huse (1969).

Mechanisms of Change

We chose an eclectic approach to create change in the organizational processes listed in Figure 1, with the basic belief that a variety of approaches to change should be used with the plant in question. The primary mechanism was consulting, counseling, and feedback by a team of four. The primary change agents were the personnel man within the organization (there have been four different ones since the OD effort began); Beer as an external-to-the-plant agent but internal to the organization, and Huse as the outside change agent. The fourth member of the team was a research assistant whose responsibility it was to interview and gather data in the client system for diagnostic and feedback uses by the change agents. [3]

We began a basic strategy of establishing working relationships with individuals at all levels of the organization. We operated as resource persons who could be used to solve specific problems or initiate small experiments in management; we tried to encourage someone or some organizational component to start implementing the concepts inherent in our model of an organization. Managers gained familiarity with these ideas through consultation and, to a much lesser extent and without full understanding, from the initial few seminars that we held. The main ingredients were a problem or a desire to change and improve, combined with action recommendations from the change agents. Soon there were a few individuals throughout the organization who began, with our help, to apply some new approaches. Because most of these approaches were successful, the result was increased motivation to change. To a degree, nothing succeeds like success!

Models for Learning

There are at least two basic models for learning. The traditional method, that of the classroom and seminar, stresses theory and cognitive concepts before action. As Argyris (1967) points out, "The traditional educational models emphasize substance, rationality. . . ." However, a number of authors (Bartlett, 1967; Bradford, 1964; Schein & Bennis, 1965) make the point that behavior is another place to start. For example, Huse (1966) has shown that one's own facts are "much more powerful instruments of change than facts or principles generated and presented by an outside 'expert.'" The process of change in this OD

---

[3] We should like to acknowledge the help and participation of Gloria Gery and Joan Doolittle in the data-gathering phase.

effort started with behavioral recommendations, was followed by appropriate reinforcement and feedback, and then proceeded to attitudinal and cognitive changes.

Figure 2 summarizes the basic concept from our experience. *Effective and permanent adult learning [Finding 4] comes after the individual has experimented with new approaches and received appropriate feedback in the on-the-job situation.* This approach is analogous to, but somewhat different from, the here-and-now learning in the T Group.

In other words, a manager might have a problem. Without discussing theory, the change agent might make some recommendations relating to the specific situation at hand. If, in the here-and-now, the manager was successful in the attempt to solve the problem, this would lead to another try, as well as a change in his attitude toward OD. This approach capitalizes upon the powerful here-and-now influence which the job and the organizational climate can have upon the individual. Indeed, such changes can occur without any knowledge of theory.

Either model of learning can probably work to produce change in the individual. However, if one starts with cognitive facts and theory

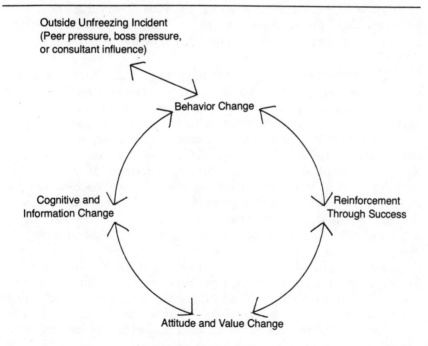

Figure 2. The Learning Process

(as in seminars), this may be less effective and less authentic than starting with the individual's own here-and-now behavior in the ongoing job situation. In any case, the process is a cyclic one, involving behavior, attitudes, and cognition, each reinforcing the other. In our case, there was an early resistance to seminars and the presentation of "Theory." However, after behavior and attitude changes occurred, there began to be more and more requests for cognitive inputs through reading, seminars, and the like. It is at this later stage that seminars and "theory inputs" would seem to be of most value.

That learning starts with behavior and personal experience has been one of the most important things we have learned as we have worked to effect organizational change. The process is quite similar to what is intended to happen in laboratory training. What we have found [Finding 5] is that *the operating, ongoing organization may, indeed, be the best "laboratory" for learning.* This knowledge may save us from an overreliance upon sensitivity training described by Bennis (1968) when he states that "when you read the pages of this Journal, you cannot but think that we're a one-product outfit with a 100 per cent fool-proof patent medicine." This finding may also be the answer in dealing with Campbell and Dunnette's (1968) conclusions that "while T-Group training seems to produce observable changes in behavior, the utility of these changes for the performance of individuals in their organizational roles remains to be demonstrated."

The Unfreezing Process. What triggers an individual to unfreeze and to allow the process to begin, if it is not "theory"? First, there are some individuals who are ready to change behavior as soon as the opportunity presents itself in the form of an outside change agent. These are people who seem to be aware of problems and have a desire to work on them. Sometimes all that they need are some suggestions or recommendations as to different approaches or methods they may try. If their experiences are successful, they become change leaders in their own right. *They then [Finding 6] are natural targets for the change agent, since they become opinion leaders that help shape a culture that influences others in the organization to begin to experiment and try out new behaviors.* As Davis (1967) points out, it is necessary to "provide a situation which could initiate the process of freeing up these potential multipliers from the organizational and personal constraints which . . . kept them from responding effectively to their awareness of the problems." Davis used "strangers" and "cousins" laboratories. In our case, the unfreezing process was done almost exclusively in the immediate job context.

An early example of the development of change leaders in our work with this company was the successful joint effort of an engineer and a supervisor to redesign a hotplate assembly operation which would eliminate an assembly line and give each worker total responsibility for the assembly of a particular product. It resulted in a productivity increase of close to 50 per cent, a drop in rejects from 23 per cent, controllable rejects to close to 1 per cent, and a reduction in absenteeism from about 8 per cent to less than 1 per cent in a few months. Not all the early experiments were successful, but mistakes were treated as part of the experiential learning process.

As some in the organization changed and moved ahead by trying out new behaviors, others watched and waited but were eventually influenced by the culture. An example of late changers so influenced was the supervisor of Materials Control, who watched for two years what was going on in the plant but basically disagreed with the concepts of OD. Then he began to feel pressure to change because his peers were trying new things and he was not. He began by experimenting with enriching his secretary's job and found, in his own words, that "she was doing three times as much, enjoying it more, and giving me more time to manage." When he found that this experiment in managerial behavior had "paid off," he began to take a more active interest in OD. His next step was to completely reorganize his department to push decision making down the ladder, to utilize a team approach, and to enrich jobs. He supervised four sections: purchasing, inventory control, plant scheduling, and expediting. Reorganization of Materials Control was around product line teams. Each group had total project responsibility for its own product lines, including the four functions described above. We moved slowly and discussed with him alternative ways of going about the structural change. When he made the change, his subordinates were prepared and ready. The results were clear: In a three-month period of time (with the volume of business remaining steady), the parts shortage list was reduced from 14 I.B.M. pages to less than a page. In other words, although he was a late-changer in terms of the developing culture, his later actions were highly successful.

The influence of the developing culture was also documented through interviews with new employees coming into the plant. The perception by production employees that this was a "different" place to work occurred almost immediately, and changes in behavior of management personnel were clear by the second month.

In other words, while seminars and survey feedback techniques were used in our work with this plant, the initial and most crucial changes were achieved through a work-centered, consulting-counseling approach, e.g., through discussion with managers and others about work-related problems, following the model of adult learning described earlier.

So much for the manner in which the unfreezing process occurred and some of our learning about this process. What were some of the normative concepts applied and why? A brief overview of our approaches and findings follows.

A NORMATIVE MODEL

Communications

In this phase we attempted to open up communications at all levels. We started monthly meetings at every level of the organization, as well as a weekly meeting between the plant manager and a sample of production and clerical employees. The aim was to institutionalize the meetings to serve as a means for exchanging information and ideas about what had happened and what needed to happen. The meetings, especially between first-line supervisors and production workers, began primarily as one-way communications downward. Little by little, qualitative changes occurred and the meetings shifted to two-way communications about quality, schedules, and production problems. This effort to communicate (which was also extended through many other approaches) was an entire year in attaining success. It was an agonizingly slow process of change. In retrospect, this was a critical period during which trust was building and a culture conducive to further change was developing. Out of this, we concluded [*Finding 7*] that *organizational change occurs in stages: a stage of unfreezing and trust building, a take-off stage when observable change occurs, and a stabilization stage. Then the cycle iterates.* In addition to the communication type of meeting described above, confrontation meetings between departments were also held (Blake, Shepard, & Mouton, 1964). These, too, improved relationships between departments, over time.

Job Enrichment

A second area of change was in job structure, primarily through the use of job enrichment, or, as it has been called in the plant, "the total job concept." We have already discussed the importance of the job for psychological growth and development—our findings in this area parallel those of Ford (1969). Our first experience of tearing down a hotplate assembly line has already been discussed. This was followed by similar job enrichment efforts in other areas. In one department, girls individually assemble instruments containing thousands of parts and costing several thousand dollars. The change here allowed production workers to have great responsibility for quality checks and calibration (instead of trained technicians). In another case, the changeover involved an instrument which had been produced for several years. Here, production was increased by 17 per cent with a corresponding increase in quality; absenteeism was reduced by more than 50 per cent.

The plant is presently engaged in completely removing quality control inspection from some departments, leaving final inspection to the workers themselves. In other departments, workers have been organized into autonomous workgroups with total responsibility for scheduling, assembly, training, and some quality control inspection (the source for the supervisor's laudatory quote at the beginning of this case study). Changes in these areas have evolved out of an attempt to utilize the positive forces of cohesive workgroups. However, like Ford (1969), we have found that not everyone in the assembly workforce responds positively to such changes, although a high majority do so over time.

Mutual goal setting has also been widely adopted. Instead of standards established by engineering (a direction in which the plant was heading when we started), goals for each department are derived from the plant goal, and individual goals for the week or month are developed in individual departments through discussions between the boss and subordinates. Our interview data clearly show that in this way workers understand how their individual goals fit into the plant goal structure and can work on their own without close supervision for long periods of time.

Changes toward a pay process more clearly based on merit (including appraisals for hourly and weekly salaried clerical and technical employees as well as for managerial and professional personnel) were made to reinforce and legitimate an escalating climate of work involvement. More and more employees are now involved in questions of production, quality, department layout, and methods. Assembly workers give department tours to visitors, including vice presidents. Organization-wide technical and product information sessions are held. Concerned more with strategy than with daily problems, the top team has for some time molded itself into a business team, meeting periodically to discuss future plans.

More recently, changes in organizational structure are taking place to move a functionally oriented organization to a matrix organization, using concepts derived directly from Lawrence and Lorsch (1969). This involves, among other approaches, the use of "integrators" at varying levels within the organization.

Systems Interaction

A systems approach requires that mutually consistent changes in *all* subsystems be made in affecting the organizational processes listed in our model. In other words, [*Finding 8*] *multiple changes in the subsystems are needed for the individual employee to change behavior and perceptions of his role.* For example, participative supervision should be accompanied by redesign of jobs to allow more responsibility, by a pay system that recognizes performance, by a communication system that is truly open, and by corresponding changes in other subsystems throughout the organization. Past attempts to change organizations through a nonsystems approach, e.g., through such single media as supervisory training or sensitivity training, have had limited success because other key leverage points have not been changed in the total system. Further, an attempt to change one subsystem too quickly or too drastically can have severely harmful results, as pointed out in the "Hovey and Beard Company" case (Lawrence, Bailey, Katz, Seiler, Orth, Clark, Barnes, & Turner, 1961). Whether structural or interpersonal changes should take precedence in a given period of time depends upon the readiness of the system to change and the key leverage points. The key concept [*Finding 9*] is that *structural and interpersonal systems changes must reinforce and legitimate each other.* Figure 3 presents this concept. The change can be in either direction in the model.

We also learned [*Finding 10*] that *systems changes set off additional interactive processes in which changes in organizational functioning increase not only outputs but also develop the latent abilities of people.* We have concluded that the real potential in organizational development lies in setting in motion such a positive snowball of change, growth, and development. For example, as assembly workers took on additional responsibility they became more and more concerned about the total organization and product. "Mini-gripes" turned into "mega-gripes," indicating a change in the maturity of the assembly workers (Huse & Price, 1970). At the same time, this freed up management personnel to be less concerned about daily assignments and more concerned about long-range planning.

To illustrate this, at the beginning of the OD effort, the organization had a plant manager, a production superintendent, and three first-line supervisors, or a total of five supervisory personnel in the direct manufacturing line. As the assembly line workers took on more responsibility, the five have been reduced to three (the plant manager and two first-line supervisors). The number of inspection and quality control personnel has also been reduced.

A Subsystem Within the Larger Organization

Up to this point in the case study we have been considering the plant as a system in its own right. However, changes set in motion here have also provided the first step in a larger plan for change and development to occur in the parent corporation (consisting of some 50 plants). As a subsystem within the larger system, this plant was to serve as a model for the rest of the corporation—as an example of how change should be planned and implemented. It was our hope that the systems approach to change would create such a clearly different culture in this plant that it would become visible to the rest of the corporation; that people from other segments of the larger organization would visit and become interested in trying similar models and mechanisms of change. Our hopes have been realized. Indeed, both authors are now applying OD concepts to other areas of the organization.

Influence is also exerted upward, with greater acceptance of these concepts by individuals at higher levels in the organization [Finding 11]. It is our perception that changes in organizational subsystems can have strong influences on the larger culture if the change is planned and publicized; if seed personnel are transferred to other parts of the system; if a network of change agents is clearly identified; and if careful planning goes into where and how change resources are

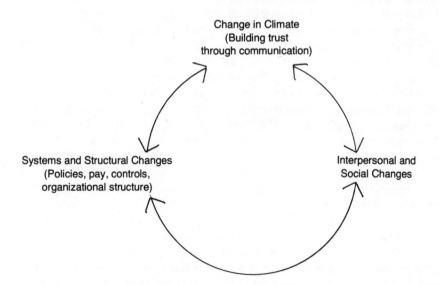

Figure 3. The Sequence of Organizational Change

to be used. Once again, top management commitment is not a necessary commitment for evolutionary change in a complex, multidivision, multilocation organization. (*Sometimes*, the tail begins to wag the dog.)

Subsystem Difficulties

However, this change process may cause some difficulties in the area of interface between the smaller subsystem and the larger system. For example, the increased responsibilities, commitment, and involvement represented by job enrichment for assembly workers are not adequately represented in the normal job evaluation program for factory workers and are difficult to handle adequately within the larger system. So pay and pay system changes must be modified to fit modern OD concepts. Figure 4 is a model which shows the effects of change in climate on individual model perceptions of equity in pay.

In addition to the larger system difficulties over wage plans, there still exists a great deal of controversy as to the importance of pay as a motivator (or dissatisfier). For example, Walton (1967) takes a basically pessimistic approach about participation through the informal approach, as opposed to the more formal approaches embodied in the Scanlon Plan (Lesieur, 1958), which "stress the economic rewards which can come from [formal] participation." On the other hand, Paul, Robertson, and Herzberg (1969) review a number of job enrichment projects and report: "In no instance did management face a demand of this kind [higher pay or better conditions] as a result of changes made in the studies." In a recent review of the Scanlon Plan (Lesieur & Puckett, 1969), the authors point out that Scanlon's first application did not involve the use of financial incentives but, rather, a common sharing between management and employees of problems, goals, and ideas. Indeed, Ford (1969) reports on the results of a series of job enrichment studies without ever mentioning the words "pay" or "salary." In the plant described in this case, no significant pressures for higher pay have been felt to date. However, there has been sufficient opportunity for promotion of hourly employees to higher level jobs as the plant has grown.

It is certainly not within the scope of this article to handle the controversy regarding the place of pay as a motivator. We do want to make the point that standard corporate job evaluation plans are only one instance of the difficulties of interface between the client plant as a subsystem and the larger system. In our experience, these and other areas have been minor rather than major problems, but they have been problems.

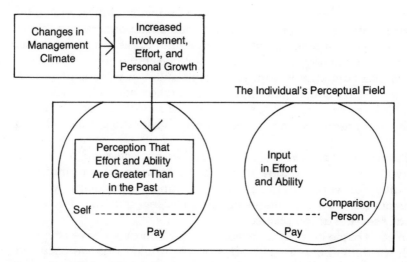

Figure 4.   Equity Model

Changes in Consumption of Research Findings

An important by-product of our experience has been [*Finding 12*] that *the client system eventually becomes a sophisticated consumer of new research findings in the behavioral sciences.* As mentioned earlier, there was early resistance to "theory"; but as the program progressed, there was increasing desire for "theory." We also found that a flexible and adaptable organization is more likely to translate theory into new policies and actions. Perhaps this is where behavioral scientists may have gone wrong in the past. We may have saturated our client systems with sophisticated research studies before the culture was ready to absorb them. This would suggest that a more effective approach may be carefully planned stages of evolution from an action orientation to an action-research orientation to a research orientation. This implies a long-range plan for change that we often talk about but rarely execute with respect to the changes in organizations that we seek as behavioral scientists.

RESULTS OF THE ORGANIZATIONAL DEVELOPMENT PROGRAM

To a great extent we have tried to share with you our results and findings throughout the article. In addition, we are retesting these concepts in several other plants. In retrospect, how much change really occurred at the client plant, and how effective have been the new approaches introduced? We have only partial answers since a control plant did not exist and since the plant was relatively new; no historical data existed against which to compare performance. However, considerable data do exist to support the thesis that change has occurred and that new managerial approaches have created an effective organization. (In addition, the second author is conducting ongoing research in another plant in the organization which has historical data. Before- and aftermeasures have already shown dramatic change: e.g., reduction in manufacturing costs for the plant of 40 to 45 per cent.)

Extensive interviews by the researcher and detailed notes and observations by the change agents indicate considerable improvement after our work with this plant. Communication is open, workers feel informed, jobs are interesting and challenging, and goals are mutually set and accomplished.

In each of the output dimensions, positive changes have occurred which we think, but cannot always prove, would not have occurred without the OD effort. Turnover has been considerably reduced; specific changes in job structure, organizational change, or group process have resulted in measurable productivity changes of up to 50 per cent. Recent changes in the Instrument Department have resulted in productivity and quality improvements. We have witnessed the significant changes in maturity and motivation which have taken place among the assembly workers. A change to a project team structure in the Materials Control Department led to a reduction of the weekly parts shortages. Following the findings of Lawrence and Lorsch (1969), the use of "integrators" and project teams has significantly reduced the time necessary for new product development, introduction, and manufacture. A fuller evaluation of the integrator role and the project organization as it affects intergroup relations and new product development is reported elsewhere (Beer, Pieters, Marcus, & Hundert, 1971).

Several recent incidents in the plant are evidence of the effect of the changes and bear repeating. An order called for in seven days and requiring extraordinary cooperation on the part of a temporary team of production workers was completed in fewer than seven days. A threatened layoff was handled with candor and openness and resulted in volunteers among some of the secondary wage earners.

New employees and managers now transferred into the plant are immediately struck by the differences between the "climate" of this plant and other locations. They report more openness, greater involvement by employees, more communication, and more interesting jobs. Even visitors are struck immediately by the differences. For example, one of the authors has on several occasions taken graduate students on field trips to the plant. After the tour, the consensus is,

"You've told us about it, but I had to see it for myself before I would believe it." Managers transferred or promoted out of the plant to other locations report "cultural shock."

SUMMARY AND CONCLUSIONS

The Medfield Project (as it can now be labeled) has been an experiment in a systems approach to organizational development at two systems levels. On the one hand, we have regarded the plant as a system in and of itself. On the other hand, we have regarded the plant as a subsystem within a larger organization. As such a subsystem, we wanted it to serve as a model for the rest of the organization. Indeed, as a result of this study, OD work is going forward elsewhere in the parent company and will be reported in forthcoming articles.

Although we have shared our findings with you throughout the article, it seems wise now to summarize them for your convenience, so that they may be generalized to other organizations and climates.

Findings

1. A clear-cut commitment to a particular OD approach is not necessary (although desirable) for a successful OD program to succeed.

2. Total top management understanding of where the OD process will lead and the state of the organization at the end is not necessary for organizational change to occur.

3. Change can and does begin at lower levels in the organization.

4. Effective and permanent adult learning comes after the individual has experimented with new approaches and received appropriate feedback in the on-the-job situation.

5. Rather than the T Group, the operating, ongoing organization may be the best "laboratory" for learning, with fewer problems in transfer of training.

6. Internal change leaders are natural targets for the change agent, since they become influence leaders and help to shape the culture.

7. Organizational change occurs in stages: a stage of unfreezing and trust building, a take-off stage when observable change occurs, and a stabilization stage. Then the cycle iterates.

8. Multiple changes in the subsystems are needed for the individual employee to change behavior and perceptions of his role.

9. Structural and interpersonal systems changes must reinforce and legitimate each other.

10. Systems changes set off additional interactive processes in which changes in organizational functioning not only increase outputs but also develop the latent abilities of people.

11. Influence is also exerted upward, with greater acceptance of these concepts by individuals at higher levels in the organization.

12. The client system eventually becomes a sophisticated consumer of new research findings in the behavioral sciences.

Perhaps the most important and far-reaching conclusion is that as organizational psychologists we have viewed our role too narrowly and with an insufficient historical and change perspective. Our research studies tend to be static rather than dynamic. We need to do a better job of developing a theory and technology of changing and to develop a flexible set of concepts which will change as we experiment with and socially engineer organizations. We are suggesting a stronger action orientation for our field and less of a natural science orientation. We must be less timid about helping organizations to change themselves. We must create a positive snowball of organizational change followed by changes in needs and expectations of organizational members, followed again by further organizational change. The objective of change agents should be to develop an evolving system that maintains reasonable internal consistency while staying relevant to and anticipating changes and adaptation to the outside environment. As behavioral scientists and change agents, we must help organizations begin to "become."

REFERENCES

Argyris, C. On the future of laboratory training. *Journal of Applied Behavorial Science*, 1967, 3(2), 153-183.

Bartlett, A. C. Changing behavior as a means to increased efficiency. *Journal of Applied Behavioral Science*, 1967, 3(3), 381-403.

Beckhard, R. *Organization development: Strategies and models*. Reading, Mass.: Addison-Wesley, 1969.

Beer, M., Pieters, G. R., Marcus, S. H., & Hundert, A. T. Improving integration between functional groups: A case in organization change and implications for theory and practice. Symposium presented at American Psychological Association Convention, Washington, D.C., September 1971.

Bennis, W. G. The case study—I. Introduction. *Journal of Applied Behavioral Science*, 1968, 4(2), 227-231.

Blake, R. R., & Mouton, J. S. *Building a dynamic corporation through grid organization development*. Reading, Mass.: Addison-Wesley, 1969.

Blake, R. R., Shepard, H. A., & Mouton, J. S. *Managing intergroup conflict in industry*. Houston, Tex.: Gulf, 1964.

Bradford, L. P. Membership and the learning process. In L. P. Bradford, J. R. Gibb, and K. D. Benne (Eds.), *T-Group theory and laboratory method: Innovation in re-education*. New York: Wiley, 1964.

Campbell, J. P., & Dunnette, M.D. Effectiveness of t-group experiences in managerial training and development. *Psychological Bulletin*, August 1968, *70*(2), 73-104.

Davis, S. A. An organic problem-solving method of organizational change. *Journal of Applied Behavioral Science*, 1967, *3*(1), 3-21.

Ford, R. N. *Motivation through the work itself*. New York: American Management Association, 1969.

Huse, E. F. The behavioral scientist in the shop. *Personnel*, May/June 1965, *42*(3), 50-57.

Huse, E. F. Putting in a management development program that works. *California Management Review*, Winter 1966, 73-80.

Huse, E. F., & Price, P. S. The relationship between maturity and motivation in varied work groups. *Proceedings* of the Seventieth Annual Convention of the American Psychological Association, September 1970.

Lawrence, P. R., & Lorsch, J. W. *Organization and environment*. Homewood, Ill.: Richard D. Irwin, 1969.

Lawrence, P. R., Bailey, J. C., Katz, R. L., Seiler, J. A., Orth, C. D. III, Clark, J. V., Barnes, L. B., & Turner, A. N. *Organizational behavior and administration*. Homewood, Ill.: Irwin-Dorsey, 1961.

Lesieur, F. G. (Ed.) *The Scanlon plan: A frontier in labor-management cooperation*. Cambridge, Mass.: M.I.T. Press, 1958.

Lesieur, F. G., & Puckett, E. S. The Scanlon plan has proved itself. *Harvard Business Review*, Sept./Oct. 1969, *47*, 109-118.

Paul, W. J., Robertson, K. B., & Herzberg, F. Job enrichment pays off. *Harvard Business Review*, Mar./Apr. 1969, *47*(2), 61-78.

Roche, W. J., & MacKinnon, N. L. Motivating people with meaningful work. *Harvard Business Review*, May/June 1970, *48*(3), 97-110.

Schein, E. H., & Bennis, W. G. *Personal and organizational change through group methods: The laboratory approach*. New York: Wiley, 1965.

Walton, R. E. Contrasting designs for participative systems. *Personnel Administration*, Nov./Dec. 1967, *30*(6), 35-41.

THE LONGEVITY OF A SYSTEMS
APPROACH TO OD

Michael Beer

The program described in "A Systems Approach to Organization Development" took place between 1966 and 1968. During this period the plant grew from about forty to approximately one hundred employees. The original plant manager was succeeded in 1967 by a manager from inside the plant who had been part of the experiment and who enthusiastically supported the move toward more participation and responsibility for production employees. From 1966 to 1969 the change effort was supported by an internal corporate OD consultant and an external OD consultant who visited the plant frequently and continued to make interventions to support the changes described. However, extensive support from both OD consultants ceased in early 1969. Shortly thereafter, a third plant manager from an older, unionized, more traditional plant took over. Three years later, a fourth plant manager from outside the plant took charge. With the exception of an attempt to rejuvenate OD activities in 1974, the plant has not had active OD consulting support since 1969. Now, almost ten years later and thirteen years after the beginning of the intervention, it is of some interest to know what has taken place.

ORGANIZATION AND ENVIRONMENT

Both the plant and the corporation have grown substantially. Today there are 180 production employees, compared with about sixty in 1968 (although recently thirty employees were laid off in a business slowdown). The salaried and managerial work forces have grown proportionally; however, no salaried employee in the plant today was part of the original management group and only a few know about the OD program between 1966 and 1968. Although the products manufactured by the plant serve the same medical and laboratory markets, they have become much more complex and sophisticated, and the market continues to be uncertain and characterized by a need for new-product development.

COMMUNICATION

Early change activities in the plant were focused on communication. A number of communication meetings and mechanisms were established to build trust and identity with the plant. Significant regression is evident in the application of these communication mechanisms. Meetings between supervisors and production employees have been intermittent and less oriented toward problem solving than in 1968. Meetings of the plant manager with a representative group of employees each week, an innovation in communication in 1966, were discontinued for several years and only recently reinstated, and then sporadically. Product-information meetings and general-information meetings for all production employees have disappeared, at least on a regular basis. Only bulletin boards posting plant performance continue as they were in 1968. A recent layoff, which would have been communicated far in advance by the plant manager in 1968, was communicated with little warning by first-line supervisors, using a typed memo as a guide. Employees are said to be poorly informed, and some rumors circulate about the future of the plant. Production employees, who received more attention than any other group in 1968, see themselves as receiving the least attention now.

JOB DESIGN

A major focus of the OD effort was the redesign of jobs to provide more interesting and challenging work (job enrichment). By and large the concepts that guided the redesign of jobs in 1968 continue to prevail in the plant: there are still no assembly lines, and workers continue to be given responsibilities for subassembly or assembly of the whole product, depending on their skill; because production employees continue to do in-process quality control, inspectors are used only for checking finished goods; in the hot-plate department there is no quality-control inspection. However, the identification of groups concerned with the manufacture of a product type seems to have disappeared, thus removing a source of task identity, feedback, and social pressures for performance. In general, it can be said that the plant has not reverted to traditional assembly-line methods, but, on the other hand, has not furthered the implementation of job enrichment.

Management seems convinced that job-enrichment approaches have yielded high quality at acceptable costs, but recent pressures have raised the viability of these concepts again. A consultant has suggested that improvements in profits and returns on investment are possible and that traditional methods may be the means to this end. Without strong management, the consultant's report may overturn the job-design philosophy that has prevailed so far.

PERSONNEL POLICIES AND PRACTICES

Despite the fact that the plant continues to be one of the only nonunion plants in the corporation, it seems to have slipped into the policy orbit of the other plants in the corporation. In 1968 both seniority and performance were used as criteria to make decisions about who was to be laid off in a business decline. Today, only seniority is used, except for people with certain critical skills. Pay levels in the plant have risen in line with union-negotiated increases in the larger corporation. The salaries of production employees are in the ninety-ninth percentile when compared with salaries in other companies in the same labor market. Some managers believe that workers are overpaid and report that workers feel the same way. Inadvertently, pay seems to have become an important part of the psychological contract between employees and the organization. It seems to have changed from effort for intrinsic rewards to compliance for money. What impact this will have on the relative importance of intrinsic rewards such as challenge and identity with goals is difficult to predict. As cost-reduction pressures increase, it will be easier and more logical for managers to rationalize bringing in assembly lines in the belief that people are paid so well that they will accept the change.

PLANT PERFORMANCE AND THE QUALITY OF WORK LIFE

Despite the fact that there has been regression in the "softer" elements of the change program—particularly communication and supervision— the plant's gross margin is very good compared to other plants in the company. Product quality is felt by management to be a competitive advantage. Turnover is almost nonexistent and absenteeism is at acceptable levels, particularly in view of the fact that the plant offers no paid sick days. Employees see the plant as more attractive than other companies in the labor market on pay, physical working conditions, and upward communication. On the other hand, older employees talk about the old days nostalgically, indicating that, despite the relative advantage in the quality of work life that the plant now holds, it is not as good as it used to be.

THE CHANGE IN PERSPECTIVE—THE FUTURE

It is interesting to note that the job changes that were "locked in" by technology (job enrichment) have been more or less sustained. This strongly supports our contention in the 1972 article that structural and technological changes can help freeze culture change. On the other hand, changes in communication and management have eroded. The corporate practice of transferring managers, the lack of OD consulting support after 1968, and the number of new plant managers not associated with and not committed to the early changes have contributed to this erosion.

The OD program in this study started with local initiative. There was no corporate commitment and none developed later; thus, no corporate strategy existed for sustaining the OD effort and spreading it to other parts of the company. A key manager, currently at the plant, reported that there was so little support for putting more energy into the OD effort that events such as the decline in influence of the corporate OD group were seen as signals of nonsupport for OD in the corporation. Without rewards for sustaining the innovations, the philosophy behind the change eroded. For a plant-level OD effort to be sustained over time, corporate support is needed to bring in managers who are sympathetic to the goals of OD. Corporate support is also needed to protect the plant from pressures to adhere to traditional corporate practices (Beer & Driscoll, 1977; Walton, 1975). In short, we are much less optimistic about the longevity of isolated plant-level OD effects than we were in 1972. A systems approach to OD within one unit cannot be successful in the long run unless the approach is also applied to the larger organization.

REFERENCES

Walton, R. E. The diffusion of new work structures: Explaining why success didn't take. *Organizational Dynamics*, Winter 1975, 3-22.

Beer, M., & Driscoll, J. W. Strategies for change. In J. R. Hackman & J. L. Suttle (Eds.), *Improving life at work: Behavioral science approaches to organizational change*. Santa Monica, CA: Goodyear, 1977.

Using Research to Guide
an Organization
Development Project

Samuel A. Culbert

This case study describes an OD project conducted within a district of religious communities. It shows how research was used to augment consultation and training and to bring to both consultants and management a more accurate perspective of the organization's problems. At a time of crisis, the district was focusing internally on issues of generation differences and skirting more fundamental issues of organization structure and purpose. The case includes (a) a discussion of the differences in problem-solving perspectives held by OD consultants and their clients, (b) a description of the specific consultant and client differences in the instance under study as well as the research and training design worked out to mediate between them, (c) a report on how research data were first analyzed to address questions raised at the beginning of the study, and then re-analyzed and used to suggest directions for future action and inquiry, and (d) a discussion of some generalizable lessons, derived from the case, for experimenting with change during times of organizational crisis.

Organization Development (OD) bridges an organization's need for continuity and its need for growth. It helps the organization change to meet the changing demands of its internal and external environments (Culbert & Reisel, 1971). A self-actualizing process for organiza-

The author served as coordinator of the research and training project described in this study. Invaluable members of this project include Lee Bolman, who supervised the statistical analysis; John McLaughlin, who coordinated the data collections and helped with analysis; and Roger Putzel, who helped with the case writeup.

tions, OD examines specific problems and conflicts in order to learn how to make fundamental, system-wide improvements in the organization. Although OD consultants prefer to help organizations grow, managers typically seek their help on immediate problems during times of crisis. Thus, the OD process usually begins with tension between the managers' desires for a specific solution and the consultants' desires to understand the system-wide issues which managers have summarized in their definition of "the problem."

INTRODUCTION

This paper illustrates how channeling the tension between the OD consultant and the manager can produce a deeper understanding of organizational problems and strategies for fundamental change. It begins with a description of this action-researcher's view of the tension and of the iterative strategy that most OD consultants incorporate in the problem-solving approaches they agree to try with managers. The body of the paper describes a case in which research was used to channel this tension and guide the OD project. The paper concludes with a model, induced from the case, for experimenting with organizational change during times of "crisis."

Tensions in the Manager-Consultant Relationship

When the relationship between the manager and consultant begins, each sees inconsistencies between the other's experience and his proposals. The manager starts with a problem he wants solved. No doubt he tried to solve it himself before requesting consultant help; his lack of success with a particular definition of or approach to a problem led him to seek consultant help. He thus appears to contradict himself by formulating his requests for help in terms of his initial definition of the problem or by asking for the kinds of approaches he has already tried. The OD consultant begins by acknowledging that he does not know the system, understand the problem, or have a standard program for helping. He thus appears to contradict himself by displaying certainty, in treating the problem as a symptom of something else, and by displaying uncertainty, in delaying action, despite immediate pressures for help. He implies that he will ultimately find his way to a solution, but he cannot specify exactly when or how.

The manager and consultant may formulate stereotypes of distrust, based on the contradictions each has seen in the other. The manager initially stereotypes the consultant as interested in change to the exclusion of continuity in operations—his major concern. The consultant initially stereotypes the manager as interested in short-term success, to the exclusion of development of the organization—his major concern. Stereotyping only aggravates each person's concern that the problem will be defined in a way that limits his contributions to its solution. The manager has the knowledge and experience needed for continuity in operations. He understands the culture and knows how to work within it to get things done. The OD consultant has the technology for analyzing systems and a conceptual perspective on the process of change. He knows how to buffer himself from the anxieties that inevitably arise during periods of system-wide examination.

As part of the organization, the manager assumes that uninvited probings in the domains of others will lead to conflict and·perhaps his own expulsion. The consultant, on the other hand, does not want his definition of the problem to be bounded by organizational structures, although he usually recognizes that solutions must take existing boundaries into account. The consultant expects to work outward from understanding the organization and the systems in which it is embedded. He wants to develop an independent perspective of the organizational components that determine, and perhaps bias, the manager's approach. He gravitates toward opportunities for growth and integration. More often than not, these opportunities are found at the boundaries between subsystems in the organization and at the boundaries between the organization and its environment.

These different perspectives and resources lead to conflict and tension which, early in the relationship, may produce overstatements of change strategy preferences on the part of both the manager and the consultant. The manager overstates his preferences in the direction of adaptational and piecemeal change; the consultant, in the direction of fundamental transposition and gross reordering. In fact, neither one knows exactly what is preferable or possible, and both need additional experience bases for proceeding.

The Iterative Strategy of the Consultant

The OD consultant has no "set" program. He has access to technologies that acquire their value when adapted to the parameters of a specific situation. He relies on an "organic" process in which problem solving takes place iteratively. Each iteration is designed to produce an output of value, and, most importantly, information to assist in the design of the next iteration. Consolidation of learning at each iteration produces an outward spiral: the activities suggested for the next iteration are increasingly broad in scope.

Discussion about project formulation usually leads to areas of agreement. The consultant and manager agree that continuity of operations is essential, that fundamental change is required for growth, and that some practices currently thought essential for continuity probably preclude growth and should be replaced. They discover that their mutual mistrust is as much a function of not knowing exactly how to proceed as it is a function of differing perspectives.

Initially lacking an independent experience base, the consultant is hard pressed to hold out for his best judgment, especially since that judgment initially depends on intuition, not "hard" facts. If the consultant holds out for a distinctly different way of proceeding and does not provide the manager a data base for understanding his position, he risks being viewed as a revolutionary. Few managers will collaborate with a revolutionary. If the consultant merely goes along with the manager's suggestions, he is in danger of becoming a counter-revolutionary who helps management avoid opportunities for fundamental change. Thus, OD consultation usually begins with the manager's assumptions and then generates the involvement and data necessary for a more adequate picture of project requirements and remedial steps. Managerial flexibility and consultant understanding will emerge on their own if this data base is pursued.

THE CASE

In the following case, management requested organization-wide sensitivity training to help members live and work together in an increasingly changing culture. Management's first formulation avoided consideration of fundamental change; in fact, it described the organization as having already changed as much as it could. Management's request for training seemed appropriate for OD technology, but the consultant lacked an experience base for trusting the client's formulation of the problem and its resolution. An extensive training program could prove to be a costly error. The consultant spent time interviewing organization members to increase his grasp of the problem. He learned enough to see a need for further study; the client, however, wanted action. Eventually the managers agreed with the consultant's counter proposal, which was to proceed on a pilot scale, with research to evaluate the results. *Research* proved essential to the consultant and client's eventual coming together. During the first iteration, data produced by research complemented the consultant's judgment, established while conducting the sensitivity training, that membership adaptation without organizational change was unlikely. Reexamination of the data and further discussions with managers comprised the second iteration. This led to a broadened and more accurate diagnosis of the organization's problems. This diagnosis specified changes which were so "extreme" that the client would never have agreed to them, nor would the consultants have been able to pinpoint them without the impartial data base provided by research.

Client Problem

The client was a district of 20 religious (Catholic) communities, each of which ran a parochial high school for boys. A decentralized operation, the district had only two executive officers and three administrators charged with the management and integration of all operations. Each of the schools and communities exercised considerable autonomy but deferred to the district officers on matters of policy. Although advised by a board of elected representatives ("directors"), the executive officers retained absolute power over the district, in accord with Vatican policy. The district, reputed to be aggressive and forward thinking, had instituted most reforms permitted by the Church after the Vatican II Council. At the time of the study (1968-69), it probably ranked among the upper 10 per cent of liberal-thinking, Catholic communities of religious living under a particular rule. Despite considerable overlap of authority, the administrative structures of the schools and their adjacent communities were considered independent of one another. An appointee (called a "superior") of the district executive officers directed the activities of each community and exercised considerable authority over the life of each community member, although he was advised by a council of elected officials. Community members were non-ordained laymen, called "Brothers," who had undergone rigorous religious training and had taken vows of poverty, chastity, and obedience. All Brothers had training as teachers; most held advanced degrees at the Master's level.

District officers and several community superiors saw their communities as splintered. Some younger community members, complaining of insularity leading to alienation, were clamoring for more communication with the outside world and for relations within the community as fulfilling as those they found outside. In short, they were beginning to accept the youth culture's definition of "community" and therefore found themselves in conflict with the established practices of their own. Increasing numbers of Brothers—the "better ones," district leaders feared—were forsaking the Order for other living arrangements, particularly marriage. Even many older members were actively weighing the advantages of their present life style against those offered by other religious communities or by life outside. Young and old agreed that deep, human encounter was missing in their lives. In the long run, district leaders feared they would be faced with the dissolution of their organization.

Troubled district leaders identified one immediate problem as a generation gap among the Brothers. The younger members saw the older ones as irrelevant to today's needs, overly ritualistic in their prayer and dress habits, and excessively obedient. "Shall we be like them 10 years from now?" they asked. The old, on the other hand, criticized the young for questioning fundamental issues in religious life: the young seemed too individualistic, selfish, and disrespectful of tradition. They initiated "too much" contact with the outside world and wanted too much change too soon—while ignoring reforms already made.

District officers and community superiors had tried to respond to these problems by changing their organizations in various ways. But, while the older members complained of too much change, the younger complained of too little. The changes had not created a sense of community. Leaders viewed the communities as still lacking in rewarding interpersonal relationships and as divided by generation differences. District officers thought themselves unable to make further organizational changes within the limits set by the Church, through the Vatican Council. They therefore requested consultant help in resolving this conflict of viewpoints by organizing a district-wide program of sensitivity training.

Consultant Response

In requesting sensitivity training, district leaders were looking for a way to deepen community relationships as well as to transcend generation differences. Much precedent supports the use of group process techniques in organizations fragmented by value differences; however, specific applications always raise questions.

The consultant recognized that most members of religious orders who attend "stranger" workshops in sensitivity training, such as the ones conducted during the summer months by the NTL Institute, report substantial personal gains. In this case, however, preliminary interviews with district members raised some doubts about their effectiveness. Even those members fully committed to change had lived in religious communities since their teens and their interpersonal styles resulted from years of community indoctrination. The consultant found clear indications that not everyone would participate in such training, and he feared that limited participation would result in further community fragmentation. In addition, uncertainty about specific designs for accomplishing management's objectives suggested proceeding slowly.

The brief study increased the consultant's respect for the client's conceptualization of its problem, but he realized that the client did not know what change was actually possible. The consultant therefore proposed beginning with a period of data collection and diagnosis. The district leaders balked: They had spent years studying the district and now wanted action. The consultant turned to formulating a plan acceptable to the client and himself.

The new proposal included group training for a limited number of communities and research for monitoring the effectiveness of different training models. The research was kept broad enough to test for new project directions—in this way learning from each step of the project was expected to suggest next steps. Most district leaders agreed to go along with the proposed plan.[1]

The resulting plan, built from the client's request for sensitivity training, was a form of team building. The training program focused on the issues of intimacy and generation differences. It was designed to teach members new ways to cope with problems they already recognized. The standard training consisted of two weekends four months apart. The interval provided participants a chance to test their understanding under daily living conditions. Although the design for the first weekend was fixed in advance, the second weekend was not planned until after the first weekend, when members of the consulting team who worked on this project could pool their experiences.

Client and consultant gave advance consideration to the broader implications of this project. They predicted that learnings developed by this progressive district might apply to other religious Orders. In the United States, six more districts of this Order, each with a parallel structure and comparable membership, and over 500 other Orders have combined memberships of more than 175,000 (Foy, 1969). At this broader level, one might well anticipate limited financial and professional consultant resources. The consultant suggested assessing a community's capacity for transferring learning and a consultant team's ability to make their training transferable. The consultant reasoned that identical units of an organization that operates in different geographical areas have much to gain if one unit can teach another. This reasoning produced an experimental design to answer questions about transferability as well as training efficacy.

Research Design

Two models for transferring learning, one pedagogical, the other epidemiological, were included in the project's design. In the pedagogical model, a community agreed to review its first weekend of

---

[1] This plan was unacceptable to at least two community superiors, who contracted with other consultants to run encounter weekends for their communities.

training and, with some minimal consultation, to plan a weekend of activities for a nearby community that had not received professional training. Through these activities the "transferring" community would develop their own experience-based techniques in order to communicate the lessons they valued in their own training. The epidemiological model considered a community receiving training as "infected." After training they would be asked to infect the men in a community adjacent to their own. The procedure for infection would come from the two communities involved. The consultant would explain the experimental design and encourage the two communities to spend time together in activities ranging from informal discussions of the infected community's experiences during training to going out to dinner or bowling together. The goal was interaction.

Four questions directed the evaluation of different forms of training:

1. Does training promote sufficient change to deepen community relationships and transcend generation differences?

2. What effect does colleague participation in training have on men who decline to participate?

3. Can one community successfully transfer its learning to another?

4. Does the act of transferring add to what was learned in a professionally led training program?

These questions, although central in evaluating the effectiveness of training, help direct the next iteration of the OD process only if training is successful. For this reason research instruments had to be broad enough to reflect change against community-wide objectives of deepening intimacy and transcending generation differences.

Table 1 details the training[2] and research design formulated to address the preceding questions. Community I received the "standard" training to see whether it would deepen relationships and transcend generation differences. Community II received the standard training one weekend; during a second weekend it designed for Community III a retreat, which took place a third weekend. Community IV received the standard training and "communicated" their training through informal interactions with the men in Community V, which was located in their city. Eventually, in April, Communities III and V,

---

[2]The training was designed and led by consultant teams composed of accredited members of NTL Institute's professional association. They included Clay Alderfer, Norm Berkowitz, Dave Bradford, Warner Burke, Sam Culbert, and Hal Kellner. As preparation for this project these consultants worked together conducting an encounter weekend for the Directors of an adjoining district.

Table 1. Training and Research Design

	COMMUNITY I	COMMUNITY II	COMMUNITY III	COMMUNITY IV	COMMUNITY V	COMMUNITY VI	COMMUNITY VII
October	Research Packet 1	Research Packet 1	Research Packet 1	Research Packet 1	Research Packet 1	Research Packet 1	Research Packet 1
November	Weekend Workshop led by professionals	Weekend Workshop led by professionals Weekend preparation for "pedagogical" transfer Conduct Workshop for Community III	Weekend Workshop led by Community II	Weekend Workshop led by professionals and instructed to be carriers in "epidemiological" transfer	Instructed to lower "resistance" in "epidemiological" model		
December							
January							
February	Research Packet 2	Research Packet 2	Research Packet 2	Research Packet 2	Research Packet 2	Research Packet 2	Research Packet 2
March							
April	Weekend Workshop led by professionals	Weekend Workshop led by professionals	Weekend Workshop led by professionals	Weekend Workshop led by professionals	Weekend Workshop led by professionals		
May	Research Packet 3	Research Packet 3	Research Packet 3	Research Packet 3	Research Packet 3	Research Packet 3	Research Packet 3

along with Communities I, II, and IV, received a second weekend in training led by professionals.[3] Communities VI and VII served as controls for the measurement of training (Community VI was from the same district and VII was from an adjoining district).

Before training, the men living in each of these seven communities received a "research packet" containing a perspective on the entire project[4] and questionnaires to be filled out, sealed, and returned within two days to the researcher working on the project. Participation in the research did not obligate a man to take part in the training. Two more packets were distributed, one about two months after the first training weekend and the other about three weeks after the second weekend of training. During the course of the year, selected community meetings were tape recorded for a process analysis of group behavior.

The self-report research packets contained questionnaires chosen for their relevance to the two objectives of the training: deepening community relationships and transcending generation differences. Training emphasized improvement at the community level. Hence research instruments focused on community functioning rather than individual gains. Questionnaires elicited data on norms (individuals' perceptions of their communities), attitudes (attitudes toward renewal, satisfaction with the district, and flexibility of individual belief systems), and relationships (propensities to give and receive feedback and perceptions of intimacy levels characterizing relationships with other community members). The next section of this paper describes the research instruments and explains how they relate to the project objectives.

Research Measures

Norms. The "Do's and Don'ts" questionnaire has been described and researched both by Callahan (1968) and by Hilfiker (1969). It measures norms (existing standards) for behavior in an organization along 12 dimensions hypothesized to relate to organizational effectiveness: awareness, authenticity, trust, inquiry, objectivity, collaboration, changefulness, altruistic concern, consensual decision making, competence-based power, emotionality as data, and individuality.

---

[3] Arranging a professionally led group experience was essential to gaining the cooperation of Communities III and V. Potentially, this second period of training would provide an additional reference point for evaluating the impact of transfer.

[4] Earlier a personal presentation had been made by the house Superior and the researcher.

Both Callahan and Hilfiker used this questionnaire to measure the effectiveness of school systems. The form used in the current investigation contained minor changes in terminology in order to focus on norms of life in a religious community.

The questionnaire asks respondents to estimate the percentage of people in their organization who believe that members "should" or "should not" exhibit certain behavior under standard conditions; respondents also check their personal preferences for each behavior. An index of community-perceived norms is obtained by tabulating the number of times a group of respondents place a majority percentage in columns related to a particular norm. An index of self-perceived alienation in a community is obtained by tabulating the mean number of times respondents mark their preferences in columns other than the one they believe a majority of community members would check. An index of accuracy in perceiving prevailing community norms is obtained by tabulating the mean number of times respondents indicate a majority preference in a column in which a majority of members actually did check a norm as their preference.

This questionnaire was used to investigate whether different generation groupings would prefer different norms and whether relationship-building activities in communities receiving training would change community norms. It was included in all three research packets.

Attitudes Toward Renewal. This research instrument, developed by McLaughlin (1971), discriminates between conservative and liberal attitudes toward change. Respondents check preferences in five major areas of change now occurring in religious communities: style of community life, liturgy, authority, apostolate, and future of religious life. Five preferences, presented for each of the areas, range from (1) no change from traditional observance to (5) a form wholly defined by function and distinctly different from present practices. Preferences for traditional practices and literal interpretation of religious doctrine are termed "conservative"; preferences, away from the established way, that emphasize "doing one's thing," are termed "liberal."

This questionnaire was used to monitor differences in values between different generation groupings. It was included in all three research packets.

Attitudes: "Satisfaction with the District." This questionnaire was developed to ascertain how much opportunity for self-development district members considered the organization to provide them. Fourteen questions, derived from ad hoc interviews with organization members were answered on a 5-point agree/disagree scale. The scores were tabulated and converted to percentages to arrive at an index of overall satisfaction with district life.

This questionnaire was used in monitoring the extent to which intracommunity conflict affected a member's feelings of satisfaction in living a religious life in the district. It was included in research packets 1 and 3.

Attitudes: Dogmatism Scale. This test was developed and researched by Rokeach (1960). It indicates "openness" and "closedness" of a respondent's belief system by measuring authoritarianism and general intolerance. The present study used Form E of the Dogmatism Scale, the one used on such populations as American college students, English college students, and English workers. This questionnaire was used to discriminate differences in rigidity of thinking among members of different generation groupings. It was included in research packets 1 and 3.

Relationships: Personal Relations Survey. This questionnaire is based on the conceptual scheme of the *Johari Window* (Luft, 1969). It was developed by Hall and Williams (1967) to measure self-reported propensities to give and receive feedback from superiors, colleagues, and subordinates. The standard form was adapted in this research to include only the section on colleagues; the terminology was adapted to describe community membership. Previous use with over 350 middle managers established a standard for comparing the scores produced in this study.

This questionnaire was used to monitor changes in attitudes that might result from the sensitivity training. It was included in research packets 1 and 3.

Relationships: "Who Knows You?" and "Whom Do You Know?" Questionnaires. These questionnaires survey the levels of intimacy that characterize interpersonal relationships in each community. The instructions to the questionnaires define five levels of intimacy: (1) Men with whom I have not intentionally shared any personal information; (2) Men with whom I have shared cordial, but not deep, personal information; (3) Men with whom I have shared moderately intimate personal information; (4) Men with whom I have shared very intimate personal information; and (5) Men with whom I have shared the most intimate of all personal information. Three items drawn from a poll of 650 statements about various aspects of the self, scaled similarly for intimacy (Taylor & Altman, 1966), described each level. The items had been scaled according to Thurstone's method of successive intervals, with a scaled value difference of at least 1½ interval separating each cluster of three used in the definitions. These items covered different topical categories and gave respondents a working definition for each category heading.

Following the definition of categories, respondents found a single page listing the names of each member of his community in the left-hand column and five adjoining columns with headings corresponding to the five levels of intimacy. The respondent could then write the name of each community member in the column indicating the intimacy level that best characterized their relationship. Each person filled out two different forms of this questionnaire, first from the perspective of "Who Knows You?" and next from the perspective of "Whom Do You Know?"

These questionnaires were included to track patterns of intimacy characterizing the communities taking part in this study. They were included in each of the three research packets.

Contact Checklist. Participants in the communities transferring and receiving learning in the "epidemiological" model received checklists for keeping track of their participation in learning transfer. The checklist was patterned after one used by Berkowitz and Bennis (1961) in studying formal service-oriented organizations. It contained space for listing specific contacts, the nature of each meeting, the initiator, the duration, the importance the meeting had for the respondent, the satisfaction he derived, and the satisfaction the respondent felt the other person derived from the meeting. This checklist was handed out with the transfer instructions and collected before the spring training session led by professionals.

Behavior: Process Measures. These measures were developed by Alderfer and Lodahl (1971) to rate two dimensions of group process: "fight-flight" and "openness." Fight-flight parallels directness and here-and-now discussion style; openness, openminded exploration of personal involvement. Each dimension is operationally defined along a 5-point scale. Judges use this scale in assigning ratings to segments taken from tape recordings of group process. Alderfer and Lodahl report high interjudge correlations: significant Kendall *taus* of .69 for fight-flight and .48 for openness. They used these measures to compare university classes, one using a T-Group format; the other, a more typical discussion style format. Their results included significantly higher fight-flight ratings of segments from the T-Group class, but no differences on openness ratings.

In the present study, each community receiving training was requested to tape record four of their weekly "business" meetings. Dates for the recordings were arbitrarily specified by the researchers to include two meetings before the training and two afterward. Speech segments were excerpted from the tapes, using a table of random numbers; coded for community, before/after training, and early-middle-late parts of the tape; and submitted to two specially trained judges for their independent ratings on the two scales. The process ratings were to assess whether sensitivity training actually changed the ways group members work together.

RESULTS OF TRAINING

The organization of the data analyses follows the consultant's line of inquiry. It addresses the earlier stated questions about training and provides other information to expand understanding of the district and design future iterations of the OD process.

Participation in the training and research was voluntary. Between one-half and three-fourths of each community participated in the training[5] and between two-thirds and three-fourths of each community contributed to the research. With one exception, the size of the community ranged between 25 and 32. Community VI, a control group, had only 15 members. Except for those in the youngest age bracket (20-25), youth correlated with participation in training and research. More men between the ages of 25 and 30 participated than between the ages of 30 and 35, and so on. In order not to confound individual variability with changes over time (due to the participation of different persons), the analyses include data produced only by those men who completed questionnaires for each of the time periods compared.

Relatively high percentages of those in communities assigned to the transfer models participated. About two-thirds of each community assigned to the "pedagogical" model participated, and three-fourths of those transferring training in the "epidemiological" model made contact with about one-half of those in the adjacent community assigned the task of absorbing learning. In the latter model, significant[6] correlations obtained between the number of times members of the trained community reported that they contacted specific members of the untrained community and the number of times those members reported themselves contacted ($r = .86$, $df = 13$). On the average, each member of the trained community reported 8.8 contacts between December and March while members of the untrained community reported an average of 6.9 contacts.

---

[5]Somewhat fewer than one-half of those in Community V participated in the weekend workshop offered in April. However, over one-half made contact with members of Community IV during the period of learning transfer.

[6]Throughout this study, the .05 level is used in determining significance.

The Participants

Data were analyzed for differences between community members who volunteered for training and those who declined. A comparison of age variances indicates that the two groups did not come from the same population ($F = 12.28$, $df = 1,74$). The mean age for those taking part in both training and research was 35.23. The mean age for those who declined training but took part in the research was 47.00. The liberalism variances registered by the two groups, as measured by "Attitudes Toward Renewal" (ATR) scores, also indicate that the groups came from different populations. Significant post hoc comparisons were found between the two groups for time 1 ($F = 11.30$, $df = 1,71$), for time 2 ($F = 9.16$, $df = 1,71$), and for time 3 ($F = 15.88$, $df = 1,71$). ATR means are displayed in Table 2. The mean scores for those participating in the training (T) are greater, in a liberal direction, than the means for the group that declined training (D).

Comparison of the satisfaction variances registered by the two groups, as measured by the "Satisfaction with the District as an Organization" questionnaire, failed to produce significant differences. The mean percentages for these groups are displayed in Table 3. Significant differences are found when an ad hoc analysis compared the pretraining means for these two groups: the first two cells in column 1, Table 3 ($t = 2.38$, $df = 72$).

In brief, those volunteering for training were younger, had more liberal values, and initially reported themselves less satisfied with their life in the district.

Norms

The data on community norms were analyzed for mean score changes over time. Communities receiving training by professionals (I, II, and IV), communities receiving learning transfer and subsequent training (III and V), and communities serving as controls (VI and VII) were also compared. Only those who took part in sessions led by professional trainers were included in analyses involving Communities I, II, III, IV, and V. Separate analyses compared community preferences for each of the 12 norms included in the "Do's and Don'ts" questionnaire as well as for perceptions of community norms. Post hoc comparisons of specific cells were carried out only when an overall analysis of variance produced a significant effect.

In summary, the number and extent of changes in norm preferences and perceived community norms indicated little impact due to professional training and transfer attempts:

Table 2. Mean Scores on "Attitudes Toward Renewal" Questionnaire and Significant Post Hoc Comparisons of Variance for Three Groupings

	Time Period			
	1	2	3	
Trained (T)	13.58	12.85	13.68	$N_T = 60$
Declined Training (D)	9.31	9.00	8.62	$N_D = 13$
Controls (C)	12.38	11.75	10.75	$N_C = 24$

Significant* Post Hoc Comparisons of Variances		
cells	F-Value	df
1,1 and 2,1	11.30	1,71
3,1 and 2,1	5.82	1,35
1,2 and 2,2	9.16	1,71
3,2 and 2,2	4.68	1,35
1,3 and 2,3	15.88	1,71
1,3 and 3,3	5.32	1,35

*$p < .05$

Table 3. Mean Scores on "Satisfaction with the District as an Organization" Questionnaire for Three Groupings

	Time Period		
	1	3	
Trained (T)	73.23	72.08	$N_T = 61$
Declined Training (D)	83.86	72.00	$N_D = 15$
Controls (C)	76.46	74.70	$N_C = 26$

1. *Time alone produced no discernible change.* Comparisons of control group variances produced no significant differences over time on preferred norms or perceptions of community norms. In each instance the means for the control groups, at time 1, approximated the means for those in the other communities. Moreover, no differences were noted among any of the variances that the two control groups produced on individual norms.

2. *Training produced little change, in fact no uniform change at all, across the three groups receiving two periods of professional training.* With respect to changes in preferences for norms, Community I registered the only statistically significant difference on the norms

of *trust* ($f = 7.07$, $df = 1,28$). With respect to perceptions of community norms, Communities I and II registered significant differences in their perceptions of *awareness* ($F = 7.51$, $df = 1,24$ and $F = 5.64$, $df = 1,28$, respectively).

3. *Groups receiving learning transfer were significantly different on only one norm (awareness) between times 1 and 2*, the period when transfer could be tested. This change took place in Community III's perceptions of the prevailing community norm for *awareness* ($F = 14.56$, $df = 1,12$).

Pooling the Data

When communities receiving training were compared with one another on the other self-report measures, analyses did not reveal any significant differences. Similarly, neither control group produced significant differences on any self-report measure. We therefore decided to consider each of these two populations as homogeneous groupings and to pool their data for further comparisons. Data were also pooled for the small number of those who declined training but completed three questionnaires since their data could not be compared on an intercommunity basis. Thus, data received from the self-report measures were compared across three groupings: those who participated in the training (T), those who declined the training (D), and those living in communities serving as controls (C).

Measures

Attitudes. Listed at the bottom of Table 2 are F values for significant post hoc comparisons of ATR variances at times 1, 2, and 3. The variances for the D grouping differ significantly at times 1 and 2 from the variances produced by the other two groupings. The variance for the C grouping differs significantly from the variance of the T grouping only at time 3, indicating that these groupings become different populations. An ad hoc analysis of the difference between the means registered by the C grouping at times 1 and 3 was significant ($t = 2.39$, $df = 46$). These analyses indicate that training does not increase the liberal attitudes toward change of those who volunteer for training. It does help them resist the tendency to become more conservative about change during the year, as the control group did.

An analysis of variance comparing the three groupings on the "Satisfaction with the District as an Organization" questionnaire failed to detect significant differences. Table 3 displays the mean scores produced by the three groupings. The mean score produced by the D grouping at time 1 appears different from the other means. Ad hoc *t* tests comparing the D grouping's mean score at time 1 with its score at time 3, and with the T grouping's score at time 1, were significant (*t* = 4.27, *df* = 13; *t* = 2.28, *df* = 74, respectively). This suggests that although training failed to increase satisfaction for those who participated, it appears to have diminished satisfaction for those who declined training, even though this latter grouping began, at time 1, with a level of satisfaction that seemed to decrease to the level of those who volunteered for training.

Relationships. The data produced by the three groupings on the "Who Knows You?" and "Whom Do You Know?" questionnaires were compared. None of the between-group or within-group comparisons was significant. Graphs of the data produced by each of the three groupings on each of the two questionnaires were similar. Figure 1 illustrates these intimacy patterns by presenting a graph for these groupings at time 1. Each community's profile resembles this one. In a

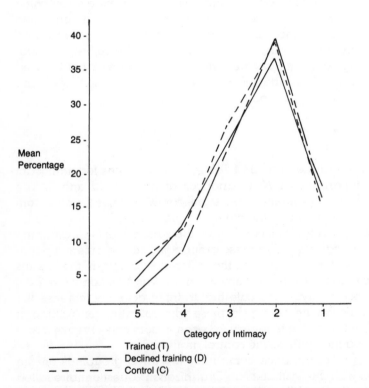

Mean Percentage

Category of Intimacy

——————— Trained (T)

—— — —— Declined training (D)

— — — — — Control (C)

Figure 1. Illustrative Intimacy: Graph of Mean Percentages for Time 1 on "Who Knows You?" Questionnaire for Three Groupings

living community of 30, the average person has one close confidant, a select few persons with whom he shares fairly intimate information, and large numbers of others with whom he shares cordial, general, impersonal information. Training did not substantially alter this pattern, even in comparisons made on a community-by-community basis.

Analysis of variance applied to the data collected on the "feedback" scale of the Personal Relations Survey failed to produce any significant effects. Analysis of variance applied to data from the "openness" scale produced a significant between-group effect. Post hoc comparisons at time 1 of the D group and the T and C groups were significant ($F = 4.55$, $df = 1,74$; $F = 8.61$, $df = 1,39$, respectively). The mean scores for the feedback and openness scales appear in Table 4. None of these means ranked above the 30th percentile when compared with the range of scores produced by over 350 middle managers.

Analysis of variance of scores on the Dogmatism Scale failed to produce any significant effects. The means for these groupings closely resembled one another and were at the average for scores of college students.

Behavior. Judges rated speech segments taken from work sessions of communities receiving training. They used the "fight-flight" and "openness" scales developed by Alderfer and Lodahl (1971). These scales provided measures of training effects on community performance. Table 5 summarizes the four-way analysis of variance made on fight-flight data from four of the five communities receiving training.[7] This analysis followed four parameters, paralleling dimensions of data collection and analysis: four communities (A), before and after training (B), early-middle-late parts of the work sessions (C), and two raters (D).[8] Analysis produced two significant effects of note, one attributed to community differences and the other attributed to training ($F = 3.92$, $df = 3,168$; $F = 3.69$, $d = 1,168$, respectively). The graph of early/late community means appears as Figure 2. Three of the four communities faced conflicts more directly during work sessions than before. The fourth community, the one which had the job of transferring their learning in the epidemiological model, declined considerably in fight-flight behavior to about the level achieved by the other communities. The last community had initially scored quite high on fight-flight; a reduction in their score might have positive implications.

---

[7]Data from Community V were incomplete and could not be included in the analysis.

[8]Reliability coefficients were calculated for the judges. These were .32 for the fight-flight scale and .53 for the openness scale. Each coefficient had 288 degrees of freedom.

Table 4. Mean Scores on Openness and Feedback Scales of "Personal Relations Inventory" for Three Groupings

Openness/Feedback	Time Period 1	Time Period 3	
Trained (T)	24.26/ 29.66	25.82/ 30.34	$N_T = 61$
Declined Training (D)	19.93/ 26.87	22.73/ 29.00	$N_D = 15$
Controls (C)	25.88/ 29.38	24.62/ 28.85	$N_C = 26$

Table 5. Four-Way Analysis of Variance for Fight-Flight Ratings on Community Work Sessions: Community X Before /After Training X Early-Middle-Late Parts of Sessions X Raters

Source	df	MS	F
Communities (A)	3	16.33	3.92**
Before/After (B)	1	15.40	3.69*
Early-Middle-Late (C)	2	.70	<1.0
AB	3	9.20	2.21*
AC	6	2.02	<1.0
BC	2	10.01	2.60*
ABC	6	2.72	<1.0
Subjects Within Groups	168	4.17	
Raters (D)	1	.9	<1.0
AD	3	2.54	1.35
BD	1	.70	<1.0
CD	2	3.75	2.09
ABD	3	3.10	1.73
ACD	6	1.37	<1.0
BCD	2	.35	<1.0
ABCD	6	.80	<1.0
D x SWG	168	1.79	

*$p < .10$
**$p < .01$

Although the absolute values of the means for the three communities that showed increases are not especially high, these increases do seem to indicate progress attributable to the training.

An analysis of the type portrayed in Table 5 was carried out with the judges' ratings on the openness scale. No significant effects were noted.

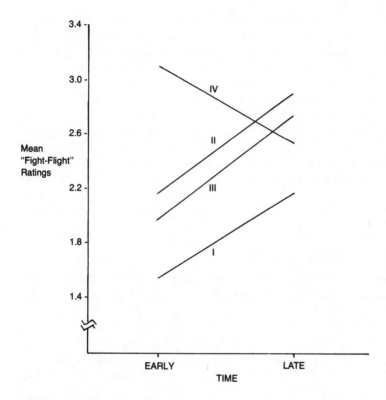

Figure 2. Graph of Early/Late Means of "Fight-Flight" Ratings for Four Communities

Open-Ended Reports

At the conclusion of the training and research, members received a supplementary questionnaire. This open-ended inquiry asked respondents to describe and explain changes which had taken place during the school year. Over 90 per cent of those who had participated in sensitivity training reported that it had helped them personally, had given them new insights into community life, and had facilitated changes for the better in district procedures. One-third of those in Community V and one-half of those in Community IV, participants in the "epidemiological" transfer, reported that these contacts had "great impact" on them, and more than three-fourths of these respondents reported that the transfer contact had "some" degree of importance.

One need not consider these favorable reports spurious, even though only meager progress was indicated by the more controlled analyses that reflected data in terms of the goals of deepening community relationships and transcending generation differences. In organizations where there is discontent, participants in sensitivity training-like activities consistently report favorable reactions and more individual gains than indices of organization effectiveness record (Campbell & Dunnette, 1968). Additional perspective is gained from the reports of the professional staff.

The staff surmised that individual progress might have been greater if the men had participated in more heterogeneous groupings, such as those which naturally occur in "stranger" groups. They saw many opportunities for change in individual behavior blocked by colleagues who acted *as if* change would threaten the stability of their interaction with the potential learner. Perhaps what participants learned could be more easily applied *outside* their home community.

Overall Evaluation of Training

The preceding findings contain little support for further use of training to deepen community relationships and transcend generation differences. Those who participated failed to change significantly in ways that could benefit their community and those who declined training became less satisfied with district life. Since training did not produce positive results, there was no way to evaluate the differential effects of the transfer models or the gains that might accrue from transferring learning.

Before presenting these findings to the client, the consultant sought additional data to guide the next iteration of the OD process. He noted that attrition rates for the district had reached a high during the year. Attrition among the five communities participating in the experimental cells receiving training were among the highest in the district. The consultant felt that the data had more to say about generation differences and members who resigned at the end of the year.

Further Analyses

Generation Differences. The Attitudes Toward Renewal (ATR) questionnaire provided a basis for further analyses of generation differences. The scores at time 1 for all who participated in the research were divided at the midpoint of possible scores on the ATR questionnaire. This produced two attitude groups with substantially different ages. The group scoring on the conservative side, below the midpoint, had 84 members with a mean age of 43.1 ($SD = 12.7$) and the group scoring on the liberal side, above the midpoint, had 64 members with a mean age of 31.5 ($SD = 7.8$). The ATR mean for the "conservative" subgroup was 9.7 (SD = 3.08); the ATR mean for the "liberal" subgroup was 16.5 (SD = 2.78). The overall correlation between age and ATR scores was negative and significant (r = .557, df = 147). These subgroups had responded differently to the self-report questionnaires, it was found, and their responses shed light on the generation conflicts.

The data on norms were analyzed by two-way (group × time) analyses of variances. Row effects indicate subgroup differences. Significant row effects were obtained for preferences of eight out of the 12 norms. Examination of means revealed that the "liberal" subgroup responded in the direction hypothesized to relate to organization effectiveness on seven of the differences; the "conservative" subgroup responded in that direction on one of the differences. The two groups proved quite similar in their perceptions of community norms. They differed only twice, with each grouping perceiving a norm in the preferential direction.

Accuracy in perceiving community norms and self-perceived alienation were also measured, using the data on norms. The two groups misjudged prevailing community norms about half the time and placed personal preferences in opposition to that which they viewed as the prevailing community norm about one-third of the time.

The data on "satisfaction" were also analyzed by a two-way (group × time) analysis of variance. The group effect was significant (F = 19.92, df = 1,100). Examination of means shows the "conservative" subgroup registering higher means, more satisfaction, during both administrations of this questionnaire, times 1 and 3.

Both subgroups produced similar relationship patterns on the "Who Knows You?" and "Whom Do You Know?" questionnaires. Their graphs matched Figure 1. On the "Personal Relations Survey," the means of their self-reported propensities to give and receive feedback were almost identical. Moreover, the groups did not differ in their scores on the Dogmatism Scale.

Those Who Resigned. Participating in all three administrations of this research were nine men who resigned from the district at the end of the school year. The pre-training ATR mean for this group, 17.44 (F = 2.87), slightly exceeded the overall mean for the "liberal" subgroup. The lowest score produced by any of these men was 14, which meant that all of them fell in the "liberal" category.

The preceding analyses present an interesting pattern of similarities and differences. "Attitude Toward Renewal" does seem to differentiate subgroups whose differences in age imply a generation gap. Since a higher percentage of younger district members volunteered to take part in the research, this age difference is, no doubt, understated. The two groups often differ in the community norms they prefer; however, they appear quite similar in their aptitudes and propensities for forming deep interpersonal relationships with other community members. In complaining about loneliness and alienation, both groups seemed to desire more intimacy and closeness. But the crucial difference lies in the consequences of this frustration for the two subgroups. Despite their complaints about the generation conflict, the "conservative" group remained relatively satisfied with their life in the district; the "liberal" group was dissatisfied to the point where many were resigning from the district.

USING DATA TO PRODUCE A NEW DIAGNOSIS

A summary of the research findings was presented to district leaders, a "management" group, at a two-day meeting convened at the beginning of the following school year. Two executive officers, members of the District Council, and approximately half of the superiors, including those whose communities had participated in the project, attended the meeting. Also present were two members of the consultant team who, in collaboration with the executive officers, had designed the meeting to include planning sessions. The objective was to move from acquired understanding of the problems to plans for next steps in improving the situation. The consultants would share their research findings and add other comments relevant to their consulting experiences. District leaders would add other information, such as attrition statistics and morale surveys of community members, and the entire group would be asked to synthesize and plan.

The consultants reported that sensitivity training had not produced enough change toward "open" communications to warrant continuation in its present form. In fact, they suggested that training might intensify fragmentation within communities. Those who declined training were older, had more conservative values concerning change, and claimed to be more satisfied with district life. Those who participated in the training gained support for their liberal attitudes. Their persistent liberalism seemed to decrease the satisfaction of those who declined training. Data suggested that training increased the directness with which district members faced conflict during community work sessions (fight-flight scores). However, this increase probably had negative consequences for community rapport, for members did not increase in their expression of more positive feelings (openness scores).

In reporting the analysis of generation subgroups, the consultants stated that the subgroup similarities seemed even more important than subgroup differences. They suggested that reported preferences for different community norms were perhaps unintentional smoke screens for more fundamental issues. They noted similar preferences for giving and receiving feedback, similar aptitudes in communication, and similar patterns of relationships formed within the communities. Even if a member objected to others with different attitudes toward change, the data indicated the presence of enough members with similar attitudes with whom he could form deeper relationships if he had the desire and/or ability to do so.

Perhaps district members shared such underdeveloped communications skills that forming relationships with one another was far more difficult than forming relationships with those outside the district. They seemed to be engaging in a power struggle to cover up their individual shortcomings. The older members were demanding that the young affirm them, as they had once affirmed those before them, by replicating their life style. The young were demanding that the old affirm them by listening to their reasons for breaking with tradition and by responding with changes in life style. As long as each group focused on changing the other, its members could avoid more penetrating self-confrontation. Thus, few members of either group had stopped to face what they needed to learn and do for themselves. Engaging in the power struggle allowed the older, more conservative, members to justify their insularity and the younger, more liberal ones their decisions to resign.

The consultants also raised the smoke screen issue at the level of district policy. Why did district leaders continue to diagnose their problems in terms of relationship difficulties? The consultants suggested that district members had lost sight of their goals and had been diverted from their mission. They therefore lacked the motivation to communicate with one another or to see how members of the other generation group were relevant to their mission. At a point of change and crisis, the consultants claimed, the district was focusing on survival and neglect—growth and renewal; compromise was leading them toward neither survival nor renewal.

The consultants raised a number of specific issues encountered during their work with the district. In contrast to the communication issues on which the training had been focused, these issues could be addressed only by considering the possibility of fundamental change. For the first time, district leaders seemed open to considering fundamental change. A description of these issues has already been published (Culbert, 1970). It includes issues at the district's interface with its environment, such as its failure to provide services for the poor—the very group it had been chartered to serve—and its policy of assuring members a teaching job for life, which supported men with outdated skills and thereby lessened the religious schools' competitive position with the public schools. The description also includes issues internal to the district, such as system maintenance and leadership. Aware that many men reported that they could not sustain themselves in communities as they were presently formed, the leaders began to realize that the total lack of assertive leadership among the young would eventually threaten the organization's survival. Each of the above issues was presented with behavioral and anecdotal data drawn from the consultant's experiences over the year.

Responses to data-based confrontation, as in this case, are always complex. While data permit different interpretations, they do not incorporate the client's biases so readily as the consultant initially does. Data typically force the client to see "give" in a system in which he saw none. Until he has tried other alternatives and reexamined his approaches, the client will persist in "making" the present system work.

It is not within the scope of this paper to specify the changes that were eventually made. Many of the issues identified at the two-day meeting resulted in fundamental change. Many problems persist.

DISCUSSION

Experimenting with Change During "Crisis"

This case generates a lesson that warrants further discussion. In framing this project within an experimental design, the consultants tried to keep the client from prematurely making a large-scale commitment. In retrospect, the client required even more protection. Data indicate that training may have aggravated the tension between those with conservative and those with liberal beliefs. Left to normal community processes, the liberal grouping probably would have mollified their demands for change, and many tensions would have subsided. Without this "give" in the system, differences and conflicts remained explicit and were confronted more directly during community meetings. This confrontation resulted in an increased defensiveness, which, in turn, contributed to the accelerated rate of attrition for those with liberal leanings and increased defensiveness, leading to greater insularity, for those with conservative leanings. For the district it meant the loss of some of its more imaginative and outgoing members.

This experience implies that organizations which experiment with change processes under crisis conditions require considerable support and protection. How can they respond simultaneously to the needs of the "cautious" majority as well as those of the "visionary" minority and still keep the organization operating? The majority require enough security so that they feel no need to suppress those who want to break from tradition, but do not know how. The minority, who feel they have contemporary vision, must have the freedom to experiment, without feeling impelled to change the other group. Neither group must lose the collaborative spirit prematurely, merely because one fears the other.

Transitional structures that give members a chance to try open-ended experiments without interrupting organizational stability are needed. Individuals need to feel out the problem, though they may be some distance from a well-thought-out solution. One organization myth must be eliminated: that one who wishes to criticize current practices must first state a well-thought-out plan for improving them. Structures are needed to support those who criticize but see no effective alternative to established practices and to support those who feel threatened when they hear confreres refer to present ways as problems. The prospect of change almost always threatens those who have lived a long time under "established" assumptions. Experience with the preceding case indicates that isolating experimental work from day-to-day operations might have reduced some of the threat. Organizational structures that remove experimentation from daily pressures should protect organizations from attrition and insularity. They certainly could make management's life easier. Members allowed to experiment in a protected setting might not confuse their frustrations in not knowing a better way with administrative resistances to overcome. And members who feel threatened by experimentation might be buffered from an onslaught of new but unsubstantiated ideas.

Transitional structures, supporting experimentation, would enhance the organization through their processes as well as through their results. If successful, new structures could attract converts from the wary. Where the experiment proved less than generalizable, it would retain merit in its means: the exercise of experimentation itself. Some organizational mechanism must govern the beginnings and ends of experiments. It must promote their initial conceptualization and monitor against their outliving their usefulness. Those forming an experimental cell should have clear, but limited, obligations to the organization. Oppressive obligation leads to new power struggles. Members starting an experiment must feel free to proceed as long as the project seems valid to them; the burden of proving a point to others should not distract or demoralize them. But they should sense when returning to traditional practices would be best.

If the experimenting group discovers a new form, demonstrably valid for a majority, then the organization has evidence to support adoption of the new form on a wider scale. Such change may leave a minority who do not wish to change. This group will then find refuge in its own experiment and, in the process, develop greater understanding of its differences with others. Having each group "field-test" its own suggestions adds flexibility as well as stability to the system.

SUMMARY

In this complex case, it is important to realize that research entered the picture at critical points of conflict and uncertainty and subsequently guided consultant and management toward a solution which included consideration of fundamental change. By agreeing to do a pilot study monitored by research, management and consultant channeled the tension between them and put their different perspectives to work constructively. Research data yielded a timely warning that sensitivity training alone would not solve the problems as management had defined them. When personal bias clouded the issue, use of research helped expose "generation differences" as a smoke screen and helped the consultants to make a credible case for fundamental change. There are many shortcomings in relying on controlled research when under the pressures of real problems. Controlled research takes time and saps resources. Nevertheless, when the situation is complex and the issues are buried, as in the present case, research can enhance the contributions of good consulting.

REFERENCES

Alderfer, C. P., & Lodahl, T. M. A quasi experiment on the use of experimental methods in the classroom. *Journal of Applied Behavorial Science*, 1971, 7(1), 43-69.

Berkowitz, N. H., & Bennis, W. G. Interaction patterns in formal service-oriented organizations. *Administrative Science Quarterly*, 1961, 6(1), 25-50.

Callahan, D. M. Conformity, deviation, and morale among educators in school systems. Unpublished doctoral dissertation, Columbia University, 1968.

Campbell, J. P., & Dunnette, M. D. Effectiveness of t-group experiences in managerial training and development. *Psychological Bulletin*, 1968, 70(2), 73-104.

Culbert, S. A. Organizational renewal: Using internal conflicts to solve external problems. *Proceedings of the 22nd Annual Meeting of the Industrial Relations Research Association*. Madison, Wisc.: The Association, 1970, pp. 109-119.

Culbert, S. A., & Reisel, J. Organization development: An applied philosophy for managers of public enterprise. *Public Administrative Review*, 1971, 31(2), 159-169.

Foy, F. A. *Catholic almanac*. Garden City, N.J. Doubleday, 1969.

Hall, J., & Williams, M.S. *Personal relations survey*. Austin, Tex.: Teleometrics, Inc., 1967.

Hilfiker, L. R. The relationship of school system innovativeness to selected dimensions of interpersonal behavior in eight school systems. Madison: Wisconsin Research and Development Center for Cognitive Learning (Technical Rep. No. 70), 1969.

Luft, J. *Of human interaction*. Palo Alto, Ca.: National Press, 1969.

McLaughlin, J. L. Measurement of attitudes toward renewal within a religious order. Unpublished master's thesis, The George Washington University, 1971.

Rokeach, M. *The open and closed mind*. New York: Basic Books, 1960.

Taylor, D. M., & Altman, I. Intimacy-scaled stimuli for use in studies of interpersonal relationships. Bethesda, Md.: Naval Medical Research Institute (Rep. No. 9), 1966.

1978 REFLECTIONS ON "USING RESEARCH TO GUIDE AN ORGANIZATION DEVELOPMENT PROJECT"

Samuel A. Culbert

I remember that writing the "Using Research" article was a heroic effort. I wrote it after the project was over when my interests were somewhere else; I had collected so much data that it took far too long to organize it to present the story I wanted to tell; and at the time I had so much to say that I was constantly taking off on side excursions and having to bring myself back. What is more, the clients, or I should say what was left of the clients, were not all that happy with my version of the story. They all but threatened to sue, and I did not even tell the whole truth. I feel confident that if I had, they would have. Now it is ten years later, and there is no need for either of us to worry because the truth has been out long enough to no longer hurt.

Our project turned out to be an escape valve for many who had "defection" on their minds. ("Defector" was what they called someone who decided to renounce his religious vows and leave the teaching order, no matter how noble the reason.) The 60s had come too fast for the organization. Imagine an organization chartered to teach the poor but running military academies for the rich in order to pay the rent. For many, leaving was the only way out. There were no longer sufficient rewards to self-justify their vows of poverty, chastity, and obedience, but they lacked the rationale that would allow them to leave without being overwhelmed by guilt. It meant renouncing their "family," their raison d'etre, and their friends. Apparently, they needed a social scientist to come in and give them absolution. We did not realize that our OD intervention was to be their way out.

As the article describes, organizational representatives sought help for the community tensions caused by the "generation gap." This was a plausible cover for an OD intervention, although a more zealous group of T-group advocates might have allowed the client's diagnosis to stick, I feel certain that the outcome would have been the same. We uncovered what we thought, and I still think, was the real problem, and to our credit we held on to it until the very end. I can still remember when two of us attended a meeting of community leaders and suggested they either sell their extra land to support their teaching the poor or to stand back and allow those who wanted to leave to do so without externally imposed guilt. At the time there were plenty of jobs in the ghetto made possible by federally sponsored community-action programs.

I still see nothing different that we could have done at the time. Rereading our study has convinced me that it is as good a write-up as I could produce, particularly considering my multiple objectives. I wanted to tell the consultation story; I wanted to describe the consultant-client tensions that I thought were inevitable in any honest OD effort; I wanted to show our restraint in not consuming more of the organization's money in training efforts which, while important for the individuals involved, were not particularly useful in terms of the organization's crisis; and I wanted to show that research provided us a platform for presenting what our clinical experiences showed and gave us a perspective that was not compromised by our earnest desire to please. What I did not say then, and can say now, is that there were any number of ways to analyze our data. I think I tried most of them, and the ones that were presented were "consistent" with what our clinical experience told us—some might even say "generated" by what our clinical experience told us. Although the latter seems a little strong, I did switch my research orientation after this study in what I would call an applied phenomenological direction.

Although I think the way we proceeded was exemplary ten years ago, I would do it differently today because now I have a much more powerful construct to guide me. Nevertheless, I would have to invent a new research format. I would need access again to the diverse realities held by different members of the client group to learn just how my understanding applied to the client's situation and which tactic to use to communicate what I learned. Today I tell client representatives something like "I need to hear how the situation appears to each of the other people involved, if only to reconfirm what you've told me and to learn how to relate what needs to be done in terms everyone can appreciate."

The construct that guides me today was introduced in an article in the *Journal of Applied Behavioral Science*'s special issue on collaboration (Culbert & McDonough, 1977). The construct is called alignment. Alignment is our way of explaining how people attend to their own self-interest while pursuing the "task requirements" of their jobs. Alignments are the "self-convenient" ways people formulate the expression of personal values, interests, and talents while avoiding defining their jobs in ways that require skills they lack. Once people have formulated their alignments and defined their jobs self-conveniently, their alignments act as "self-beneficial" lenses which color what they see. Alignments determine the unique meaning each person attributes to each organizational happening. Give five people the same job and they do it differently. Five people with somewhat different self-pursuits can observe the same organizational event and report it differently. It all depends on one's alignment.

Alignments explain the inevitable consultant-client tension. Both want the situation structured in a way that allows them to personally succeed. Research in one form or another is essential for the consultant to reconstruct the situation and to perform a client service that allows clients to feel that they participated in the process. An organizational situation can be constructed in any number of ways, and the consultant's job is to help clients come up with one that unlocks the organization from a crucial problem and allows everyone to contribute to the organization in ways that are both personally meaningful and externally valued. This issue is taken up in detail in the Culbert and McDonough (1977) article. Certainly, the particular design we developed in order to diagnose more deeply and to search for an alternative to running sensitivity training and team-building sessions for literally hundreds of community members fit the consultants' alignments, mine in particular. We took a lot of pride in giving the clients valuable and efficient consultation in a form that produced scholarly research and colleague interaction.

The project also fit the alignments of the people who hired and coordinated with us. Most of them left the organization, and the few who did not seem to have stayed for personal reasons rather than the service and self-sacrifice their religious order emphasizes. I am still in contact with some who left. Most of those I knew who left chose service professions such as teaching and counseling; all have married and most have families.

Alignments can also explain the liberal/conservative split upon which the study was based. The data show that the "conservatives" were mostly older people who, although criticized for trying to resist change, were trying to hold on to structures that gave their lives meaning. In retrospect, it was an impossible situation. Each group was attempting to persuade the other to go along with a definition of reality that fit its alignments only. Such situations do not work in academia, they do not work in business, and they do not work in religious communities. There is no amiable solution to an organizational conflict in which each group's definition of reality comes at the expense of the self-respect and success of the other. Such a conflict of alignments, and the war of opposing values it evokes, today would probably keep us consulting at the level of structural and organizational analysis rather than at the level of personal growth and interpersonal communication.

This is where the consultation finally took us anyway. Eventually, we learned enough to see the situation for what it was; we learned how to present it to them; and the result was understandable. In the original write-up I hedged about this point because too many people knew the name of the organization and I did not want to violate its integrity by specifying that I thought the organization was disconnected from its underlying purpose—serving the poor. I did not see their personal trade-offs of poverty, obedience, and chastity as paying off. But the theory of alignments tells us that there were other trade-offs that made running military academies for rich kids worthwhile for some people. Some trade-offs were probably defensive, such as fear of going into the uncloistered lay world after years of living the protected life of a monk. Others were probably self-expressive, such as having the organizational position from which to have one's views recognized and acted upon. But to me, from my priviledged position as an academic monk who, with tenure, can never be turned out, the disconnection between spoken organizational and secret personal aims reeks of careerism, yet alignments tell me why it exists. People have interacted with their jobs to make them maximally expressive of personal values, interests, skills, and the need to avoid looking incompetent, and the organizational mission comes second.

REFERENCES

Culbert, S. A., & McDonough, J. J. *Ego patrol*. Unpublished manuscript.

Culbert, S. A., & McDonough, J. J. Collaboration vs. personal alignment: An experiment that went awry. *Journal of Applied Behavioral Science*, 1977, *13*(3), 351-59.

Toward a Self-Renewing School

Alfred Alschuler

*This case study describes the use of OD strategies to introduce psycholog-
ical curricula in a community college. The author hypothesizes that the
success of the intervention was due to the combination of three factors:
favorable historical antecedents, the nature of the intervention, and continuous leadership by key administrators before and after the intervention. The interdependence of these three factors is analyzed.*

There is an apocryphal story of an educational reformer who
began as a classroom teacher, tried unsuccessfully to get administrative support for his innovations, and decided he needed to be in control
of the school if reforms were to begin. When he became principal, the
increased authority allowed him to inaugurate more sweeping
changes, which in turn caused broader-based community resistance.
Nevertheless, his energy and ideas were respected, especially from a
distance, and he was invited to become superintendent of a system
ripe for change. But there too he was defeated in his visionary reforms,
this time by state-mandated curriculum requirements and laws that
officially defined his "open campus" high schools as illegal, school-
enforced truancy. Impatient for the freedom to create his own rules, he
started a private consulting firm that actively lobbied for new laws

This article is adapted from *Motivating achievement in high school students: Education for human growth*, by Alfred Alschuler. Englewood Cliffs, N.J.: Educational
Technology Publications, 1972. I wish to express my admiration for the work of the entire
faculty at Jamestown Community College. In addition, I extend my appreciation for the
participants in the Bergamo workshop for their time and honesty during the interviews.

permitting communities to redesign their school systems. The logic of this well-intentioned educational reformer is as consistent as his history of escalated failures. His story is equally exciting and depressing: both the promise and the risk in dealing with the metasystems surrounding the learning process are clear. At each level there is more power over the systems that cradle the classroom, but less direct influence over what happens in it. Only a calculus of power could identify the precise distance from the classroom at which system leverage maximizes influence on specific acts of teaching-learning.

Our five-year research project began humbly enough.[1] We designed, tried out, and assessed some methods of increasing adolescent achievement motivation as a prototype for other psychological curricula currently being developed for schools (Alschuler, Tabor, & McIntyre, 1970). We decided to be as practical as possible as early as possible in order to avoid the frequent failure of researchers who are either personally unable or professionally unwilling to translate their laboratory successes into institutionalized procedures. We chose to do our research in classrooms.

As part of the entry *quid pro quo* with our "laboratory" schools, we agreed to train some of their teachers as research collaborators. Everyone considered it an advantageous arrangement, since it would create an indigenous corps of teachers to carry on the motivation training after the inevitable departure of the researchers. To our mystification, however, motivation training ceased when we left—in spite of enthusiastic teachers, in spite of proven results and promises of administrative support. The complexities of counterbalancing pressures in the system of schooling mocked our good intentions.

Knotty, recalcitrant, and frustrating as the school system is, it now appears to contain a deep wisdom and supra-individual rationality, which if given a voice would say, "I will guard my children against ill-conceived reforms by being exceptionally difficult to change. I will yield to you, but only if you back your proposed innovations with the persistent energy that comes from firm convictions in their value. If the reforms command that much dedication, I will allow them . . . but slowly."

Out of respect for the powerful, institutionalized conservatism that we witnessed but did not fully understand, we affirmed the obvious (a rather refreshing act for those of us long rewarded for complicating reality): setting up motivation training in schools requires more than the fallout effects of action research. At the same time we were reluctant to engage in that potentially endless escalation of the quixotic

---

[1]The Achievement Motivation Development Project was supported by the U.S. Office of Education (OEG-0-8-071231-1747), Bureau of Research.

reformer. We thus settled on a compromise; fortunately, in retrospect, a good one: We would work only on the system immediately beyond the classroom, the one that exerts itself most frequently and forcefully on the teaching-learning processes—the school in which motivation training is to be instituted.

This article describes the organizational development strategies used to introduce psychological curricula in Jamestown Community College. The first section describes the 18-month period following a week-long workshop, attended by 24 of the 65 college faculty members, in which we tried to create system support for our educational innovations. After it is clear that there are sufficient "results" to be worthy of further explanation, I will analyze the contribution of three intertwining causes that appear to account for most of the subsequent changes—the college's readiness for change, the workshop intervention, and the continuing leadership of key individuals. These three forces for change were coordinated through a productive combination of organizational development strategies and psychological education. The relationship between these two approaches deserves, and will receive, attention in the concluding paragraphs of this study. At best, however, case studies yield enlightened commentary rather than definitive conclusions. Only one conclusion is clear to me: decoding the puzzle of school reform requires the services of a genius cryptographer—probably several of them.

DEVELOPMENTS AFTER THE WORKSHOP

The objectives of the workshop were as simply stated as they were hard to attain. First, we wanted to introduce motivation training to the college in such a way that it would still be a course offering for students a year to two years later. Second, in order to facilitate additional innovations, we wanted workshop participants to learn about other available courses, techniques, and orientations in psychological education. We spoke in terms of developing a "self-renewing" system where an established climate of change would encourage all members to build new instructional bridges between the abilities of students and the demands of life after school; but even while the words were in our mouths, we knew there would be a gap between the ideal of a self-renewing school and the results of the workshop. The only question was the size of that gap.

Fifteen months after the workshop I returned to Jamestown with a colleague to find out what had happened.[2] During a week in which we

---

[2] My thanks to Dr. Daniel Callahan for his help in interviewing faculty members and in analyzing the changes.

interviewed all but three of the participants[3] and a sample representative of the rest of the faculty, we hoped to identify most of the workshop's major effects on school policies and procedures, classroom activities, and individuals' public roles and private lives. We were less interested in the detection of "statistically significant results" than in the discovery of significant social changes that we hoped would render statistics superfluous or pale outlines of reality at best. The composite description of "results" that follows is as faithful to the interviews as possible, and introduces and defines the phenomena examined more fully in the second section of this case study.[4]

A New Spirit

The workshop ended on Friday. Registration for the second semester courses began the following Monday. Its participants—the 24 faculty members and three students—were still glowing from the invigorating affection they had won, in part, by learning together but particularly by facing up to and knocking down a number of the long-standing interpersonal barriers, misunderstandings, and distrust that typically are an integral, though covert, part of every school's operating procedures. These personal irritations and kinks in a system drain energy. This is so much the norm in most institutions that when some of the problems are resolved, even temporarily, there is a strong counter-reaction of delightful surprise and exuberantly expressed affection. In the eyes of the faculty who had not gone through the fear, pain, tears, and eventual acceptance of former adversaries, the dramatic changes were not understandable. Second semester registration shocked them. As usual, it was held in the grim gym, the only place large enough to hold all the tables with all the forms to be signed. But in contrast to the usual dehumanizing routine and the steady mumble of many simultaneous voices, the workshop faculty had transformed registration into a reunion. "Creedence Clearwater" and "Country Joe and the Fish" played loudly over the PA system, as they had during the workshop. Members greeted one another with hugs rather than the ritual words. Their warmth spread to students, now ushered in in the style of a happy airline stewardess from one registration table to another. The blooming determination of workshop participants to maintain and spread their good feelings was matched by "the others'" suspicions

---

[3]Only 21 of the 24 faculty were interviewed. One was on sabbatical and two chose not to be interviewed.

[4]This description has been read by the participants we interviewed. Except for a few minor corrections (e.g., an additional $100,000 in grants was obtained after the interviews but before the description was completed), it was endorsed without dissent.

and their rock-hard norms against public display of affection, however innocent and mild, in school.

Institutionalizing this momentum immediately became a twofold problem. First, the motivation course and other specific innovations had to be instituted. Second, the climate of friendly, cooperative support had to be spread from the new "in" group to the uninitiated "out" group. The record is fairly clear. Three semesters after the workshop, 207 of the 1,350 day students had taken the five-day achievement motivation course. The course instructors had disseminated the motivation training outside the college through four workshops for 122 faculty members and students elsewhere. Within Jamestown Community College itself there had been 115 participations (one person in one program is a "participation") in nine outside workshops in psychological education, on such topics as "Public Knowledge and Private Concerns," "Growth-Oriented Groups," "Value Clarification Techniques," "Synectics," "Advanced Training in Psychological Education,"[5] Most of the 65 faculty members participated. In addition, in-house seminars and mini-workshops for Jamestown faculty were conducted by participants who wanted to share and spread what they learned from the outside workshops. Using a very crude statistic, 444 extensive "participations" by faculty and students followed the original workshop experience of 24 faculty members and three students. Thus, the rough "spread" ratio was 16 : 1.

New Policies

There were also new policies affecting the whole school, some of which had required faculty approval. The motivation course was taught by five members of the Dean of Students' counseling staff. One staff member had been reassigned from the psychology department to concentrate full time on psychological education programs within the school. Another had been assigned half-time, and several faculty members had been given released time to work in this area. The reallocation of personnel, like the redistribution of money, is evidence of an important change in priorities. The faculty also formally approved Achievement Motivation Training as a three-credit course. Another decision, made by the Academic Standards Committee shortly after the workshop, was the adoption of a "no flunk out" policy in which students who were dropped for academic reasons could return to school if they took an Achievement Motivation course. Gentle

---

[5]These workshops, like the original workshop on Achievement Motivation Training, were conducted by the Center for Humanistic Education at the State University of New York at Albany.

coercion or not, this policy kept the back door open and helped a number of students.[6] By public decision the faculty also chose to give up its minutely legislated prerequisites for graduation. Within the required 48 credit hours in liberal arts and sciences, students were now almost completely free to choose their courses. Further, all faculty committees were opened to students, a clear public declaration of trust in the good judgment of their younger partners in the educational process.

Innovative Projects and Grants

During this same year and a half, various faculty members sought and obtained $277,000 in special grants for new projects; e.g., "Institutional Grant for Science," "Multimedia Learning Center for Career Students," "Law Enforcement Education Program," "Education Opportunity Program," "Greater Sensitivity for the New Technologies in Medically Oriented Careers," and a planning grant to find ways of incorporating drama into philosophy, psychology, and anthropology. Not one outside grant had been obtained in the 18 months *prior to* the motivation workshop. Several other new projects that did not require special funding were conducted. Three of the workshop participants created a multimedia, experience-based English course. Four teachers synthesized what they had learned in several advanced workshops and presented their own "Process Teaching Workshop" to the faculty. In the fall following the workshop, the Dean's staff organized a special small-group experience-and-discussion orientation program for new students. During the summer a year and a half after the workshop a faculty group planned a "Developmental Studies Program" which used motivation training, among other procedures, to provide special help for "problem" students entering college under New York's open-enrollment plan. Over half of the original workshop participants were key members in lobbying for policy changes, obtaining grants, or planning and conducting special projects, which have had at least an indirect effect on everyone at Jamestown Community College.

Classroom Techniques

The greatest variety of workshop applications and the most direct effects on students occurred in the classroom. Nineteen of the 21 teachers interviewed 15 months after the workshop had tried two or more procedures learned in the workshop. Music, milling, touching,

---

[6]The following year some students were dropped for academic reasons without recourse to the motivation course. Thus, there is now a *partial* "no drop out" policy.

name games, and other warm-up, get-acquainted exercises were used the first day of class. As much as 50 per cent of class time was spent in examining the relevance of the subject matter to the individual lives of the students. Negotiations with the students to decide collaboratively the course content were undertaken. Changes in the teacher's role from director to facilitator of student-chosen projects occurred. Individualized student-selected pacing was adopted. A six-step psychological learning sequence to plan courses was used. Videotapes were replayed for feedback on group processes. A mini-free university in class (a kind of carnival with different learning booths) was created. Role playing, fantasy trips, sensory awakening techniques, value whips, and other techniques to get experientially into poetry and literature were tried. There were more personal anecdotal illustrations in class; changes in the grading system to encourage team learning projects; individual learning contracts; more systematic use of attention-getting techniques; more time spent talking with individual students outside class; student-made examinations and group tests; use of permanent subgroups in class for fun and work. Most of these changes reflect greater inclusion of students' needs in the conduct of teaching. Whether through explicit negotiation or techniques that tap students' deeper concerns, nearly every teacher had taken steps to make broader human contact with his students.

Difficulties in Changing

Such changes are seldom quickly achieved or instantly rewarded by the acceptance of students, who finally attain their secret goal of recognition as fully human beings in the learning process. From the first gush of registration day some students stiffened at what they experienced. The logic of their feelings made an "is" into an "ought"— "schooling is not like this, therefore this is not the way it ought to be." The immediate reaction of many was confusion over what the new relationship rules were to be. Some wanted the anonymous security of distance and structured instruction. For 12 years they had learned from undeviating experience that learning is primarily content not process, abstract not personal, receptive not proactive, and authoritative rather than uncertain in some primal and ultimate sense. For some students, their teachers' attempts to humanize learning was "weird" and to be at best "endured" until things got back to normal. In turn, a number of teachers lost courage when their bold steps toward students produced a student retreat in equal measure.

A straightforward listing of the number and variety of innovations may be persuasive; but, for all their accuracy, numbers miss an important personal dimension and lie by omission. Some pain accompanied each outstanding success like a shadow the sun. The workshop experience of what learning among peers could be like revolutionized faculty expectations and made the continuing reality of their classrooms a daily reminder of unattained goals. One teacher reported,

> For two months after the workshop I was depressed. In school, by comparison to the workshop, there was less meaning, less contact with others, and less intimacy. There was an emptiness and a real identity crisis for me. It raised a lot of questions about teaching, relationships, and trust. It didn't impair my teaching, though. Now I have warmer relationships with the kids, my own and the students, but it took me a while.

Or, again, from another teacher,

> I felt disorganized and depressed for a while last spring. Some students wondered what was bothering me. I wasn't less effective as a teacher, but I was just examining all aspects of my relationships. First, I recognized my attempts to manipulate and control students, especially in individual conferences. So I tried to be less directive and allowed students to take more initiative. We still get there, but it's more relaxed. Now, I just feel more comfortable. It's easier to accept them where they are without lecturing or moralizing to them. It's easier to really listen to different points of view. But for a while last year I couldn't concentrate on a lot of new techniques because I was "hung up" on myself.

One professor admitted with bittersweet pride of being a "teacher of literature" accustomed to the pleasures of his discipline and dedicated to stimulating this same appreciation in his students. Gentleness and good intentions shine through his formal bearing and measured, absolutely correct grammar:

> The workshop convinced me I had to get closer to my students. I wish I could do easily some of the things I see others doing. I'm saddened at my inability, but I can't do these things. I have adopted the attitude of knowing my strengths, developing my weaknesses, but stopping when it threatens my strengths.
>
> At first we worked in small groups to minimize lecturing and maximize class discussion. It seemed to fail; so I abandoned it. I just can't open up in class. However, I can open up in my office. I seek out students and their previous teachers to find out what interests them most. I encourage them to see me after class in my office where I can "hook up" the course with their ultimate interests. That way, they can satisfy my expectations at the same time they satisfy themselves. Last year perhaps I saw three students each week in my office, mostly about the mechanics of expression. This year I see an average of 15 students each week in my office and we talk about their interests. I find that I enjoy this contact very much.

Most teachers, like this budding Mr. Chips, have persisted, in spite of initial difficulties, to the point where changes are more satisfying to students and to themselves. None of the teachers interviewed said this had occurred immediately or without some disappointments. Nor were they as successful as their ultimate hopes.

Overall Evaluations

Some of the most poignant observations were from faculty who did not attend the workshop. Their reactions were mixed:

> For years there has been a polarization for the faculty based on cliques. People from both cliques went to the workshop and came back with the urge to unite. The most pleasant unity in eight years is now present.

> * * *

> People who didn't go felt left out. It divided the faculty into two groups. The major problem is the communication gap between those who went and those who didn't. Explanations were tried, but they didn't help. Sometimes they made it worse.

> * * *

> People came back with enthusiasm, and there's a much friendlier atmosphere.

> * * *

> I was disappointed with the people who came back from the workshop. Their religious fervor was contrived and unreal. It was brainwashing. There is suspicion about the faculty who went and came back the "workshop warriors."

> * * *

> I'm new here. The faculty seems to have fewer tensions than other places. I never felt like I was in an "out" group. It stirred up a lot of talk about teaching students.

> * * *

> It hurt some people.

> * * *

> It helped some people. My daughter went through an achievement motivation course and it had a good effect on her.

> * * *

> The counselors are not doing their job now. (They are teaching motivation courses instead.)

Even among those who attended, there was some division in their overall evaluations, although the majority opinion was a positive one.

> Not all the results are beneficial. There is more tension. Some of it is from letting more feelings be known and being unsure of reactions. I have the

feeling that students are becoming less responsible. They are going off on the emotional side. It interferes with their classwork. Hard work is good for the soul.

* * *

There is a better feeling in the school now. I don't see the tremendous bitterness in faculty meetings or in the teachers' lounge anymore. I feel as if I belong to a community now. Other faculty were resentful at first, but that's died out now.

Participants reported numerous changes in personal lives, which will not be reported here out of respect for their privacy. However, their number, tenor, and range were similar to the changes described above. Most comments were positive, but there was enough pain reported to command continued reflection on the responsibilities of workshop trainers and the risks inherent in any change they facilitate.

AN HISTORICAL ANALYSIS

In the interviews with participants I was surprised by the amount of progress they seemed to have made. Yet there was something curious about their reports. I asked them about the effects of the workshop, and they described everything that had occurred as if the workshop had been THE cause, rather than a cause for some of the changes. One teacher even said, "The workshop shook this place. All the things that have happened were started and made possible there."

It is irrational to assume that the college was an inert system brought to life by the workshop. Furthermore, a mass of accumulating data gently instills humility in change agents: The most important determinants of change are not the quantity, quality, or delivery of educational input but the characteristics of the learners, e.g., their belief that one can control one's own destiny (Coleman, 1966), their motivation and intelligence (Luborsky, Chandler, Auerbach, Cohen, & Bachrach, 1971), their value of achievement (Alschuler, 1972). Perhaps there are institutional equivalents of these personality characteristics, e.g., in a system's conviction that changes are possible, important, desired, and wise. The starting point may have been before the workshop; perhaps the possibilities for change were embedded in existing but unactualized repertoires of the faculty members. From this perspective, the workshop would simply have triggered the sustained changes. To explore this interpretation, the school's history before and after the workshop must be reviewed. What were the signs of readiness? What were the conditions preceding the workshop that made possible sustained development after the workshop? Like a review of

scientific literature before devising experiments, the aim of the historical analysis that follows is to uncover hypotheses, not to test them.

Jamestown Community College sits at the bottom of a gentle hill on
the edge of a quiet town in western New York. The buildings in the
center of Jamestown are taller than one expects in a rural community.
Their color is darkened with age, however, and points to a more active
past. The rich rolling farmland within sight of the town epitomizes an
integration of rural and urban ways of life. There is a tiny "inner city,"
with noticeable but minor racial problems. Some youths use drugs, but
there is no epidemic of hepatitis nor deaths from overdoses. The
economic crisis across the country is cause for careful spending in
Jamestown, but there have been no layoffs nor angry revolts of
teachers or taxpayers. The tidal waves of urban change have only
rippled into Jamestown. It remains a good place to raise a family: rural
enough for fresh air and clean water, yet close enough to Buffalo for
cultural life; small enough to walk outside at night safely, yet big
enough to have its own college and an array of human relationships.

"The College" is the oldest community college in the state, but
after this early achievement it never attempted anything sufficiently
controversial to create talk across the state. Nor has there been strong
external pressure for change—a cry for community control, a funding
crisis, the shifting borders of a segregated minority—as found
elsewhere. For 20 years, Jamestown Community College did its job of
preparing students for a vocation or a four-year college. For 12 of these
years, the college was administered by a rather authoritarian president. The first sign of change was the hiring of a new Dean of Students,
Roger Wingett. He left a middle-sized New York university after 10
years of advancement from Director of Residence Halls to Dean of Men
and Acting Dean of Students; predicting (correctly) a stormy, politicized work climate there, Dean Wingett decided to accept a new post
at Jamestown. He landed in the middle of another stormy, politicized
work climate. Faculty trust of the authoritarian president was at such a
low ebb that they resorted to the Taylor Law in negotiating salaries.
Hired by the president, Dean Wingett was the prime candidate for
Red-Herring of the Year. Even his innocuous decision to improve park-
ing regulations was struck down by the faculty as usurpation of their
prerogatives. Effective functioning required the dean to act collaboratively, to be trustworthy and open—in a climate whose first and last
question was always "Which side are you on?" It was his considerable
accomplishment to remain his own man and earn general respect.
Major innovation at this time, however, was a distant luxury.

In the spring of the dean's second year, a prolonged and bitter
struggle over the president's firing of a faculty member divided the

institution and united the faculty in opposition to the president. But Dean Wingett saw opportunity in this adversity. At the height of the turbulent spring semester, he encouraged and then publicly supported the creation of a constructively still "backwater." One of his staff members, Robert Oddy, collected a volunteer group of 15 faculty members, students, and administrators to meet weekly with the aid of a series of encounter-tapes, a commercially available set of audio-taped suggestions of group methods for developing openness, trust, authenticity, and generally enhanced more satisfying human relationships. It was a judiciously small testing of the college's readiness for change of this kind, since there are always faculty members who believe "psychological education" is insidiously deceptive jargon for brainwashing. The encounter-tapes were a mild success, leaving the participants pleasantly engaged and sufficiently unsatisfied to want more.

The following August the President resigned, giving 30 days' notice. A former chairman of the board of trustees, a retired banker, was named Acting President and the new school year began in a quiet hiatus blessed by all. The Acting President devoted himself to untangling the snarled college finances, disclaimed expertise in educational matters, and warmly deferred policy decisions to his deans and faculty. For Dean Wingett, it would have been politic to coast, building relationship capital with faculty members until the new president had been chosen and his style, direction, and stance were known. Nevertheless, he sought a way of continuing the interest aroused by the encounter-tape sessions. He contacted the Center for Humanistic Education at the State University of New York at Albany to inquire about workshops, requested and obtained supplemental funds from the Acting President, recruited about two-thirds of the 65 faculty members through individual conversations, and set up interviews between faculty volunteers and workshop staff members to explore needs, goals, and possibilities.

This is the lonely grit of change agentry: The Dean worked in an educational leadership vacuum, in the absence of major institutional precedents, without either visible support or opposition from the faculty. Neither diagnostic super-brilliance nor blind faith activated the Dean, but instead unactualized convictions:

> At that point we were an institution that talked about creating an educational climate that was satisfying to students. "Education" was passing us by. We needed to examine what we were doing and what we were giving to students. The student body is always changing. We must try to understand these students and relate to their needs. For me, we *have* to be changing our educational models continuously. I am committed to changing, and it wasn't going on here.

Absence of Genotypic Problems

The Dean's efforts touched a number of hidden strengths, which can be appreciated when the problems confronting the college are contrasted with the problems of most schools. In an extension of Talcott Parsons' theory of social systems, Miles (1967) describes four genotypic properties of school systems and their resulting endemic problems. My retrospective hypothesis is that it is the *absence* of these typical obstacles at Jamestown College that constituted its comparatively high state of institutional readiness for change.

1. *Goal Attainment*. Educational goals are usually vaguely stated, multiple, conflicting, emotionally loaded, and difficult to measure. It is therefore nearly impossible to use outcome measures as levers for introducing change. In their absence, decisions are often made on moral or ideological grounds, which stimulate value conflict. It is not surprising that there are frequent retreats to the one justification that touches everyone—money: "See how much we care! Look at how much we spent!" or "See how frugal we have been this year."

2. *Technology*. Teachers perform out of sight of other adults and are judged on once-removed criteria, e.g., average class grades on standardized tests. They get little feedback on the effectiveness of particular procedures. Awareness and direct use of relevant knowledge about the teaching process is rare, and diffusion of new practices is difficult, in part because there are virtually no internal R&D functions in schools, as there are in industry. Various constituencies are in regular conflict over who is most expert, and the quality of teachers is uneven. All this causes administrative overloading.

3. *Pattern Maintenance*. Most teachers are not linked to a common fate, in the sense that they must rely on each other to accomplish a single common goal, like players on an athletic team. They have a low degree of interdependence.

> It is important to note that a low degree of interdependence ordinarily makes a system much more difficult to alter, since if changes occur in one part (e.g., in one teacher's practices), there are no meaningful channels or linkages by which they can travel to other parts of the system. This state of affairs may lead to internal integration problems centering around teacher morale: feelings of isolation, depression, and nonconfirmation by peers (Miles, 1967, p. 12).

Nor do most schools spend much money to help teachers learn, grow, develop, or innovate. This is considered to be an individual matter, protected by the norm of.academic freedom. The same is true at an organizational level: there is little investment of time or money in the improvement of a school's operations.

4. *Integration.* Although public schools are essentially noncompetitive with other schools in the area, they are nonetheless highly vulnerable to criticism at any point, at almost any time, by nearly every one of their constituencies. The Board of Education or Board of Trustees is often the epitome of these conflicting groups, and sound decisions are difficult to get. In this context, frequent survival mechanisms are *passivity* and *defensiveness.*

> In many school systems the main stance of the chief administrator in the face of system vulnerability and varying demands from the environment is a withdrawing, passive one. The tacit view of the school is that it has little power to initiate, develop, grow, push things, or be disagreeable to anyone or anything. Setting up barriers of various kinds, withdrawing into ritualistic use of existing procedures, justifying existing policy, and the like also seem to appear rather frequently as a response to pressure from outside (Miles, 1967, p. 19).

Although this may increase the ease of pure system survival, it does not make for great leaps forward in improved technology and higher goal attainment.

Consider the contrasting situation in Jamestown Community College. There were no emotionally loaded debates over vague, confusing, multiple, and conflicting goals. There were relatively steady goals of preparing students for vocations or transfer to four-year colleges, and Dean Wingett's clear yet open commitment to examine "what we were doing and what we were giving to students." By personally going to all faculty members and appealing for volunteers when initiating new practices like the workshop, Dean Wingett honored their strong tradition of faculty decision making. They reciprocated by accepting, albeit conditionally, his goal statement. *Voilà! Goal clarity* and *maintenance* of decision-making patterns.

Dean Wingett saw himself and presented himself as an agent of change, not as an expert on all that is new in education. He therefore *avoided conflict* about who was most expert. He sought only to provide exposure to *new practices and technology* in an adult-peer learning context. His focus on a faculty group project was aimed at reducing role invisibility and nonconfirmation by peers and stressing the *norms* of professional development and innovation.

In contrast to the frequent defensive, passive mode of school administrators, the Acting President supported *every* recommendation made by the Dean of the College and the Dean of Students for their special areas. His stance and work on college finances facilitated internal *integration* amid general calm. In the absence of preempting external threats, the Acting President's support fostered adaptations that contributed to the system's survival as an effective institution of learning.

In this context, what the workshop did was increase existing interest, partially satisfy aroused curiosity about new technology, and continue the conversion of faculty solidarity, formed in opposition to the ex-president, into a consolidated group proposing innovations. The workshop intensified and quickened the system's self-renewal that began inauspiciously in the stillness after the storm of the previous spring. To clarify how the workshop catalyzed, but did not create, the subsequent changes, it is necessary to examine the evolving relationships between the outsiders who conducted the workshop and the Jamestown insiders who participated.

Phases in the Evolving Relationship Between Change Agents and Participants

Their collaboration passed through the ten-step sequence that typically fosters organizational development in schools (Schmuck & Miles, 1971). I have divided these steps into three phases which marked major turning points in the relationship: engagement, intervention, and institutionalization. In each phase the existing forces for change were slightly transformed, as we tested whether the match between Jamestown's needs and our technology was sufficient to justify further collaboration. Mutual willingness was balanced by mutual caution.

Engagement.

1. Middle or top management of an organization becomes interested in OD and feels that the organization has problems which can be met through training.

2. Management invites an outside OD consultant to visit the organization.

3. After the outsider's entry, legitimation, and contact with a variety of roles and groups, the organization works out a contract with the outsider specifying the nature of the projected relationship, its goals, and procedures.

4. The outsider, working with insiders, collects data about the organization.

5. These data form the basis of a joint diagnosis of the points of difficulty in the organization (Schmuck & Miles, Chap. 1).

In our first meeting with Dean Wingett, we indicated that a preliminary diagnosis of the college would help us all decide what, if any, intervention would be appropriate. We asked him to solicit as many volunteers as possible from all factions within the faculty and key administrators to meet with us.[7] In our interviews we discovered the standard number of interpersonal impasses and their typical institutional outcome: the creation of ingenious detours around problem relationships, as if stalemated relationships have benign rather than corrosive effects. We also identified extensive ignorance about the norms actually favoring innovation. Almost everyone accepted the myth that "Jamestown Community College is traditional and uninterested in change," but simultaneously and privately hoped for change. The actual norm was as invisible as each individual's fantasy life. Finally, we found that many of the teachers wanted to increase their students' motivation, a need tailor-made for our expertise in new methods of strengthening achievement motivation.

In conveying our impressions to Dean Wingett we also said that the college seemed to be getting along "pretty well" in comparison with other colleges. No outstanding problem seemed to demand intervention, and such efforts *could* create temporary disequilibrium. When the Dean indicated'that he was committed to innovating with us or without us, we decided to go ahead with him. Together we called a meeting of all participants to set appropriate expectations for a workshop. This meeting began to transform private plans into public norms, raised hopes that communication blocks between key individuals would be addressed and perhaps resolved, and promised a variety of new techniques for increasing student motivation. In this way the entire engagement process intensified interest in innovation at Jamestown Community College.

Intervention. The sixth step in the typical organizational development sequence is "a first intervention, usually some form of intensive meeting involving several key roles" (Schmuck & Miles, 1971). A capsule outline of our five-day workshop is presented in Figure 1.

The flow of activities in this psychological education course follows a sequence for whose effectiveness there is considerable empirical evidence (McClelland & Winter, 1969; Alschuler, 1972). Since the components of this course have been described elsewhere in extensive detail (Alschuler, Tabor, & McIntyre, 1970), I will concentrate here on describing its rationale. In order for any learning to occur, students must be attending. We attempted to *sustain attention* the first night by creating moderately different interpersonal norms in order to emphasize the degree of openness, supportiveness, and trust that might be transferred back to the college. Most of Monday and Tuesday *provided*

---

[7]Dr. Harold Skorpen and Edward Maurer collaborated in all phases of conducting this workshop.

	Sunday	Monday	Tuesday	Wednesday	Thursday	Friday
Morning		Role play on how to be an effective group member	An exercise in fostering pride and a sense of accomplishment in others	Free time for reading and deciding on Free University activities	Free University— 5) Principles of organizational development 6) Planning a motivation course	Integration Sharing perceptions of how participants had changed
After-noon		The Origami game: an experience simulating high achievement motivation	Blindfolded activities: more practice in helping --------- Film: "The Need To Achieve," summarizing all background information	Free University— 1) Ethical issues 2) Mental health 3) Classroom rule structures	Small-group and large-group planning	
Evening	Dinner Introductions Microlab to set norms of openness, trust, and directness	Lecture and practice in using the achievement planning pattern --------- Staff open planning session	The disarming game simulating the problems in establishing trust --------- Staff open planning session	Free University— 4) Exploring the uses of imagination ----------- Staff open discussion ----------- Encounter group for some volunteer members	Group divided by choice into Party group and Encounter group	

Figure 1. Summary of Workshop in Psychological Education and Achievement Motivation Training

intense experiences of achievement, affiliation, and power motivation, which permitted participants to meaningfully conceptualize the nature of these motives during the lecture and film on Monday and Tuesday. A secondary purpose of these activities was to provide all participants with new data about one another's styles, motives, and concerns.

During the Free University sessions on Wednesday and Thursday, the conceptualized experiences were *related to* other psychological education *techniques and* to the participant's own *needs* and ideals. This created an initial access to useful but seemingly unrelated innovations. Application of these ideas began on Wednesday and Thursday nights, when participants met in voluntary encounter groups to deal with interpersonal relationships that were hindering effective communication and decision making within the organization. On Thursday afternoon, participants made further specific plans for group projects, team efforts, and individual applications. Since all key decision makers and informal leaders of the college attended the course, numerous potential administrative problems were identified and resolved then and there. Friday morning was reserved for reviewing significant personal changes and group plans.

The course provided the technology for which participants were ready, time and space boundaries that insulated members from typical distractions, and impartial outsiders who encouraged commitment to engage in team projects and resolution of interpersonal difficulties. The workshop dealt equally with innovations that would increase the productivity of the organization and organizational norms that would enhance the survival of all members in the system.

Institutionalization. Just as an individual must consciously practice a new skill before it becomes internalized and automatic, a system requires a period of active effort and support before new norms, policies, practices, and procedures become institutionalized. This is often a time of some success, some personal frustration and misunderstandings, resulting from the enthusiasm of persons not yet practiced in their "practice." If enthusiasm is the only factor counterbalancing personal difficulties and system hindrances, sustained change is far less likely. Support from outside change agents is necessary, but it must be gradually transformed from external sources into internal resources. The trick is to leave on time—not too soon, because guidance is needed in the early phases, and not too late, because that retards the essential self-reliance. It was during this transformation period that Dean Wingett, his staff, and the other deans provided critical leadership in coordinating outside support with the development of inner strengths. The final steps in an organizational development effort as described by Schmuck and Miles (1971) identify the events but miss the people who create continuity throughout these seemingly discrete activities:

7. The intervention is evaluated via new data collection. Often future success of the effort depends on the degree in which key figures have been freed up to be more open, concerned, and creative about organizational improvement.

8. Next steps in intervention are planned following this, and so on.
9. The OD function itself becomes institutionalized within the organization. An OD department is formed and it takes central responsibility for continuing the OD process.
10. The internal specialists become increasingly professionalized, responsible for their own continuing professional development and growth (Schmuck & Miles, 1971, Chap. 1).

After the workshop, Dean Wingett, now joined by others, continued to do what he had done before—lobby for faculty decisions through personal contacts, promote new group projects, seek additional funding, and maintain his commitment to change: "I don't know what precisely we shall be doing a year from now, but I hope we have made improvements and are doing things differently." Through his daily contacts his awareness of the talents and problems of faculty members enabled him to manage an appropriate continuation but gradual decrease in the involvement of the Center for Humanistic Education. During the early months after the workshop there were numerous consultations by telephone, by mail, and in person. Several advanced workshops were planned to accommodate specific needs and to train additional faculty members. With increased expertise, the Dean's staff took on the responsibilities of an internal organizational development team.[8] The momentum was increased later that spring when a new president was chosen: By publicly declaring himself in favor of innovation and by energetically leading the search for more outside seed money, he quickly validated the faculty's vigor.

An incident late that summer illustrates how the continuing process of institutionalization introduced major programs and changed minor interactions. One result of the workshop was a decision by the deans and the faculty to sponsor an Educational Opportunity Program. During an intensive preregistration orientation program, modeled after the 5-day course, one of the janitors discovered about 15 black students asleep in the lounge at 7:30 a.m., quite against the rules. In a sequence of events reminiscent of Henny Penny, he brought a buddy to confirm the reality of what he saw. They then ushered in the supervisor, who went to the Dean of the Faculty, who, in turn, came, saw, and conquered the situation by *joining* the whole group for coffee and doughnuts. Dean Schlifke had been to the workshop—and was "more open, concerned and creative about organizational improvement," it was said.

---

[8] Duane Faulkner has been a key member of the team and deserves clear recognition for his extensive efforts.

SUMMARY

This historical analysis of the sources of change at Jamestown Community College strongly suggests three factors necessary for sustained change: (a) a high level of system readiness prior to any organizational development effort, (b) a combined effort of organizational development and psychological education, and (c) the continuous leadership of key individuals within the organization before, during, and after the participation of outside change agents.[9] From this perspective, the five-day workshop was something less than Prince Charming awakening the college with a five-day kiss, and something more than an inert tool of the Jamestown faculty. However, the contribution of the workshop, in comparison with readiness and leadership factors, is a matter for empirical testing. Nonetheless, each factor appears to be a *sine qua non* for creating a self-renewing school. Their interdependence is clear in the mutually enhancing nature of organizational development and psychological education, two terms I have used *almost* synonymously. Differentiating these concepts and defining their interdependence is an appropriate stopping point in this analysis.

OD and Psychological Education

It is a bitter paradox of the Alice-in-Wonderland world of public education that it is devoted almost exclusively to fostering growth in students, yet remains itself highly resistant to change. New curricula, dedicated teachers with good ideas, "hot-shot" administrators who take on schooling because it is a dragon worthy of their finest efforts, each makes a dent. But the problem is bigger than the individuals. It is in the system of schooling, the fixedness of rules, role relationships, procedures, policies, norms, goals; the coercive hierachy of requirements; the raised guillotine of standardized testing. It is the system that must be changed before, after, above, and beneath all else. This is the mission of organization development in schools: to foster self-renewing systems. That it can be done is illustrated by the changes at Jamestown Community College.

The successful practice of organizational development depends also on psychological education. The roles, rules, role relationships, procedures, and norms of systems have a meta-individual permanency. They tend to continue regardless of who occupies the role or who plays by the rules. Though these stable system properties can be

---

[9]Again, Duane Faulkner has been a key member in most innovations after the workshop and deserves credit here along with others who have been mentioned.

legitimately abstracted in thought and spoken about as if they are tangible, in fact they have reality only so long as they are given life by the role occupants, the rule-follower, and so on. In short, the approach to organizational development is always through individuals, clarifying or changing the goals individuals share, improving the stable patterns of communication among role inhabitants, altering their shared expectations, helping the leader to lead differently, improving the efficiency of problem solving done by groups of individuals, facing and resolving conflicts between people, collaboratively redefining roles. Not surprisingly, most of the OD methods, (training, process consultation, confrontation, data feedback, problem solving) are at most extensions of psychological education techniques developed originally for promoting self-renewing individuals. Perhaps now it is more accurate to say there is a common pool of techniques from which OD specialists and psychological educators draw. Using these techniques, the organizational health of educational systems can be increased through individuals; using these techniques, the psychological health of students can be improved in schools. Only the focus is different. OD attempts to increase the health-giving properties of schools available to all who pass through them. Psychological education attempts to increase the health that individuals must carry with them through any institution.

REFERENCES

Alschuler, A. *Motivating achievement in high school students: Education for human growth*. Englewood Cliffs, N.J.: Educational Technology Publications, 1972.

Alschuler, A., Tabor, D., & McIntyre, J. *Teaching achievement motivation*. Middletown, Conn.: Educational Ventures, Inc. (209 Court St.), 1970.

Coleman, J. *Equality of educational opportunity*. Washington, D.C.: Government Printing Office, 1966.

Luborsky, L., Chandler, M., Auerbach, A. H., Cohen, J., & Bachrach, H. M. Factors influencing the outcome of psychotherapy: A review of quantitative research. *Psychological Bulletin*, March 1971, 75(3), 145-185.

McClelland, D. C., & Winter, D. G. *Motivating economic achievement*. New York: Free Press, 1969.

Miles, M. B. Some properties of schools as social systems. In Goodwin Watson (Ed.), *Change in school systems*. Washington, D.C.: National Training Laboratories, National Education Association, 1967.

Schmuck, R. A., & Miles, M. B. *Organization development in schools*. Palo Alto, Calif.: National Press, 1971.

COMMENTARY ON "TOWARD A
SELF-RENEWING SCHOOL"

Alfred Alschuler

If self-renewal were valuable in itself, we would applaud cancer and the Neo-Nazi party. The first question we need to ask is what should be renewed. Nearly a decade after the Jamestown project, I see clearly that I confused "doing a good job" with "doing good works."

It was easy to be confused. Jamestown Community College provides local training for jobs and access to higher education. What could be more American? So long as the organization or individual is not obviously evil, why not apply one's professional techniques to the task of self-renewal? I took pride in my skills and camouflaged this egocentrism slightly by describing effective general strategies, tactics, and tools. As a well-educated, reasonably well-paid, white male member of several "old boy" networks, I merely was doing what came naturally. I ignored the question of values entirely.

I choose not to confess here the events that placed tasks on a ladder of importance. I have come to see that while I was helping to renew a rural, predominantly white college, many urban desegregated schools were on the verge of collapse. While I facilitated the realization of greater potential, many ethnic minority students were being systematically excluded from the entire educational process by discriminatory suspension practices and lack of native language instruction. As I taught individuals how to increase their achievement motivation, whole groups were being deprived of opportunities to achieve. I fiddled in Jamestown while urban schools burned.

My shift in focus may be part of a developmental sequence. Certainly I have witnessed numerous students in our graduate programs in humanistic education, counseling, juvenile justice, and human services initially preoccupied with learning the tools of their trade: being able to design good research, obtaining statistically significant results, writing papers that earn the plaudits of their professors, reading the most important books, finding crucial information, and acquiring the essential skills of effective helping. Their professional self-concepts are tightly tied to the skills they have as judged by their professors and signified for all to see by their terminal degree.

Then comes a period of "practicing their profession and using the tools of the trade." One's professional image is determined not by what they have, as judged by their "superiors," but by what they can do, as judged by their clients, students, employers, number of publications, tenure status, rank, income, or reputation. The issue is not "how to do" but "how much to do." The Jamestown project was conducted during this phase in my own development.

In the next phase one's "calling" becomes more important than one's vocation, service more important than work, the problems one chooses to solve more important than trivial successes, and the affection one expresses more important than the effectiveness one demonstrates. The abiding question is "what to do," not how or how much.

Currently I see teaching, consulting, organization development, and psychological education as several means through which love can be expressed. Any technique or work, however effective, done without love is not good. Any problem or project that has increasing loving relationships as its essential goal is good. Obviously, I do not advocate that everyone should endorse the same value. Other colleagues are using their skills in the service of different values: justice, liberation, or truth. Recognizing our limitations, we continue to work as hard now as before in striving to actualize our values. However, I suspect that for many other professionals, as well as for myself, the basis for determining these values has shifted in the course of their careers from specific external authorities to internal universals.

As I look back on the Jamestown project, I think that if I had been ten years older, I probably would not have done the project at all. Combating hate, conflict, violence, vandalism, oppression, and systematic dehumanization in our nation's public schools has priority.[1] If I were to do it again, I would try to reduce the amount of interpersonal conflict within Jamestown Community College after the workshop, which I accepted at the time as the price to be paid for any significant organizational self-renewal. Loving cooperation is more important to me now than is self-renewal.

---

[1]One attempt to translate this priority into action is described in A. Alschuler et al. Collaborative problem solving as an aim of education. *Journal of Applied Behavioral Science*, 1977, *13*, 315-327.

A Structural Approach
to Organizational Change

Robert A. Luke, Jr.

Peter Block

Jack M. Davey

Vernon R. Averch

Management strategies of organizations often rest on the assumption that close control of individuals—through various forms of reward and punishment—is the most effective way to accomplish objectives. The change effort described herein is keyed to the concept that education, training, and support can also enable an organization to accomplish its objectives. The case explains the process by which the management—attitudes, behavior, and structures—of a retail food organization underwent a change from close control of employees to a form of training and consultation for employees.

Measured by indices of profit and productivity, as well as indices of employee attitude and morale, the project was successful. The case also demonstrates that such a change in management strategy requires the involvement and commitment of people at all levels and that, in the final analysis, the real change agent is the client himself.

The authors would like to acknowledge the effort and contribution made to the program by Charles Johnson, Alan Steiger, and Edward Weiss, the Management Development Team.

This is a report of an OD program which resulted in significant delegation of authority and changed the attitudes of several key executives from a belief in close, continuous supervision to the view that most lower management will work productively without close supervision if given the opportunity and training. The innovative features of this case are twofold: First, the change was accomplished by structural alterations; and, secondly, the consultants were more architects than trainer-intervenors. The real change agents in this case were line executives. The consultants worked closely with these executives to shape and mold a new structure, but it was the latter who were actually responsible for the changes.

OD consultants often define their role as conducting events, training programs, and personal consultation in order to change a client's attitude about people and his relationships with them:

> Organization Development is a response to change, a complex educational strategy intended to change the beliefs, attitudes, values and structures of organizations so they can better adapt to the dizzying rate of change. Whatever the strategy, organization development almost always concentrates on the values, attitudes, relations and organizational climate—the "people" variables—as the point of entry rather than on the goals, structure and technologies of the organization (Bennis, 1969, p. 2).

By way of contrast, the OD effort reported here focused on changing the structure of the organization, i.e., the role responsibilities and relationships of organizational members and their centers of accountability, from which behavioral changes and, finally, attitudinal changes flowed. The program significantly altered the chain of command by creating new roles, modifying existing roles, and changing the managerial style of middle and top management. The project proved an effective means of developing managerial personnel and enabling personnel at several levels of management to gain more control over their jobs and environments.

Lawrence (1958) and Dalton, Barnes, and Zaleznik (1968) report on similar structural change programs, which were completely designed and carried out by top management of the organizations under study. Their reports are a researcher's description and analysis of structural change efforts and, as such, provided useful guidelines to the consultants involved in this case. Beer, Pieters, Marcus, and Hundert (1971) report on a program initiated at Corning Glass Works, which resulted in a new organizational role—an integrator—that greatly facilitated the problem-solving capabilities of multifunctional task forces. Beer and Huse (1972) demonstrate that structural and interpersonal changes can support and reinforce each other in a systems approach to organizational change.

BACKGROUND

The client organization is a large retail food chain with annual sales of $800 million and a work force of about 18,000. In 1969, a new top management team initiated an OD program to improve employee training. For two years, the program emphasized training events designed to effect attitudinal and behavioral changes (Averch & Luke, 1971). This effort aroused the interest of several top executives, who believed OD would make a contribution to the company. These executives allowed the OD staff to attend, as members, key meetings.

The senior author's participation in one of these meetings, the Store Operations Meeting, led to the development of the project described here. A monthly Store Operations Meeting is chaired by the Corporate Vice President of Store Operations, his staff, and the person (Store Operations Manager) charged with overall store performance and second in authority to the Divisional Vice Presidents. These meetings, attended by the four Divisional Store Operations Managers, test ideas for new work systems and design methods for implementing them in the stores.

During the September 1970 meeting, concern was expressed about the slowness with which a grocery management system for ordering and stocking merchandise was being implemented in the stores. In an earlier field test it had proved to be an efficient management system. Training Store Managers to use this system was delegated to the District Manager (DM), the direct supervisor of 10-15 stores. A lengthy discussion of his role revealed that though he was supposed to be a trainer and resource person, as well as supervisor of the Store Manager, a DM actually devoted his time to inspecting stores and personnel to make sure that company standards were met. DMs did not view training as a priority. They merely outlined the new system and told Store Managers to implement it. Results were therefore sporadic.

During the October meeting, the group considered ways of helping the DM implement the grocery system. Three alternatives were proposed. One was to create a new job, that of a grocery specialist who would work for the DM and put in the system. This was a typical method of introducing new procedures: create a specialist in that area and charge him with implementation. The second suggestion was to assign a current store manager to spend half his time training other managers in the system. The third alternative, suggested by the OD staff, was to change the role of the DM from a line executive to a consultant without line authority, and make him available to managers in all areas of store operations, including system implementation.

The rationale for this suggestion was that the close, inspection-like supervision of Store Managers by the DM and Specialists resulted in an overload for the Store Manager, who was often in a position of trying to please his many bosses. He therefore had minimal control over his store and little time for training or implementing new work methods. With less direct supervision and more training available from a consultant, it was hypothesized that Store Managers could more effectively manage their stores.

Historically, the company had relied on close supervision at all levels. The idea that Store Managers could manage their units effectively without direct supervision seemed absurd to several members. However, the chairman and one Store Operations Manager (the third author), who volunteered a district of 15 stores, felt the consultant concept might be a way of developing more competent Store Managers. The OD staff was asked to develop a proposal for a consultant structure, which is outlined in Figure 2. Figure 1 depicts the traditional DM-Specialist structure.

The basic functions in running a store are twofold. Merchandising consists of developing sales programs that yield an acceptable profit, attract customers, and ensure product variety. Store Operations, as the name implies, is concerned with the mechanics of getting work done—scheduling employees, stocking shelves, ringing registers—in a way that is economical but still attractive to customers. Under the traditional structure, three lines of authority reach the store. Merchandisers develop the sales program, which is passed by their assistant, the Coordinator, to Specialists, and then to department heads. Operational responsibilities are initiated by the Store Operations Manager and transmitted to the Store Managers by the District Manager, who is also responsible for overseeing the grocery merchandising program. The Store Manager therefore left the perishable department of his store to his department heads and their Specialists, and restricted his activities primarily to the grocery and front-end departments. This limited his ability to manage the entire store. In addition, his boss, the District Manager, when visiting the store, would inspect for problems—dirty floors, poor appearance of personnel, inadequate check-out service, incorrect prices, and so on. With the traditional structure and DM role, a Store Manager was primarily concerned with maintaining standards and overseeing the grocery department; he had little time or sense of priority for training, management, and new systems in the organization.

In the consultant structure, the roles of District Manager and Specialists were changed from supervisory to consultant to the Store Manager. Department heads were to report to the Store Manager, while the managers reported directly to the Store Operations Manager. The Management Development Coordinator (MDC)—the title dreamed up for the ex-DM—and the meat and produce specialists, now called consultants, were to function as a team, under the leadership of the MDC, to consult with and train managers in all areas of store management. Within the limits of overall company policy, the manager now had the final say about in-store priorities. The consultants had no line authority; the Store Operations Manager now supervised and evaluated in-store performance.

METHOD

This structural change is similar in type and intent to that described by Lawrence (1958). In that case, top management designed the change without behavioral science consultation. In this case, however, the first, second, and fourth authors served as OD consultants to the project. The third author was the major client and change agent. He frequently referred to "our view from the cat bird seat," and that is an accurate description of our relationship to the project. Our primary roles were as consultants to him, the MDC team, and Merchandisers.

Following the November 1970 Operations Meetings, the four authors developed the consultant model and a method of implementation, which was presented for approval at the January 1971 Division Managers' Meeting—a monthly meeting of the top 25 executives. The Division Vice President and the President agreed to try it on an experimental basis and to review the results in six months.

To test the new structure's effectiveness in developing a range of managers, we selected an average district composed of managers with varying competencies. To have chosen only the best managers obviously would have stacked the deck. We also selected a current DM for the MDC role, to see if a DM could in fact operate effectively as a consultant. The Operations Manager and senior author jointly interviewed four DMs (selected by the Operations Manager as most promising) and independently selected the same man. The new consultant was the youngest DM, with the least amount of time "on the road," but was the only one of the four who asked some hard questions about the merit of the whole idea. He had been with the company for 12 years, having worked his way up to DM from clerk.

We felt that the selection of the MDC was critical to the project. Lawrence (1958), in describing the management-initiated program at Food World, concluded that the ability of DMs to adapt their managerial style to the new rules was largely responsible for the success of the program in several districts.

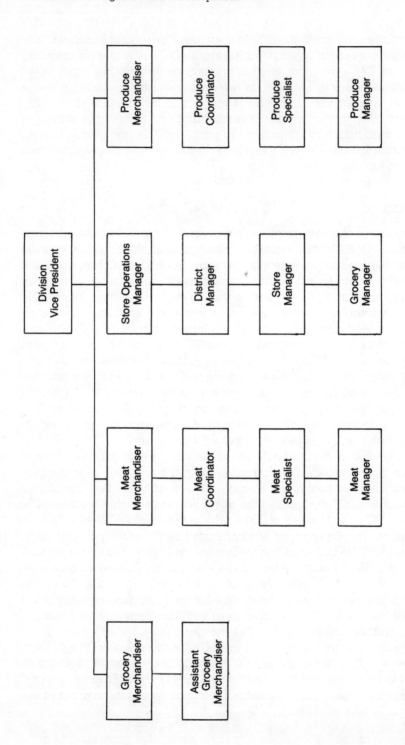

Figure 1. Traditional District Manager-Specialist Structure

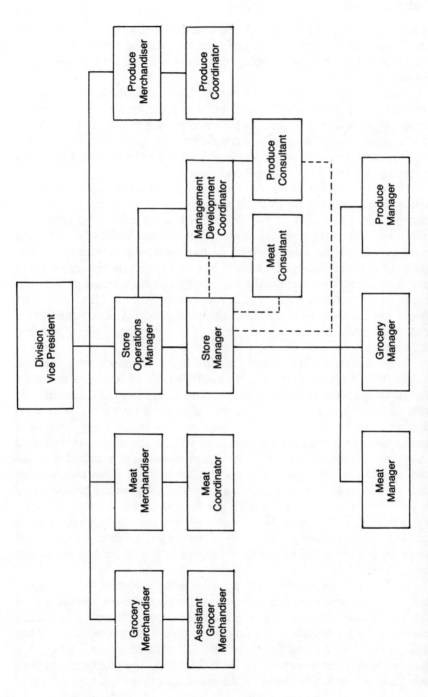

Figure 2. Proposed Consultant Structure for Store Management Development

Training Needs

The next step was to select meat and produce specialists to serve on the MDC team as consultants for perishables. This selection was left to the MDC because it was important that he have confidence in his assistants.

All three new consultants were highly competent in store operating methods, but we felt they needed training in human relations and consultation skills to perform their new roles effectively. Their training in management had been solely a function of their experience: When a person is promoted to District Manager, he is simply given the keys to a company car and told to supervise his stores.

In February 1971, the new consultants attended a week-long sensitivity training program to accelerate their team building and to increase their awareness of the impact of their behavior on others. In their new roles, they would have no line authority for influencing managers and would therefore be more dependent on their own interpersonal competencies. In addition, the new structure would facilitate their use of interpersonal skills and awarenesses gained at the program. By definition the consultant role meant that the MDC members would not be as subject to hierarchical constraints of organizations, which typically discourage the use of interpersonal skills learned at T Groups.

The consultant skill training for the MDC members was done on the job, following their return from the T Group, while they were still a District Manager and Specialists with line authority. The OD staff rode with each man on his visits to a store, observing his style and method of working with store personnel. Between stores, at lunch, and over end-of-the-day cocktails, we analyzed with them why they handled situations as they did, what their objectives were in particular stores and whether or not they were accomplished, and what impact they had on the people with whom they worked. We would occasionally suggest different forms of behavior for them to try out the next day and we would then analyze the results. At the end of this month-long process, all three knew, in terms of their own behavior and recent experience in the stores, what it meant to be a consultant rather than a boss.

While the consultant training was taking place, the OD staff, under the leadership of the Operations Manager, held meetings with divisional executives to map guidelines and establish evaluation measures (to be reported later). A week before implementation of the experimental consultant structure, the OD staff conducted a two-day team development workshop for the MDC team, the managers in their new district (we felt the MDC team should work with a new group of managers rather than having to undo relationships with their current managers), and the division management. The purpose of the workshop was to establish the MDC's credibility and accelerate the relationship building between MDC team members and their new store managers, who did not believe the company was actually committed to allowing them to manage their stores with the consultant resources of the MDC team. The workshop included typical relationship-building activities and role plays designed to demonstrate how the MDC team and division management would respond to problems in the experimental district. Figure 3 shows the ground rules for the consultant district and those for traditional districts. The differences were major and called for new behavior at all levels of the division.

One change not explicitly reflected in Figure 3 is the Divisional Perishable Merchandisers' loss of control over the specialists (see Figures 1 and 2). Formerly, the merchandiser or coordinator closely directed the activity of specialists; under the consultant structure, the consultants on perishables reported to the MDC. Much of the resistance to the consultant structure came from Divisional and Corporate Merchandisers, and one reason was a loss of staff from their organization.

THE CONSULTANT STRUCTURE

Start-Up

The consultant structure, thoroughly planned and written out, went

Ground Rules for Consultant District	Ground Rules for DM District
1. Consultants will make appointments for store visits and develop a quarterly contract with each manager.	DM visits stores unannounced to inspect for adherence to company standards.
2. Store managers' performance will be evaluated by the Store Operations Manager. MDC team will have no evaluation responsibilities for managers.	DM evaluates a manager's performance and conveys his evaluation to the Store Operations Manager.
3. Store Managers are responsible for total store results.	Store Manager responsible for results in grocery and front-end departments only. Perishable specialists responsible for results in meat and produce departments.
4. Consultants' performance would be evaluated by Store Operations Manager on the basis of their ability to perform as consultants and on the basis of managers' opinion of their helpfulness.	District Manager and Specialists' performance evaluated by Store Operations on the basis of results in the stores.

Figure 3. Differences in Ground Rules for Consultant Vs. Traditional District Store Management

into effect in April 1971, the beginning of the June quarter. It was immediately beset with major problems.

Two weeks later, the Division decided on a major sales promotion for these stores and felt the managers were not capable of handling the promotion without supervision. It sent teams of people from the office into the stores for three weeks to oversee the promotion. The MDC team was taken off the road and put to work in a store being remodeled. In the Division's eyes, the business needs were more critical than the experiment, though they did protect the status of the MDC team by avoiding asking them to play a supervisory role during the promotion. Nevertheless, this reintroduction of supervision of the stores was a clear message to all that the Division felt uncomfortable about the managerial competencies of the store managers. Although that was probably an accurate judgment, the promotion plan considerably heightened the managers' skepticism about company commitment to the consultant structure. The first and third authors had their first real confrontation over the issue of the company's commitment to developing managers. This episode marked the beginning of a productive discussion about how managers can be developed on the job without causing serious damage to the business. Following the promotional effort, which lasted four weeks, the MDC team really began its consultant role.

The team members had to establish their credibility with the managers all over again, and it is to their credit that they were able to do so. At this point, the success or failure of the project was very much in their hands. Rather than ignoring or pooh-poohing the managers' feelings, as would be typical, the MDC team dealt directly with them while beginning to develop working contracts.

Problems began to occur in the meat and produce departments and store-wide payroll, a predicted consequence of the learning curve experienced by the managers as they take over management of their stores. Store Operations responded by holding weekly group meetings in which the managers were told of the problems and exhorted to improve. Store Operations described them as "hammer and tong" meetings. After several such meetings, little improvement was noted, and Store Operations was becoming increasingly frustrated in not being able to get the managers to improve. The OD staff suggested that Store Operations instead perform their control and management role through individual performance appraisal sessions with the managers. The Operations Manager agreed to try this approach. He discontinued the weekly meetings and conducted an hour-long review with each manager at the manager's store. (He felt he would get better results by going to the store instead of calling the managers into the office.) During the first half of each review, the Operations Manager went over the figures, identifying areas that needed improvement and complimenting managers on areas that were doing well. The second half of the review was the manager's time to talk about his problems. These reviews represented the first time an Operations Manager had ever spent an hour with each manager in a district on his performance, and the experience was highly satisfactory for both. The managers were ecstatic at being able to talk nose-to-nose with their Operations Manager, and the Operations Manager reported he developed a much better understanding of the managers and conditions in their stores. The performance reviews remain as the primary control vehicle for Operations and represent one example of management's loosening up its supervisory control patterns.

The district received an inordinate number of visits from corporate executives, many of whom came "not to praise Caesar but to bury him." The consultant approach was viewed very skeptically by many, who would report problems and apparent examples of the structure's failings to the Divisional Vice President and the company's Executive Vice President. The OD staff's response was to ask these people to chart the results—sales, gross profits, payroll per cent, and so on—in the consultant district and in the control district[1] rather than relying on periodic "eyeballing" to evaluate the effectiveness of the consultant district. With the exception of the meat department, which everyone, including the managers, acknowledged would take the longest to learn to manage, there were no differences in financial and performance results between the two districts. As the second author was fond of saying, "At least we're up to the level of no difference." This was considered a success of sorts, in view of the fact that the betting around parts of the company was that the consultant stores would simply go under.

At this time the MDC members were encountering two major problems. The managers were not asking for help. In the early stages, the opportunity to manage their own stores went to their heads, and they would call the consultants only on minor problems or to bail them out of serious situations that usually could have been prevented by earlier planning with their consultants. In addition, the Merchandisers continued to see the produce and meat consultants as their staff and would ask them to go to stores to resolve particular problems. This put pressure on the consultants: to be consultants rather than bosses, they could not carry out the orders of the Merchandisers. Merchandisers

---

[1]The Division Vice President identified a control district which he felt was most similiar to the consultant district among the other five districts.

and Coordinators were supposed to communicate directly with the Store Managers within the new structure, but this was inconvenient for the Merchandisers—and old habits die hard.

A major review meeting, involving the Division Management, Corporate Merchandisers, the MDC team, and the OD staff, was held in July. All the above problems were thoroughly discussed and the following modifications made:

1. The MDC members, still acting as consultants and not supervisors, could take more initiative in pointing out problems and suggesting solutions, but it was still the manager's decision to act on the consultant's recommendations. A consultant was given the option of not working with a manager if he felt a particular manager was avoiding him.

2. The Corporate Meat Merchandiser agreed to design a management training program for the managers. This represented the first such training program for Store Managers by a Merchandising office.

3. The ground rule was established that when a representative of Divisional and/or Corporate management visits a store, he will inform the manager of his observations and can suggest that the manager call his consultant. Previously, top-echelon visitors would order the manager to make changes on the spot or inform Store Operations but not the manager.

The meeting also cleared the air, and the consultant structure operated more according to plan for the remainder of the six-month period, with one major problem still unresolved. Division management, and particularly Store Operations, continued to feel uneasy about the managers' developing competencies. They therefore retained many of the former functions of the DM, such as calling stores weekly to adjust their labor budget or sales projections or inspecting the stores for appearance and adherence to standards. During the transition period, while the managers were developing, Store Operations still had to meet their responsibilities; as a result, the Operations Manager became a "high-priced DM" for about six months. This put an enormous workload on Operations, for they still had five other districts to manage; and they had to be convinced, through the efforts of the Store Managers, that the latter could adequately manage their stores. The managers' positive response to the performance reviews was the first indication Operations had that this might be possible; and toward the end of the six months, Operations saw more and more improvement in the stores. Hence, at the end of the six months, Operations people were on the verge of becoming believers.

Six Months Later

At the end of the six-month trial period, the consultant structure was operating according to plan. Operations continued to retain the controls the DM previously exercised and there continued to be no difference in the performance between the two structures. The consultant structure was designed to replace close supervision with training, on the hypothesis that this would develop the capabilities of Store Managers. As we have seen, the "hard" measures demonstrated no difference between consulted managers and supervised managers, though it is important to remember that the Divisional office still maintained a high degree of control over the managers' budgets. Hence, at this point, the performance data are inconclusive.

To assess the impact of the experiment on the Store Managers, the OD staff administered a nine-item questionnaire to managers in the experimental and control districts. The questions were intended to assess the managers' feeling of support from management, the degree to which their abilities were being used, and the degree to which they felt involved in decisions. The baseline data were collected in April 1971, two weeks before the start of the experiment (Table 1). The postmeasure was taken in October 1972 (Table 2).

Table 1 shows that, prior to the experiment, the supervised managers gave higher than average responses to six of the nine items. In comparison to the soon-to-be consulted managers, supervised managers felt their boss (DM) complimented them more on a good job, they were more knowledgeable about DM standards for evaluation, received more help in problem solving and support with higher management from this DM, felt problems were being more confronted, and that their skills and abilities were being used better. Consulted managers felt they were slightly more consulted on decisions, received slightly more encouragement from their DM to exercise judgment and initiative, and saw a career with the company as somewhat more attractive.

Table 2 shows the amount of change in the two groups' average responses to the same items six months later. At T_2, "boss" was interpreted to mean MDC team by the consulted managers. Table 2 shows rather clearly that, from the managers' perspective, the consultant structure had accomplished its primary developmental goal of increasing the utilization of managers' skills. The consulted managers show a noticeable positive increase on all but one item while the supervised managers show a decrease on six items and slight gains on three.

It is important to mention that during these six months, the Division encountered a severe decline in sales, experienced a large union wage settlement, and underwent a rather traditional cost-cutting program. In all districts except the consultant district, this meant that supervisors were exercising much closer control over managers. Managers in the consultant district were given guidelines for reducing costs but had more leeway in their execution than did the supervised managers. The closer supervision of the supervised managers may well explain the decreases on those items measuring support from management, career attractiveness, and the degree to which they were consulted on decisions.

The OD staff also conducted open-ended interviews with the MDC team and consulted managers, which demonstrated that the managers neither wanted nor appreciated the traditional DM function. In response to the question, "What do you miss under this style of working that you had when you had a District Manager?" 13 said they missed "nothing"—and that's their word. Many volunteered that they did not

Table 1. Average of Consulted and Supervised Managers' Responses to Project Evaluation Questions at T[1]

Items	Consulted Managers (N = 15)	Supervised Managers (N = 15)	Difference
1. How often does your immediate boss encourage you to show initiative and exercise judgment? (never/always)	4.57	4.44	+.13
2. To what extent does your boss compliment you when you have done a good job? (never/always)	3.57	4.11	−.54
3. To what extent do you know the standards your immediate boss uses to evaluate your performance? (never know/always know)	3.72	4.00	−.28
4. How would you rate the help your immediate boss provides you in solving problems? (never helpful/always helpful)	3.86	4.34	−.48
5. To what extent do you feel your immediate boss backs you up with higher management? (never/always)	4.29	4.44	−.15
6. To what extent do you feel problems are being faced rather than ignored? (never faced/always faced)	3.72	4.22	−.50
7. How well do you feel your skills and abilities are being used? (not used/used very well)	3.57	4.23	−.66
8. How would you rate the extent to which you are consulted when decisions are made which affect your work? (never/always)	4.28	4.00	+.28
9. How attractive does a career with the company appear? (unattractive/quite attractive)	4.43	4.22	+.21

miss "the aggravation of do-it-my-way," "being treated like a child," "getting my ass kicked," "never knowing what he [the DM] is going to do when he comes around," "bone-crushing meetings," and more. Many consulted managers talked about a new-found sense of pride in their work and a new feeling of wanting to advance in the company. To a man, they expressed a great deal of respect and affection for the Operations Manager, whom many had previously spoken of in less glowing terms; and they felt that his performance appraisals were helpful in their development as store managers. In short, the consulted managers were "turned on."

CONSEQUENCES

Reactions of the Consultants

All three continue to miss the authority and control they had as members of a DM team and some of the traditional prestige and status

Table 2. Amount of Change in Consulted and Supervised Managers' Average Responses to Project Evaluation Questions—T^1 to T^2 a

Items	Consulted Managers (N = 15)	Supervised Managers (N = 15)	Difference
1. How often does your immediate boss encourage you to show initiative and exercise judgment?	+.18	+.37	− .19
2. To what extent does your boss compliment you when you have done a good job?	+.76*	−.08	+ .84
3. To what extent do you know the standards your immediate boss uses to evaluate your performance?	+.61*	+.01	+ .60
4. How would you rate the help your immediate boss provides you in solving problems?	+.97*	−.14	+1.14
5. To what extent do you feel your immediate boss backs you up with higher management?	+.21*	−.64	+ .85
6. To what extent do you feel problems are being faced rather than ignored?	+.63*	+.08	+ .55
7. How well do you feel your skills and abilities are being used?	+.55	−.03	+ .58
8. How would you rate the extent to which you are consulted when decisions are made that affect your work?	+.14	−.20	+ .34
9. How attractive does a career with the company appear?	+.01	−.22	+ .23

*Indicates items on which consulted managers scored lower than supervised managers at T_1 but higher at T_2.

a Parametric tests of statistical significance are not applicable to the data for reasons of sample composition; i.e., neither district represents a probability sample. However, using the nonparametric sign test, the probability of the consultant managers' rate of change being higher, on 8 of 9 items, occurring by chance is .04.

associated with authority. Nevertheless, they also feel they have gained in-depth experience in dealing with people and in effective problem solving. Members of a DM team have formal line authority—or a club, as it is more popularly known. Whether or not the club is used, its mere existence does make managers listen more carefully and respond more quickly. Without the club, the consultants have had to rely on their interpersonal skills to accomplish work. Evidence of their effectiveness is shown in Table 2, question 4. Consulted Store Managers perceive the consultants as more helpful on solving problems than control managers perceive their DM team to be, which suggests that the consultant structure has developed capabilities for interpersonal competence and problem-solving training through the new role and behavior of the MDC team.

The report itself was submitted to the Division management and to the President. This, and the fact that the consulted stores were at least holding their own in terms of performance, enabled management to agree to continue and expand the experiment. Within six months, two additional consultant structures were implemented.

Personnel Changes

One consequence of the initial consultant structure, which continued from October 1971 to February 1972, was that each manager's performance was much more visible to Operations since it was far more intimately involved in the stores and with the managers. It became apparent that two managers, who had the most years of service with the company, were unable to manage a store effectively without direct supervision. They made the least use of the consultants and found it most difficult to make decisions on their own. They were transferred out of the district and replaced by men who Operations felt could manage their stores independently of close supervision. Operations put two other managers who were having difficulty into each other's store. One went from a high to a low volume store, usually considered a demotion, and, with fewer responsibilities, performed quite well. The manager who went from a lower to a higher volume store, usually considered a promotion, suprised Operations by doing an outstanding job. Hence, 13 of the original 15 managers were still in the district a year later and were doing at least an adequate job.

Cutting the Umbilical Cord

By March 1, 1972, the Division management felt confident that this group of managers could manage their own stores. At their initiative, Operations decided to go the whole route. For the first time in the company's history, a group of managers were given sole responsibility for meeting their quarterly sales and labor budget. Usually, Operations, through the DM, would call managers weekly, asking them to increase or decrease hours or sales projections. Until now, Operations had used this approach with the consulted managers. For this quarter, however, the managers were to receive no instructions but would review their budgets with the Operations Manager at the end of the 4th, 8th, and 13th week. Sometime in the future, as managers acquire more competence—and Operations more confidence in their competence—managers may be able to run their budgets for a quarter or even a year.

Performance Results

A district's quarterly performance is measured by the percentage of increase or decrease in sales, its increase or decrease in sales per man hour (number of labor hours divided into sales), and its increase or decrease in labor per cent (labor dollars expended expressed as a percentage of sales), when compared to the same quarter in the previous year. Improvement, or lack thereof, is a major indicator for measurement of the value of new programs.

Applying these measures to the June 1972 quarter, we find the consultant district had the smallest decrease in sales (sales throughout the division declined 1971-1972), the smallest increase in labor per cent (all labor per cents increased), and was one of two showing an increase in sales per man hour (Table 3). As a district, the consultant district had the best showing for the June 1972 quarter. Table 3a shows the performance of the districts on the same measures for the June 1971 quarter. Table 3b compares the rank-order improvement position of each district for the two quarters. As a total district, it is interesting to note the consultant district was in fifth position in 1971 (clearly in the bottom half) but had attained the number one position by 1972. At the end of the first year of the experiment, the consultant district had outperformed the other five from 1971 to 1972.

Table 4 compares districts' performances against their June quarter, 1972, budget. The consultant district is the only district to meet or exceed its budget in all three categories. This suggests that the consulted managers were better able to manage their budgets than were their supervised colleagues.

On the basis of these results, Operations believes managers can assume major responsibility for profit goals, and it has taken the necessary steps to implement that view. (Gross profit responsibility is usually tightly controlled by the Merchandisers.)

Table 3. Rate of Change in Sales, Sales Per Man Hour, and Labor Per Cent in the Consulted District and Supervised Districts During the June 1972 Quarter Compared Against the June 1971 Quarter

District	Sales	Sales Per Man Hour	Labor Per Cent
1.	−19.7%	−$3.26	+1.5%
2.	− 4.3	−$1.19	+1.0
3.	−12.8	+$1.20	+1.2
4.	− 6.0	−$2.13	+1.1
5. (Consulted)	− 5.4	+$1.38	+ .4
6.	−11.6	−$ .20	+1.0
Division Average	−11.7	−$ .58	+ .9

Table 3a. Rate of Change in Sales, Sales Per Man Hour, and Labor Per Cent in the Consulted District and Supervised Districts During the June 1971 Quarter Compared Against the June 1970 Quarter

District	Sales	Sales Per Man Hour	Labor Per Cent
1.	+10.0%	+$1.32	+.9%
2.	− 8.6	+$4.12	+.4
3.	+ 7.9	+$2.94	+.3
4.	+25.0	+$2.28	+.4
5. (Consulted)	+ 9.8	+$ .49	+.9
6.	− 7.3	+$ .38	+.7

Table 3b. Comparison of the Districts' Improvement Rank-Order Positions in June 1971 (Table 3a) and June 1972 Quarter (Table 3)

District	Sales		Sales Per Man Hour		Labor Per Cent		District Rankings*		1971—1972 Difference
	1971	1972	1971	1972	1971	1972	1971	1972	
1.	2	6	4	6	5.5	6	4	6	−2
2.	6	1	1	4	2.5	2.5	3	2	+1
3.	4	5	2	2	1	5	2	4.5	−2.5
4.	1	3	3	5	2.5	4	1	4.5	−3.5
5. (Consulted)	3	2	5	1	5.5	1	5	1	+4.0
6.	5	4	6	3	4	2.5	6	3	+3.0

*Determined by ranking of sum of ranks for each year.

Table 4. Performances in Terms of Sales, Sales Per Man Hour and Labor Per Cent, in Relation to June 1972 Quarterly Budgets of Consulted District and Supervised Districts

District	Sales	Sales Per Man Hour	Labor Per Cent
1.	+5.0%	−$1.45	+.3%
2.	−6.5	−$ .52	+.3
3.	−3.7	−$ .13	+.1
4.	−2.9	−$ .69	+.1
5. (Consulted)	+ .1	+$ .49	−.2[a]
6.	−4.8	+$ .59	−.1

[a] A savings against the plan in labor dollars of $15,534.

CONCLUSIONS

Attitude Change

Perhaps the most significant change associated with the consultant structure is not the change in behavior and performance of the managers, but the change in attitudes about supervision. Not all executives are convinced, but the Operations Manager, the Divisional Vice President, the Corporate Vice President of Store Operations, and the President now believe that 75-80 per cent of current managers can contribute more to the company if they are supported and trained rather than merely closely supervised. The possible consequences of this attitude shift for the management philosophy and structure of the company are obvious. It is also important to underscore that this change in attitude occurred as a function of these executives' direct experience with a situation intimately familiar to them. It is unlikely they would have occurred as the result of a specific OD attitude-training intervention in this company.

Behavioral Changes

Changes in behavior took place at the level of Store Manager, who made more decisions, became more involved in perishable departments, and made regular requests for help; at the level of District Manager and Specialist, who identified problems, suggested solutions, and trained managers instead of simply inspecting their performance; at the level of Store Operations Manager, who now meets with his managers on a regular and individual basis to plan with them and discuss their performance instead of relying on a District Manager to convey his orders and giving managers no performance feedback; and at the level of Divisional Vice President, who took an obvious risk in allowing the project to start in the first place and supporting and developing it throughout the first year. Again, these behavioral changes did not occur solely out of a belief that individuals should gain more control over their lives or that training and feedback are inherently good things. They were required to support the change in structure, which was deemed necessary because the old structure was not helping the company move as fast as it wanted in developing managers and implementing systems. One moral, therefore, for OD practitioners might be that form follows function, not vice versa.

Resistance, Risk, and Ethics

The executives most opposed to the consultant structure also tended to be those executives who (1) were the firmest believers that "everyone needs a boot in the ass," or (2) lost staff and therefore power under the consultant structure—the Merchandisers, or (3) both. Most executives had worked their way up from stock boy level under a management structure of close supervision. For many, the consultant approach disconfirmed the merit of a management style which they had skillfully learned and mastered over the years and on which a large measure of their positive self-concept undoubtedly rested. Similar discomfort was noticeable among other District Managers, who, seeing the amount of company interest in and support of the MDC team, began to wonder about the security of their positions. It was also evident among most Merchandisers, who, actively or passively, resisted the consultant project.

Although the Store Managers responded enthusiastically, the consultant structure meant new evaluation criteria for them. Just doing well what their bosses asked of them no longer sufficed. The two managers who could not manage without close supervision were demoted as a result. Hence, there was an element of risk in the project for managers, and the project was imposed on them; they really did not have the option to say no.

The risk was high for the MDC team as well. They too had risen through the ranks to their current positions of District Manager and Specialist, and one reward for their efforts was the authority and prestige of line positions. The consultant structure removed their line authority, a fact which we have seen they continued to lament, and thereby removed some prestige from them in the eyes of many. Had the project failed, the MDC members stood to lose the most. Though they were given the formal opportunity to decline, all three would have found it difficult to decline a new position for which they had been hand-picked. So, in reality, their freedom of choice was also limited. In their case, and in the case of the managers, the success of the project has enhanced their individual standing in the eyes of company executives. By virtue of their pioneering, visible positions, the MDC team and managers received far greater attention and positive evaluation by management than have their colleagues in other districts. In their case, the risk paid off. Nevertheless, the consultant project raises important ethical questions for both executives and the OD staff. For example, how much should others be asked to risk for the sake of change that executives and OD staff feel will benefit the company and contribute to people's development and autonomy? To spare the reader a long discourse on ethical dilemmas for which there are no definitive solutions, suffice it to say that the planning, design, experience, and evaluation were conducted in an open atmosphere which allowed all the opportunity to voice their views and exert influence. Of course, we did not realize a totally democratic situation: strands of vested interest and political pressures were evident (e.g., let's not speak out publicly about a program the President, Division Vice President, or Operations Manager—depending on what level one is in— endorses). We did fully share intentions and plans, and we asked critics to support their views with data and applied the same criteria to our enthusiasm. As a result, we like to think the project was conducted ethically, though we are fully aware that some coercion and imposition occurred.

IMPLICATIONS FOR THE OD CONSULTANT

Unlike many OD programs which use training interventions— T Groups, team building, workshops focusing on management by objectives, and others—the OD staff saw its role as that of an architect, i.e., one who makes himself familiar with the client's problems and needs and works with the client to design a structure to meet the need, but leaves the final acceptance decision to the client. We proposed a new structure, offered some training experiences (the off-site T Group and 2-day team building laboratory), recommended new behavior (that the MDC be a consultant, that the Operations Manager conduct performance appraisals), and continually evaluated results. In each case, the client made the final decision, and, as a result, our influence on the system was determined by the client's perceptions of how well our designs or recommendations met his needs.[2] This is not a model of subservience, for our recommendations and urgings are consistent with our beliefs in the value of training and of increased autonomy as well as authentic confrontation and evaluation; and they are clearly different from recommendations that most executives would have made to speed up the implementation of the grocery system. The architect style did seem to enable the client to own the changes rather than merely to rely on our expertise and recommendations.

The use of any OD strategy is a design question, and we present for the reader's consideration the model of architect to be included with other models of training and consultation for system change.

FUTURE DIRECTIONS

As this report is being written, June 1972, the Corporate Human Resources and Store Operations staff is preparing a proposal that will

---

[2]Not all our recommendations were accepted. Training the MDC team and manager to conduct in-store meetings, performance appraisals with employees, and a team development workshop for the Division management are examples of recommendations that were not accepted.

create a management division task force for each of the four divisions. The task forces will be composed of a vertical slice of current management and will plan the management structure and needed training supports—both interpersonal and technical skill development training—required in each division. If accepted, the task forces will represent the company's first commitment to involving in management planning those who will be affected. It will also represent its first commitment to using the Human Resources staff in management planning. Prior to this proposal, all such planning and decision making were done by a select few executives who met in private. Under the terms of the proposal, the task forces will be coordinated by members of the Human Resources and Store Operations departments.

Hence, though the initial consultant project proved successful, its contribution to the company does not rest only in its demonstration of the structure's effectiveness as a management development program. More importantly, the structure has had an impact on the attitudes of many organization members who now accept McGregor's (1960) theory that people in organizations seek challenge and responsibility to the benefit of themselves and the organization. If the consultant structure experience will also change the *process* of management, it will have been successful beyond our wildest expectations of October 1970.

POSTSCRIPT[3]

The division management task forces met through the summer of 1972 and developed the following management structure: The role of Store Operations Manager would be deleted and two new *staff* roles created for each division—Sales Manager, charged with coordinating the division's sales program, and an Administrative Service Manager, charged with coordinating the quarterly budget-setting process. Each role reports to the Division Manager. In place of District Managers, a new role was created, that of a Zone Manager, who reports directly to the Division Manager and has line responsibility for sales, budget, profit, and personnel functions throughout 18 to 20 stores. The Zone Manager's role is clearly that of a line manager and as such can introduce the needs of his particular area into the Division's planning in the areas mentioned above. Working for the Zone Manager is a produce trainer, meat trainer, and grocery trainer, each of whom serves as consultant staff to the 18-20 Store Managers in the same way

---

[3]This article was completed in June 1972. The authors are pleased to report that during the intervening year the company has continued to make major changes in its management structure, building on the consultant experiment.

as did the Management Development Team in the consultant structure. In addition, face-to-face quarterly performance appraisals are now in effect between each two levels from Corporate Senior Vice President to Store Clerk; and an incentive bonus plan, based on performance and store conditions, has been introduced for Store Managers.

The changes made by the task forces have resulted in a more direct line relationship between stores and the division office, considerably reduced the number of people exercising line authority over the Store Manager, and retained the practice of training and development as a management strategy. Full implementation of the structure is one to two years away. A recent study indicates a 15 per cent improvement in productivity for those stores now operating under the structure and a generally high level of acceptance of the structure by those participating in it. The consultant structure, as described in this case study, has been eliminated as the new structure takes effect.

REFERENCES

Averch, V., & Luke, R. Organization development: The view from within. *Training and Development Journal*, 1971, 25(9), 38-42.

Beer, M., & Huse, E. A systems approach to organization development. *Journal of Applied Behavioral Science*, 1972, 8(1), 79-101.

Beer, M., Pieters, G. R., Marcus, S. H., & Hundert, A. T. Improving integration between functional groups: A case in organization change and implications for theory and practice. Symposium presented at American Psychological Association Convention, Washington, D.C., September 1971.

Bennis, W. *Organization development*. Reading, Mass.: Addison-Wesley, 1969.

Dalton, G., Barnes, L., & Zaleznik, A. *The distribution of authority in formal organizations*. Boston: Division of Research, Harvard Business School, 1968.

Lawrence, P. *The changing of organizational behavior patterns*. Boston: Division of Research, Harvard Business School, 1958.

McGregor, D. *The human side of enterprise*. New York: McGraw-Hill, 1960.

REFLECTIONS ON "A STRUCTURAL APPROACH TO ORGANIZATIONAL CHANGE

Robert A. Luke, Jr.

In rereading the article, I am struck by the absence of references to power and the implicit naive assumption that power played no role in the change process but that the key was organizational architecture. Of course, power did play a role. First was the formal power conveyed to any consultant through the support and backing of top management; although we called ourselves architects, in retrospect, a better word would have been manager, although we were marginal to the system. As managers, we had the luxury and opportunity to experiment without the constraints other managers had such as meeting budgets and overseeing company policy at all levels in the organization. As marginal managers, we chose to use our power by challenging the system—not as rebels or cabalists but as planners, confronters, and exposers, if you will, of the ever-present organizational phenomenon of pluralistic ignorance, which tends to prevent people from deviating visibly from company policy short of resigning. Put another way, I think we served as energizers and legitimizers for a small and courageous group of middle managers who, although they were familiar with the writings of McGregor, Maslow, et al., felt that they had too much to lose by rocking the boat. In this respect, we used our power essentially to serve as a conduit of information—continually monitoring sales, profit, and morale among various levels in the organization. Although not everyone was pleased at first, the norm was soon established that people could solve problems across organizational levels for mutual fun and profit. Once that norm had been established, the experiment was completed.

Today I have more insight into the power of consultants and the importance of being aware of the phenomenon and making selective choices about how to use it. I find that a useful role for consultants is actually to manage internal resources, not so much to aim for a specific type of change, but more to test the organization's willingness to identify, confront, and solve problems both in the areas of tasks and people—i.e., to assume a 9,9 stance (using Grid language, Blake &

Mouton, 1964), which Warner Burke has so aptly characterized as "tough love."

REFERENCES

Blake, R. R., & Mouton, J. S. *The Managerial Grid*. Houston, TX: Gulf, 1964.
Burke, W. W. Personal correspondence.

Social Intervention in Curacao: A Case Study

David E. Berlew

William E. LeClere

This article describes an effort to apply behavioral science technologies to facilitate the social and economic development of the Caribbean Island of Curacao, Netherlands Antilles. A period of rising tensions, culminating in a labor dispute which erupted into a night of rioting, burning, and looting, preceded the intervention.

The project had two major elements: (1) motivation training, designed to encourage residents to view themselves as "origins" rather than "pawns" and enable them to set life and career goals and plan effectively to achieve them; and (2) an "outlet program," which involved the Island's leaders in creating new educational and job opportunities for individuals whose aspiration levels were raised by the motivation training. The intervention is evaluated, and several problems and issues relevant beyond the Curacao case are discussed.

INTRODUCTION

In early May 1969, McBer and Company,[1] a Cambridge-based consulting firm, received an inquiry from the Chamber of Commerce and Industry of Curacao, Netherlands Antilles, about "achievement motivation training" as a means of encouraging indigenous business enterprises. An article in the April 25, 1969 issue of *TIME* Magazine,

---

[1] McBer and Company (previously called the Behavioral Science Center) was founded in 1965 by David C. McClelland and several associates to apply behavioral science concepts to current social and organizational problems.

Reproduced by special permission from *The Journal of Applied Behavioral Science.* "Social Intervention in Curacao: A Case Study," by David E. Berlew and William E. LeClere, Vol. 10, No. 1, pp. 29-52. Copyright 1974 NTL Institute for Applied Behavioral Science.

which described the use of achievement motivation training to stimulate small-business development in India and in economically distressed sections of the United States, had prompted the request (McClelland & Winter, 1969; Timmons, 1971).

On May 31, 1969, the *New York Times* reported a major outbreak of violence on Curacao. According to the report, a labor dispute between a group of plumbers and a Shell Oil contractor unexpectedly escalated from a lockout into large demonstrations by laborers and their sympathizers. Shots were fired, and several prominent political leaders on the Left were wounded, which led to widespread burning and looting of businesses in downtown Willemstad, the capital and only city of Curacao.

In September 1969, the senior author traveled to Curacao to explore with leaders of the Chamber of Commerce and Industry the feasibility of a small-business development project. According to correspondence from the President of the Chamber, the disturbance of May 30th had heightened the urgency for encouraging more Antilleans to become directly involved in the mainstream of commercial activities on the Island.

Impressions from Pre-entry Meetings

The following journal excerpts describe the first 24 hours of this first visit to Curacao:

> At 8 p.m. (a few hours after my arrival) I met with the Board of Directors of the Chamber of Commerce and Industry. The President listed four objectives to which the Chamber was committed: (1) to encourage Antilleans to become associated with existing businesses, (2) to increase the amount of commercial activity on Curacao by encouraging Antillean business activity, (3) to create new jobs, and (4) to give Antilleans a sense of participation in their community.
>
> We spent the next two hours reviewing current business and social conditions on Curacao and the prerequisites of an effective small-business development program. I emphasized that while we believe achievement motivation training to be one essential element, the availability of capital and training in business skills are also critical. We ended the Board meeting by planning strategy for a meeting scheduled the next morning with 40 government, community, labor, and business leaders. Our approach, we decided, would be (a) to describe "new behavioral science technologies" such as achievement training; (b) to engage those present in a discussion of how these technologies might relate to the problems of Curacao; and (c) to discuss how we might proceed to apply these technologies, if they were perceived as relevant.

Although the morning meeting was held in the Chamber building (hardly neutral turf), nearly everyone invited showed up. I introduced myself as a "technologist"—someone who did not know much about their specific situation but who was knowledgeable about some new social or change technologies which they should know about and might find useful in solving their problems. During my initial presentation I described achievement motivation training, various types of group training, and "psychological education"; in response to questions, I also discussed community and organization development. Fearing that people might too readily see "cures" to their problems, I tried to be very objective and factual, presenting research findings whenever I could. The meeting lasted over four hours, and each group present appeared to find something relevant to its specific needs, which went well beyond the business development needs of the Chamber. The meeting ended with what seemed to be a general feeling that these new "technologies" were highly relevant and an effort should be made to apply them to the problems on Curacao.

The remainder of the three-day visit was spent interviewing government, labor, community, and business leaders. A number of impressions emerged from the visit.

Civil Disturbance a Catalyst. The demonstrations and looting of May 30th, the first civil disturbance on Curacao in years, frightened people badly (even the looters themselves, many of whom returned stolen merchandise). Island leaders expected more violence and did not know how to prevent it or to get at the root causes. Actively seeking help, they favored Americans because they viewed us as pragmatic and experienced in problems of urban unrest (as compared with the Dutch). They were also highly impressed with a recent Texas Instruments' new plant start-up on Curacao. The crisis atmosphere had made them ready, even eager, to use new ideas and approaches if someone showed them the way.

Factions. Leaders of different Island factions had surprisingly similar visions of Curacao's future, but they were generally unaware of their shared dreams. The important left-wing groups were not highly radicalized (despite their Castro-type fatigue uniforms), and highly militant groups attracted few followers.

Intergroup Relations. There was excellent leadership within Island groups but rarely *across* groups or factions. Financial resources to support a large-scale change program existed but were very unevenly distributed among key factions.

Economic Forecast. Curacao's economic potential permitted a "win-win solution," i.e., more for everyone, as opposed to a straight transfer of wealth from the "haves" to the "have nots." Although two major industries were reducing their work forces, Curacao had only begun to exploit its potential as a tourist attraction and its access to the European Common Market, as part of the Dutch Commonwealth.

The project staff[2] decided that while a small-business development project similar to those conducted in India and the United States was highly relevant to Curacao, there was much more that could be done to help the Island solve its problems. Moreover, since the business community had been the target of the rioters on May 30th, we felt that a unilateral effort by the Chamber of Commerce and Industry to recruit black Antillean businessmen would meet considerable resistance.

There was one problem, however. Since we could identify no organization on the Island which had the trust of more than one or two major Island factions, we decided we would not become involved unless a new organization with representation from all major factions was formed. In response to our concern, the "Fundashon Renovashon" was incorporated as a foundation to ". . . accelerate the social and economic development of Curacao through the better utilization of the Island's human resources." The Steering Committee of the Fundashon Renovashon comprised representatives from government, labor, business, and community organizations.

Three weeks after this first visit, McBer submitted a proposal to the Fundashon Renovashon (rather than to the Chamber itself); one week later it was formally accepted, and shortly thereafter work began.

BACKGROUND

Curacao is an arid Caribbean island located approximately 40 miles off the coast of Venezuela. The largest of the Netherlands Antilles, it is approximately 40 miles long and 12 miles wide, with a population of about 140,000 residents. Aside from its natural harbor, it has few natural resources and is poorly suited to agriculture.

Discovered by the Spaniards in about 1499, the entire Indian population was seized into "red slavery" and exported to the mainland or other islands. In 1634 the Dutch took Curacao from the Spanish; soon after the island became a slave depot for the Dutch West India Company. Today, the overwhelming majority of Curacaons are descendants of African slaves brought to Curacao by the Dutch.

---

[2]The authors would like to acknowledge the contributions of our colleagues on the Curacao project, namely: David H. Burnham, David A. Kolb, Harry Lasker, David C. McClelland, Ronald McMullan, Norman Reynolds, and Roy Thompson.

When the British briefly ruled over Curacao twice in the early 19th century, they required English to be spoken. In addition to Dutch and English, most Curacaons speak "Papiemento," a blend of the African, Dutch, Portuguese, Hebrew, and English influences that have formed this island culture.

Development of the Venezuelan oil industry had great impact on the Island economy. In 1917 the first oil refinery was established on Curacao, thus beginning the dominance of the Island's economy by the oil industry. Crude oil was shipped from Venezuela into the great harbor at Willemstad, refined, and then shipped by large tankers to markets in North and South America and Europe. Approximately 60 per cent of all employment on the Island depends on the Dutch-owned Shell Oil Company refinery. In 1918 some mining of potash began on Curacao, but the operation recently became uneconomical and is being phased out. In 1968 Texas Instruments opened an assembly plant on the outskirts of Willemstad; it now employs approximately 1,500 workers, many of whom are women.

Long a popular stop for cruise ships because of its picturesque harbor and duty-free shops. Curacao has recently built several international-class hotels, some with casinos, adding a more stable element to the tourist industry.

The Netherlands Antilles gained substantial independence in 1954, but remained a Commonwealth member of the Royal Dutch Empire. Dutch remains the basic language of its government and commerce, although Papiemento has been adopted as its official language. Most Curacaon professionals are educated in Holland, for there are no institutions of higher education in the Netherlands Antilles. The Queen of the Netherlands appoints the Governor-General of Curacao, and the first black Antillean Governor-General assumed office in 1970.

As noted earlier, the overwhelming majority of the Curacaon population are black, and of African descent; political power rests in their hands. The most significant minority groups are either Dutch citizens or Antillean descendants of Dutch citizens who came to the Island as seamen or soldiers or to assume governmental, professional, or managerial positions. They still hold many high posts as civil servants and as managers of Dutch-owned enterprises. There are two small but active Jewish communities on Curacao, both prominent in banking and commerce.

Curacaons have had a reputation over the years of being an unusually attractive and peace-loving people. From the freeing of the slaves in 1863 through 1969 there is no record of racial disturbance or disorder on the Island.

THE INTERVENTION

The Fundashon Renovashon program had three goals:

1. An increase in the rate of economic growth
   New jobs
   New businesses
2. Individual and social development
   More jobs and better jobs for black Antilleans and other under-employed and unemployed groups
   More black Antillean businesses
   A heightened sense of efficacy and independence among black Antilleans
3. Community development
   Greater awareness of goals shared by most Curacaons
   Better coordination among Island factions
   Improved individual and institutional capability to achieve goals.

The program consisted of two major elements (see Figure 1). The first element was *Motivation Training*, intended to train individual Curacaons to think of themselves as "origins" rather than "pawns," to set goals realistically and plan effectively for goal achievement, and to work effectively in groups.

Our strategy was to adapt existing training models to the Curacaon culture and prepare a cadre of Curacaon trainers and consultants to apply them. The training models adapted included McClelland's (McClelland & Winter, 1969) achievement motivation training; efficacy training—a modification of achievement motivation training developed by Richard deCharms (1968, 1969) and his associates; and group dynamics training, emphasizing participative leadership, conflict management, and the dynamics of competition and collaboration (Schein & Bennis, 1965).

The second element of the program was the *Outlet Program*, designed to create new educational and job opportunities to ensure socially and economically productive outlets for individuals whose aspiration level was raised by the motivation training. Outlet Program activities were directed at increasing the Island leaders' ability to work collaboratively in creating a better community.

Demonstration Programs

In late 1969, two four-day motivation training programs were conducted on Curacao. Each included heavy emphasis on efficacy and

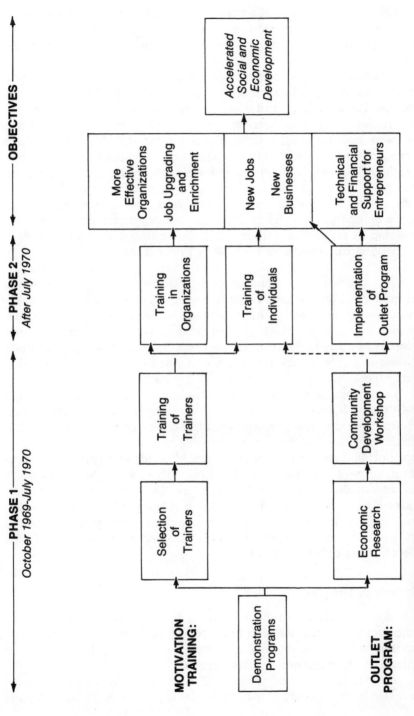

Figure 1. Intervention Plan: Major Activities and Objectives

individual achievement (life planning, goal setting, and action planning), with a secondary focus on interpersonal skills and group building. The final half-day of each program explored the relevance of the training to Curacao.

Approximately 50 persons attended the two demonstration programs, including all members of the Steering Committee of Fundashon Renovashon and representatives from business, labor, government, churches, barrios, and major political groups. The training was well received and to a great extent fulfilled the functions intended; i.e., the demonstration programs provided Fundashon Renovashon Steering Committee members with an excellent orientation; and gave individuals in decision-making positions an opportunity to experience the "new technology" firsthand and to evaluate its relevance to their groups and to Curacao. The programs also served as a first step in recruiting, screening, and training a cadre of potential Curacaon trainers and consultants for Phase 2 of the Motivation Training.

Two incidents are worth reporting. During a simulation exercise an influential businessman and a left-wing leader performed exceptionally well as a team. The businessman, who had previously "despised" the radical leader, gained a new respect for him and later referred publicly to the radical leader as "his friend"—bringing upon himself a public attack by "his friend," who could hardly afford a public association with a conservative businessman.

In addition, the participation of the editor and a key staff member of Curacao's ultra-left newspaper in a demonstration program convinced them that the program could help the poor of Curacao. The radical left thus implicitly agreed that it would not discredit the program at its outset; nor, however, would it actively support the program, since it was supported by the Establishment. Nevertheless, it indicated it would attack the program any time it met with its disfavor. (Indeed, at a later date it did attack the Fundashon Renovashon program as "CIA inspired," an accusation that was openly debated in the city square. The attack was both mild and short-lived and had little effect that we could ascertain.)

Motivation Training

The Motivation Training element of the intervention consisted of four major activities: the selection and training of a cadre of trainer/ consultants, training individual Curacaons, and training the members of Curacaon organizations and institutions.

A list of trainer candidates, both nominees and volunteers, was compiled and carefully screened to identify individuals with leadership potential and time to spend several weeks a year in training-related activities. Twenty candidates representing most of the major factions on the Island were selected. Included were businessmen, social workers, youth leaders, behavioral scientists, civil servants, and labor leaders.

Trainer candidates were given three weeks of intensive group training, reading assignments, and a monitored training experience over a period of five months from February to July 1970. Our objective was to develop their skills to the point that they could deliver pre-designed semistructured training programs to achieve specific behavioral objectives. We hoped that several trainer candidates, because of professional training and experience or natural aptitude, would be able to go beyond prescribed training designs and serve as group and organizational consultants.

As part of their training, the candidates adapted existing training designs and materials to Curacaon culture and organizations and supervised the translation of materials into Papiemento. In July 1970, 18 trainers were certified as having reached a preestablished level of proficiency.

Because of the personal interests and goals of the Curacaon trainers and their organizations, training was planned and conducted for groups of individuals including the underemployed and unemployed, teachers and youth leaders, union and cooperative members, and policemen. A major thrust was training individual entrepreneurs and potential entrepreneurs (primarly blacks) as a way of creating new job opportunities on Curacao. This involved three elements. First, owners of small businesses as well as potential entrepreneurs would be recruited for one-week achievement motivation training programs. Second, the Chamber of Commerce and Industry would establish a Small-Business Development Center to provide business-skill training and consultation to individuals who completed motivation training. Finally, individuals who completed motivation and business training and developed a realistic plan for starting or expanding a business would be given a government-guaranteed bank loan.

Using the results of similar projects as guidelines (McClelland & Winter, 1969; Timmons, 1971), the projected output, based on training 1,060 existing or potential small businessmen during the five-year period 1969-1974, was 5,215 additional jobs (i.e., jobs over and above the normal expected increase).

Many of the attitudes and behavior patterns inculcated through motivation training, such as taking the initiative and setting and working toward self-development and career goals, would not be welcomed by traditional Curacaon organizations; indeed, a frequent reaction to Motivation Training was, "I want to change, but it will get me in trouble in my organization." Although it was unrealistic to undertake major organization development projects, we knew that Curacaon trainers sponsored by local business organizations and public institutions would have opportunities to conduct "in-house" training programs. Thus we exposed these trainers briefly to concepts and techniques related to team building, management style, job enrichment, and career development to help them function more effectively in an organizational context.

Outlet Program

The Outlet Program consisted of a research phase, a workshop for community leaders, and an implementation phase.

The project staff conducted a brief study of the economic potential of Curacao and obstacles to its economic and social development. Our first objective was to become knowledgeable as quickly as possible about current economic and social conditions on Curacao. Of paramount importance was whether or not it was realistic to expect to create significant new opportunities for Curacaons. If indicators pointed to an extended period of economic decline, we would be trying to raise expectations and levels of aspiration during an opportunity famine—a set of conditions that can lead to violent revolution (McClelland, 1971). Fortunately, the economic outlook for Curacao is relatively bright.

Second, we wanted to gather together, or at least catalog, existing economic data, reports, and forecasts for use during the Community Development Workshop. It was not our intention to draw conclusions from the data, but to digest and organize them so that they could be readily used by community leaders for problem solving and planning.

Community Development Workshop. An intensive five-day Community Development Workshop was held in January 1970 for a group of 30 business, labor, community, and political leaders. The objectives were to:

Identify common goals for Curacao and Curacaons, but also acknowledge the legitimacy of group-specific goals

Determine the major assets and obstacles to the social and economic development of Curacao

Develop concrete programs of action to overcome or avoid obstacles to development and an Outlet Program to open new economic opportunities for Curacaons.

The development of a tangible Outlet Program was especially critical since the impact of the Motivation Training was directly tied to it.

A list of workshop participants was carefully drawn up by the Steering Committee to include the heads of major businesses and industrial corporations, banks, political parties, and labor and credit unions as well as government officials responsible for social and economic planning and development. Each person on the list was sent a written invitation, followed by a personal visit from a member of the Steering Committee.

The Fundashon Renovashon was successful in attracting to the Workshop a large percentage of economically powerful Curacaons. Participation by the politically powerful was limited, however; although the Prime Minister opened the Workshop and the Minister of Labor and Social Welfare attended the first day, both appointed staff to participate in their place. This was deeply resented by some non-government participants, and as a result they may have felt somewhat less optimistic about what the Workshop might accomplish. A brief description of the five-day Community Development Workshop is presented in Figure 2.

Implementation of Outlet Program. The output of the Community Development Workshop was the implementation plan for the Outlet Program. Four action teams were formed, each composed of individuals personally committed to working on certain types of problems. By the end of the Workshop, the action teams had formulated group goals and detailed plans for reaching those goals. Each team's plans had been reviewed by the other Workshop participants, responsibilities had been assigned, schedules established, and criteria for measuring progress identified.

The following statements, taken from documents submitted by each action team to the Fundashon Renovashon a few weeks after the end of the Workshop, will convey a general picture of the planned Outlet Program.

One action team concerned itself directly with creating new job opportunities. As its members viewed the problem:

> It is estimated that there are at the moment 8,000 unemployed persons and that yearly 550 will be added to these. For 1970 this committee estimated that 1,500 new jobs would become available, but it is necessary to create in the coming five years a total of at least 10,500 jobs if tensions are to be relieved.

This action team stated as its short-term priority goal ensuring the creation of 1,700 new jobs in Curacao by January 1, 1971: in tourism (400 jobs), industry (800 jobs), small business (300 jobs), and a government work project similar to WPA (200 jobs).

The second action team ". . . undertook to study and carry forward plans to establish an Economic Development Corporation on Curacao

	Day 1 Articulation of a Shared Dream	Day 2 Identifying Obstacles and Testing Collaborative Strategies	Day 3 Dynamics of Community Problem Solving	Day 4 Forming Action Teams and Developing Commitment to Results	Day 5 Planning for Action
Morning:	Projection to 1975: What would you like Curacao to be? What are facilitating factors? What are obstacles? What priority actions and decisions must be taken soon?	Reaching consensus on obstacles to collaborative community problem solving	The Critical Situation Exercise: An exercise in which a real community problem is identified and solved. The process of problem solving is intensively analyzed.	Identifying priority action steps Defining commitment	Goal setting and planning in action teams Group review of action team goals and plans
Afternoon:	Reaching consensus on strengths	The dynamics of competition and collaboration	Same as morning	A model for goal setting and planning	Replanning by action teams Closing
Evening:	Analysis of leadership Dream sharing	Free	Introduction to community goal setting	Establishing individual priorities Forming action teams	

Figure 2. Design of Five-Day Community Development Workshop

to promote the establishment of industry and tourist facilities, to create 10,000 jobs in the next five years, to make feasibility studies, and to obtain (or assist in obtaining) financing."

An action team concerned with education had as its overall goal to ". . . bring post-school education to as large a segment of the Curacao population as possible." The team recommended a large number of specific education programs aimed primarily at adults, including weekly educational programs on television, radio, and in the newspapers (covering topics such as civics, responsibilities of citizenship, and motivation), crash courses for elementary school dropouts, leadership training courses, teach-ins, weekend workshops for members of the labor movement, and home economics courses. The focal point of the team's action plan was a three-month Antillean Institute of the Social Sciences planned for the summer of 1970 for 100-300 adult students from all walks of life, with 10-20 full- and part-time instructors, including educators, businessmen, government executives, labor leaders, and a few visiting scholars from the United States, Holland, and the Caribbean.

The fourth action team, concerned with social benefits, comprised three union presidents and a government planner. Their goal was to ". . . provide an adequate social benefits program for the Netherlands Antilles." Specifically concerned about old-age pensions, widow-orphan pensions, unemployment compensation, sickness-accident insurance, and medical and general insurance, they wanted to accomplish their goal by obtaining participation for the Netherlands Antilles in the Dutch social security system.

Termination of Phase 1

When Phase 1 (see Figure 1) ended in July 1970 the Fundashon Renovashon was to carry on with minimal support from the consultants. The authors met with its Steering Committee several times during the spring of 1970 to help plan for the transition to Phase 2. Most of our efforts involved helping it set goals for the coming year, develop strategies for reaching those goals, and identify ways of raising additional funds to sustain the organization.

The final Phase 1 intervention consisted of a July 1970 workshop with the trainers and Steering Committee members to finalize training targets and related support systems for 1970-71. The meeting ended with the certification of the 18 Curacaon trainers, an event that received full television and press coverage.

Formal involvement of the authors and McBer and Company with Curacao and the Fundashon Renovashon was thereby concluded. One part-time McBer staff member remained on the Island to conduct his own doctoral research and for a short period worked directly for the Fundashon Renovashon to help set up an information system which would provide feedback for a systematic evaluation of the program. This same staff member, who later took up residence on Curacao, continued to work with the trainers on his own time.

EFFECTS

It is difficult to describe the effects of the Curacaon intervention, partly due to a lack of quantitative data, but also because many important effects were either unanticipated or elusive. Things happened which were exciting and which seemed terribly important at the time: A Dutch industrialist and the black president of his industry's union, who had never spoken with each other, spent a week together planning a better community, conducting a competition/collaboration exercise, and a half-day later watching the Workshop participants work together to avert a walk-out and probably a general strike; educators discovered alternatives to traditional Dutch practices they knew to be inappropriate for Curacaon children.

There were as many disappointments: the peripheral involvement of top-echelon government officials; the gradual dissolution of the group developed by the Community Development Workshop; the government's failure to follow through on a program to guarantee loans to qualified small businessmen; the Fundashon Renovashon's inability to sustain itself as a viable organization.

The intervention can also be evaluated in terms of the plan and objectives shown in Figure 1. The five Phase 1 activities were relatively successful. The demonstration programs were very well received and served their intended functions. Trainers from a variety of backgrounds and factions were recruited, screened, and trained and for the most part reached the level of proficiency required to carry on the motivation training; some were qualified to do much more. The Community Development Workshop brought together Island leaders who had never met as a group and taught them to problem solve and plan together. Despite the pall caused by the absence of top government leaders, the Workshop ended on a high note of optimism for both participants and consultants. The economic research, despite a very small budget, successfully collected, collated, and presented a wealth of economic data from a wide variety of sources. Unfortunately, the written document elicited a certain amount of blame placing and defensiveness and on balance made little contribution.

Although Community Development Workshop participants did not function effectively as a group during most of Phase 2, the action teams continued to work toward their goals with varying degrees of success. An economic development corporation was formed in late 1970 and became operational in December 1971 with 1½ million guilders (approximately $750,000) as capital. The education action team was instrumental in establishing a highly successful social science institute for three months during the summer of 1970, attended by over 400 students. The program dealt primarily with current problems of Curacao and was marked by unprecedented freedom of expression and open debate. This same action team also initiated a variety of other adult education programs.

It is more difficult to describe the activities of the action team concerned with job creation because it was concerned with several areas of the economy and because several individual members held positions such that their decisions could significantly influence the number of available jobs (for example, the General Manager of the Shell refinery, who made decisions regarding the pace and extent of automation). Although the team eventually drifted apart, individual members and subgroups made significant achievements. One member, with the help of a UN expert he brought to Curacao, was instrumental in establishing a handicraft cooperative. Another member, a leader in the Chamber of Commerce and Industry, worked actively to promote the establishment and expansion of Antillean-owned businesses.

By July 1970, the Fundashon Renovashon could carry out achievement motivation or "entrepreneurial" training for businessmen or potential entrepreneurs. By Fall, a Small-Business Development Center had been established under the sponsorship of the Chamber of Commerce and Industry, and a small-business consultant from the United States hired to work with individuals who wanted to start or expand businesses and train Curacaon counterparts. The Island government agreed to take over the Center once it was operating, and also agreed in principle to a business development loan program that would guarantee 50 per cent of private bank loans to small- and medium-sized businesses. Under these conditions local banks indicated their willingness to make higher than normal risk loans to trained candidates with carefully prepared business plans.

By February 1971 the Small-Business Development Center had trained 79 candidates for business loans, 30 of the candidates had started new businesses, and 69 new jobs had been created. Unfortunately, the government did not implement the loan guarantee program, and when 30 per cent of the new businesses failed in the first several months, the banks reverted to their former loan policies.

Although considerable interest in motivation training and in other forms of "psychological education" was stimulated on Curacao, the

Motivation Training element of the intervention did not go according to plan. From November 1969 through June 1970, the Fundashon Renovashon sponsored training for approximately 250 individuals from a wide variety of social and occupational groups. During the period July 1970 to March 1971 another 300 people were trained. There was little activity during the remainder of 1971: the Fundashon was unable to raise the funds required to underwrite the costs of training. In late 1971, the Fundashon Renovashon decided to continue training but at a slower pace and with a greater share of the training costs borne by the participants. On this basis, monthly training sessions were scheduled to begin in 1973, with increased emphasis on recruiting businessmen and potential businessmen in order to have a more direct impact on the creation of new businesses and new jobs.[3]

In May 1971, one of the Fundashon Renovashon trainers founded a private training enterprise with the assistance of one of our project staff members. During its first year of operation, this organization provided laboratory training for 500 Curacaons. At least 11 of the 18 Fundashon Renovashon trainers have moved to new positions as full-time or part-time trainers, and considerable "training in organizations" has been conducted by this group and the private training organization noted above. Although the specific number of Curacaon trainers and those trained by them is not known to the authors, the increasing use of behavioral science training and techniques on Curacao represents a significant cross-cultural transfer.

PROBLEMS AND ISSUES

The examination of problems and issues will be divided into two parts: the relationship between the client and the consultant, and the design of the intervention.

Obligations of Consultant to Client

Structuring the Relationship. The following are pertinent facts related to the early development of the client-consultant relationship:

> McBer was first contacted by the Chamber of Commerce and Industry of Curacao, a semipublic, predominantly white organization of businessmen and industrialists. Their stated objective in making contact was to obtain help in establishing more small-business enterprises owned and operated by Curacaons.
>
> The explicit objectives of the Chamber as communicated to the consultant were to (1) encourage more Antilleans to become associated with

---

[3] At this writing, the authors do not have information on how successfully the modified training plan has been implemented.

existing businesses, (2) encourage the establishment of more Antillean businesses, (3) create new jobs, and (4) give Antilleans a sense of participating in their community.

On the morning of his first full day on Curacao, the consultant was asked to conduct an already scheduled meeting with 40 labor, government, community, business and industrial leaders, sponsored by the Chamber of Commerce and Industry and held in the Chamber building.

At the meeting, the consultant presented himself as someone who did not know much about their specific situation but who was knowledgeable about some new change technologies which they might find useful. Most of the participants appeared to be intrigued, then excited, about possible applications of these technologies.

These facts can be interpreted in a number of ways. The business community may have wanted to initiate a community development effort and chose a business development program as most familiar and feasible. With the arrival of a consultant who appeared to know something about community as well as business development, they decided to invite inputs from the rest of the community, something they were happy to do as long as the final plan included a business development element. If this interpretation is correct, then the consultant acted appropriately in leading a meeting which in effect redefined the identity of the client and broadened the focus of the intervention.

The same facts are also subject to the interpretation that the Chamber was only interested in supporting a business-oriented program; they felt they needed the approval of the community and they expected the consultant to "sell" the project to the community leaders. If so, the consultant sold them down the river by treating the community, rather than the Chamber, as the client, and thus left the Chamber with no choice but to support a community-oriented program or appear parochial and self-serving.

Regardless of the correct interpretation, a critical choice point was passed with important implications for the nature and success of the intervention. If the correct path was taken, it was the result of good luck and good instincts.

What were the effects of the decision that was made? Only about 50 of 550 individuals trained in 1970-71 were potential candidates to start or expand businesses on the Island. Only three or four of the 18 trainers placed a high priority on training small or potential businessmen. Project funds were used up in nine months; if the intervention had been more focused, they might have been spread over a longer time period, and the rather abrupt termination that occurred might have been avoided. Several businessmen got caught up in the community-oriented project, but some key members of the Chamber became less involved when the original goals were subordinated. The business community that provided most of the funds for Phase 1 did not support Phase 2; it might have, if there had been more evidence that its original objectives were being aggressively pursued.

On the other hand, in the short run, more people and a greater variety of organizations and factions gained from the intervention in terms of individual development and better intragroup and intergroup relations. A variety of concrete plans for alleviating the Island's problems were developed, and some were implemented. Finally, the business community had an opportunity to take the lead in community development, and a number of individuals worked extremely hard and sacrificed a great deal to fulfill that responsibility.

What could or should have been done to ensure that the choice was the correct one and that the original goals of the original client, the Chamber of Commerce and Industry, were met?

Chamber or Community? There were at least three questions that should have been answered, or at least explored, before a decision was made. First, how flexible were the goals of the members of the Chamber of Commerce and Industry? Were they inextricably committed to a small-business development program, or was that simply the best community development program they had come up with? Second, how open were they to influence by the community? Were they seeking ideas and collaborators, or just approval to run "their" program? Third, who did *they* perceive the client to be? The Chamber or the community? Would they accept the consultant's view that the community was the most appropriate client? It is unfortunate that these issues were not carefully explored before a chain of events was started from which there was no turning back.

Business or Therapy? If in the course of psychotherapy a patient gets into trouble, the therapist sees him through; he does not desert the patient. Responsible group trainers have a similar rule of thumb: do not open up problem areas unless they can be worked through in the time available. The therapeutic relationship assumes that the therapist has more insight than the patient into how much and what kind of treatment is required. Although the client or patient can always break off treatment, under normal conditions the therapist has the greatest influence in deciding whether or not a patient is ready to terminate therapy. It is also assumed that concern about his fee does not influence the therapist's decision.

In the normal business relationship, the buyer decides what he wants, how much he wants, and when he doesn't want any more. The seller may try to influence the buyer, but it is the buyer's decision.

What about the relationship between the buyer and seller of social intervention services, as in the Curacao case? Should it be a straight business transaction, with the buyer perhaps listening to the advice of the seller but ultimately making his own decision about what he wants and how much of it? Or is it a therapeutic relationship wherein the buyer cannot be expected to understand enough about the treatment or service to know how much to buy, and the therapist or consultant should be expected to specify the precise kind and amount of service that will be required for a cure?

The relationship between McBer and Company and Fundashon Renovashon was structured as a business relationship. The buyer read about a particular product and contacted what he believed to be the sole distributor. The seller visited the potential buyer, displayed his wares, and conducted a quick diagnosis to determine whether his product fit the buyer's needs or needed adaptation. The buyer asked for a proposal, and the seller provided one, complete with the description of the 12 tasks that would have to be carried out, the time and money required to complete the tasks, and a schedule for task completion. The proposal and terms were formally agreed to.

It was a good proposal from a business point of view. The tasks were well defined, they were in the right sequence, and man-day estimates for completing them were surprisingly accurate. But they weren't perfect. The first modification occurred when one demonstration program proved insufficient. So a second was conducted and turned out to be critical for gaining community acceptance. The client was not willing to "pay extra" for this second program, but he knew its importance, and so he agreed to a shifting of man-days and funds in order to fund it. Two or three more minor modifications were made, and several tasks that would have enabled the consultant to provide some continuing support to the Fundashon Renovashon, the trainers, and the community leaders' group during Phase 2 were eliminated. (We did not leave the patient stranded, but neither did we see him through to a cure. We stopped before we wanted to, when there were still things we could do which we knew would help.)

The question remains: Is social intervention like the Curacao case business or therapy? Is it ethical or professional to contract to do a piece of work for a certain amount of money, knowing that you cannot anticipate all that may happen or the amount of treatment that may be required to work through problems that surface? Is it even professional to start a job you are not certain you can finish?

On the other hand, there is something "clean" about a business relationship, a contract to do a defined task according to a given schedule for a certain fee. As much as the therapeutic relationship protects the client from being stranded, the business relationship protects him from an unnecessarily protracted relationship and psychological dependence.

There is a third possibility, which lies somewhere between the business and therapeutic relationships, with some of the advantages of both. One characteristic of such a relationship might be the separation of diagnosis from treatment, the equivalent of the psychiatric evaluation interview. A short diagnostic or feasibility study as a prelude to writing a proposal or deciding whether to do a job is common in the consulting world and has clear advantages for both buyer and seller. Another characteristic might be a contingency fund of perhaps 25 per cent of the value of the contract, over and above the estimated cost of completing the work, as an explicit reminder to both parties that all events cannot be foreseen and that both share the responsibility for evaluating their impact and, if necessary, dealing with them. If there is a good relationship between consultant and client, they should be able to negotiate the use of contingency funds. If trust is low, an expert third party should probably be involved.

Still a further characteristic of the relationship might be the requirement for long-term commitment. It is hard to give if you are the buyer, and hard to get if you are the seller, but it may be necessary for the protection of both parties. It might be a more palatable arrangement to the buyer if it was not required that the same consultant be involved for the full period. It might even be advisable to specify qualified alternative consultants at the beginning of the relationship, or specify an expert third party who would make such a designation. Thus consultants might place their clients in other competent hands much as psychotherapists recommend other therapists when the relationship fails to develop.

Design of the Intervention

The Curacao intervention may have been unusual in that it was based more on a motivational model derived from individual psychology than on concepts from social psychology or sociology. The motivational model seemed particularly relevant for a number of reasons. First, during initial interviews, black Antillean leaders expressed great concern over the lack of an Antillean identity. Specifically, they worried about an almost total lack of initiative by black Antilleans, which they attributed to centuries of dependency, first as slaves, then as Dutch subjects. It was this information that led us to the concept of efficacy and deCharm's distinction between "origins" and "pawns." Second, the lack of an entrepreneurial tradition among black Antilleans suggested that achievement motivation and the development of entrepreneurial spirit should play an important part in the intervention.

It was obvious that the use and distribution of power would have to be a major concern of the intervention. McClelland's (1970) distinction between "the two faces of power" seemed particularly pertinent. Individuals with high needs for "personal power" feel stronger by making others weaker. They view the amount of power available as a limited commodity and interpret events in "win-lose" or zero-sum terms. Individuals with high "socialized power," on the other hand, satisfy their needs for power by influencing group members to work toward group goals. They tend to view the world in "win-win" or non-zero terms. McBer and Company (1970) had recently conducted an experimental program in which community leaders had been trained in socialized power. The results were promising in that the trained leaders became more effective institution-builders, their organizations were more active in carrying out community-related projects, and members of their organizations felt a greater sense of participation.

The motivation training model, then, gave us a series of interrelated concepts for analyzing problems and designing or adapting training inputs to remedy those problems.

Unfortunately, we never fully understood the complexities of power on Curacao, although we did come to appreciate its singular importance. A trained sociologist living on Curacao describes one aspect of the problem:

> And that's one of the reasons for the success of the program on Curacao: the willingness of the people to listen. Consultants are accepted because of a funny cross-mixture of the voodoo culture and the Dutch educational system where the people basically believe in voodoo, in magic, in fortune telling, in destiny, and all those things. The motivation training course is seen as something that gives people increased mental powers to control the direction of their lives. And to that extent it's consonant with what I call the voodoo cult. On the other hand, anyone who is a university professor is, by definition, the master. . . . People don't even question the validity of the ideas. So I think the consultants' initial speeches to the community were accepted immediately, whereas they wouldn't be necessarily in other systems.

As Americans, we never really understood this strange combination of the European and the African. It is fascinating to hear a white Antillean educated in the United States tentatively (because he is afraid you may laugh at him) describe occult experiences he has had; it begins to add possible new dimensions to events. For example, when we described the existence of "powerful new change technologies" to the meeting of 40 community leaders during our first visit to Curacao, we inadvertently created a new basis for competition among groups. In a culture where power needs are exceptionally high, where the word of the expert is revered, and where belief in the occult is still alive, we described a powerful "new technology" and promised them control over it. The various Island factions may have agreed to form a single community organization not because of a new feeling of community spirit and cooperation but because if they could not have the new magic for themselves, they at least wanted to stay close to the source so it would not be used against them. Indeed, the magical power of trainers was a continual theme throughout the intervention.

We know that on Curacao personal power need is very high (much higher than achievement motivation, as measured in fantasy) and socialized power need is very low. We also know that many individuals translated achievement motivation training into power terms and used achievement strategies to achieve power goals. Our failure to understand and deal with these issues more fully was clearly the weakest aspect of the intervention.

EPILOGUE

The following is a statement taken verbatim from a taped interview with an American living on Curacao, conducted at a Harvard University Social Intervention Seminar on January 11, 1971. Although the informant was involved in some parts of the intervention, he remained a critical observer. Perhaps this statement will help to put what was for us a fascinating and rewarding experience into perspective for the reader.

> *Question:* What difference has the motivation training intervention made in Curacao at this point?
>
> *Answer:* It's too early to answer that question. In terms of the exposure of people to training it was just a millisecond. We have tried to set up an organic process which feeds on its own successes and builds. We have successfully closed the loop in that system so we could cut the umbilical cord, and it will live. Whether the system will grow has to be seen. It will continue to have an impact and a growing influence on the society. The biggest impact to date comes from the [Community Development Workshop] group where something really did happen. A lot of people are still talking about it. It affected a lot of very key people on the Island in an important way. One of the definite effects is a moderating effect. It made the system more able to cope with its problems. Now a lot of people could argue that that's kind of reactionary. I think you could argue just as easily that it's taking people who have talent and power and putting them out in potential positions to do more for people in the society. I have no reason to believe that a revolution would cure Curacao's problems because in the vacuum a revolution creates Curacao will still need institutions and people to solve basic problems. This intervention asks people to analyze what they want, when they want to do it, and then to do it, or try to do it.

That can create revolutionaries as well as solutions. But unless some of the people start thinking in these terms, nothing in the system is going to improve anyway.

REFERENCES

de Charms, R. *Personal causation*. New York: Academic Press, 1968.

de Charms, R. Origins, pawns, and educational practice. In G. S. Lessor (Ed.), *Psychology and the educational process*. Glenview, Ill.: Scott, Foresman, 1969.

McBer and Company Publications Series. Influencing community change. October 1970, No. 4.

McClelland, D. C. The two faces of power. *Journal of International Affairs*, 1970, *24*(1), 29-47.

McClelland, D. C. *Motivational trends in society*. New York: General Learning Press, 1971.

McClelland, D. C., & Winter, D. G. *Motivating economic achievement*. New York: Free Press, 1969.

Schein, E. H., & Bennis, W. G. *Personal and organizational change through group methods*. New York: Wiley, 1965.

Timmons, J. A. Black is beautiful—Is it bountiful? *Harvard Business Review*, November-December, 1971, pp. 81-94.

PROBLEMS AND ISSUES IN THE CURACAO CASE: A NINE-YEAR PERSPECTIVE

David E. Berlew, William E. LeClere, and Victor Pinedo, Jr.

With the added perspective of time and the insight of one of the Curacaons directly involved in the project, we now know something more about the long-term effects of the Curacao intervention. Some of the most striking include:

- The apparent long-range impact of the project on the professional and personal lives of the Curacaon trainers;
- The continuing effects of the work begun by action teams after the Community Development Workshop;
- The ongoing individual efforts of members of the steering committee to improve the quality of life in Curacao;
- The range and number of unintended consequences that can be connected with activities initiated in conjunction with the intervention.

In the intervening years, virtually all of the trainers have undergone major career changes. At one time or another, at least twelve of the eighteen part-time trainers have moved into some kind of full-time educational or training activities, although only two were educators or trainers at the beginning of the project. Approximately half of the team members have been engaged in training activities, some with Fundashon Humanas, two with a government training center, others with a teacher-training institute, and several in private industrial organizations. Many who did not move into training went through other significant career changes that they attribute at least in part to the individual self-assessment and planning they engaged in while being trained as trainers.

Although the community leaders assembled for the Community Development Workshop never again met as a group, several of the action teams continued to function, and institutional aftereffects continue to be evident. The Economic Development Corporation has played an important role in several major community projects. The handicraft cooperative continues to flourish and to provide new jobs and economic activities for a considerable number of Curacaons. The education action team, in addition to sponsoring social science institutes, brought new educational television programming to the island and stimulated innovative teacher training through the years.

Individual members of the steering committee have pursued the general Fundashon goals through other institutional affiliations, in spite of the termination of Fundashon Renovashon. A job creation and training center was established, largely through the efforts of one committee member, and several continued community-development plans were implemented, with individual members of the steering committee playing prominent roles. One committee member has become a consultant to government and industry on economic matters; others have reached prominent positions in the government and pursue community-development goals from those positions.

The many unintended long-range consequences are perhaps best illustrated by the creation of Fundashon Humanas which, adding ego development and Gestalt training methods to the motivation model (Pinedo, 1978), has trained thousands of supervisors and managers at Shell Oil and become a major training/consulting organization in Venezuelan industry and government systems. Many additional Curacaon and Venezuelan trainers have been trained, and, through the ripple effect, the change technologies introduced some nine years ago have spread beyond our capacity to track and quantify them.

Two major elements in the original intervention plan can be seen as failures: (1) the inability of Fundashon Renovashon to survive as a continuing community-development force and (2) the failure to link achievement-motivation training to an ongoing small-business-development center to stimulate Antillean-owned small businesses.

FUNDASHON RENOVASHON

The Fundashon was created in response to the consultants' desire that a new organization with representation from all major factions be formed. The artificial genesis of the organization may have doomed it from the outset. However, given the willingness of the Chamber to establish such an organization, the consultants may have been able to give it a greater chance to prosper.

One problem was that the specific motivation and goals of the steering committee were not clarified at the outset. It is difficult today to recreate all of the environmental factors that influenced the business and community leaders of Curacao in 1969. In addition to general agitation in Europe and the United States, black awareness was sweeping the Caribbean, accompanied by shootings in the Virgin Islands, disturbances in Jamaica, and intense concern over the actions and intentions of Cuba. Curacao seemed ripe for trouble, with Dutch-owned Shell Oil as the major employer, Dutch or Dutch descendants controlling many crucial institutions, and the Jewish communities visible in business and commerce. With the exception of tourism, much of the economy seemed to be static or declining, and unemployment was rising and threatening to continue to rise with cutbacks at Shell and the pending closing of the potash mines. To their credit, the leaders of these dominant institutions in Curacao had the foresight to see that something had to change. The initial requests for assistance went out some weeks before the burning and lootings (still referred to in Curacao as the events of May 30).

What exactly should be changed was another matter. Beyond the laudable goal of trying to "accelerate the social and economic development of Curacao through better utilization of the Island's human resources," the committee had difficulty specifying and prioritizing objectives and action steps. There was never unanimity on what direction the project should take. McClelland's (1969) theories on individual and community change, as well as many other behavioral science approaches, were explored. Significantly, just prior to McBer's first visit, many community leaders and almost all steering committee members had participated in a Managerial Grid® seminar (Blake & Mouton, 1969). This double exposure to the wonders of behavioral-science technologies may have contributed to expectations of what behavioral-science-based training could accomplish. Committee members did agree on a general approach (behavioral-science training) to some general goals (to accelerate social and economic development), but they had difficulty setting priorities. Thus, the Community Development Workshop, for all of its obvious success, further compounded the problem by dispersing scarce resources (community leaders of stature and power) into five unconnected action teams with no interaction and, ultimately, no central focus.

In retrospect, we believe that the consultants should have spent far more time working with the committee and broadening the representative nature of that group because the lack of active participation by government and political leadership made the Fundashon entirely dependent on the private sector for resources. Also, credible, black, Antillean leadership was probably underrepresented, and the political Left was totally unrepresented. Resources that were spent training trainers should have been spent strengthening the human organization of the precariously created, multisector Fundashon.

SMALL BUSINESS DEVELOPMENT

Obviously, the attempt to extend the goals of the project beyond its initial focus was the major factor in the failure in the small-business area. In addition, we were probably overly optimistic about the economic potential for small business. In the years since the intervention, the tourist industry has stagnated, and much of our projection for small-business growth assumed continued growth of tourism. Clearly, our economic study was inadequate and/or we drew erroneous conclusions during the Community Development Workshop. If we had more accurately foreseen these developments, we probably would have pulled back from this part of the project ourselves, but because we were not clairvoyant we at least should have seen that more of the training team had a professional or personal commitment to small-business development. Only three or four of the eighteen saw this as a high priority.

We also should have made the skills-training element (added at our suggestion) more an integral part of the program, and we were probably naive to think that because McClelland's achievement-motivation training (McClelland, 1969) worked in India and the United States that it would work in the Curacaon culture. Subsequent research (Lasker, 1978) suggests that until a certain ego level is reached by trainees, achievement-motivation training is difficult if not impossible. This is consistent with some of McClelland's own speculative comments around the "non-change" problem among a minority of his experimental trainees in India.

And finally, the loss of guaranteed loan support by the government brings us to the failure of the consultants and the steering committee to see the need to slow down and do what was necessary to achieve political and government involvement at high levels in order to ensure linkage between private and public sector resources.

CONCLUSIONS

We continue to believe that our earlier analysis was accurate as far as it went, but a larger and more discreet diagnosis contract should have been executed before training was introduced. A contingency clause in the contract would have made eminent good sense for a project in which so many variables were unpredictable. Besides acknowledging our inadequacy in dealing with the power issues in Curacao, we would have done well to have tried to confront them, understand the issues, and help Curacaons acknowledge and understand them as well. Perhaps the technology to do so was not available at the time.

Subsequent research and development have resulted in at least three training models that could be used today in similar circumstances (Berlew & Harrison, 1976; McClelland & Burnham, 1976; & Oshry, 1976).

REFERENCES

Berlew, D. E., & Harrison, R. *Positive power and influence program.* Boston: Situation Management Systems, Inc., 1976.

Blake, R. R., & Mouton, J. S. *Building a dynamic corporation through Grid organization development.* Reading, MA: Addison-Wesley, 1969.

Lasker, H. M. *Ego development and motivation: A cross-cultural, cognitive developmental study of achievement.* Unpublished doctoral dissertation, University of Chicago, 1978.

McClelland, D. E., & Burnham, D. H. Power is the great motivator. *Harvard Business Review*, March-April, 1976, pp. 100-110.

Oshry, B. Power and systems: An overview; Power and the control of structure; Power and powerlessness: Good and lousy gardening. *Social Change: Ideas and Application*, 1976, 6(2, 3, 4). NTL Publications.

Pinedo, V., Jr. Loevinger's ego stages as the basis of an intervention model. In J. W. Pfeiffer & J. E. Jones (Eds.), *The 1978 annual handbook for group facilitators.* La Jolla, CA: University Associates, 1978.

Head Start Parents in Participant Groups[1]

Paul Wohlford[2]

Sensitivity training groups have rarely been conducted with low-income people. A modification of the laboratory training method, here called the "participant group method," was used with low-income parents of Head Start children to demonstrate under what conditions participant groups might be helpful to parents and their children. Eight groups met twice a week for eight weeks to help parents increase their children's language skills or to help them with their child-rearing problems. Parent trainers

[1]The author is indebted to Margaret Darden, Leona Eldridge, Jean S. James, James M. Kolarik, Elizabeth Phillips, Irving D. Strachan, Nancy Thompson, Joseph A. Trunfio, Birdie White, and Maxine R. Wooten, who gave of themselves as Parent Trainers and made the Parent Project possible. The author wishes to thank Gracie Miller, Associate Director of the Economic Opportunity Program, Inc. and Helen Stolte, Miami Head Start Project Manager, and Head Start staffs for their splendid cooperation. Finally, the author wishes to thank Dr. Herbert M. Dandes, the Associate Investigator, for sharing preservice training and supervision duties; Leslie H. Danford, for conducting the Language Development training; Dr. John W. McDavid, Dr. Carl E. McKenry, and Dr. Virginia Shipman for their assistance. The Parent Project was supported in part by a research grant titled, "Changing Parental Attitudes and Behavior Through Participant Group Methods," from the Office of Economic Opportunity (CAP CG-8003) to the University of Miami, for which the author was the Principal Investigator.

[2]Requests for reprints should be sent to Paul Wohlford, Ph.D., Division of Manpower and Training Programs, National Institute of Mental Health, 5600 Fishers Lane, Rockville, Maryland 20852. This article was written by Dr. Wohlford in his private capacity prior to his present affiliation. No official support or endorsement by the National Institute of Mental Health or the Department of Health, Education, and Welfare is intended or should be inferred. The author wishes to caution the reader: The author was—and still is—biased favorably toward both participant group methods for effecting prosocial behavioral change (e.g., Wohlford & Stern, 1968; Wohlford, 1973) and careful research to help to understand such change (Wohlford, 1972).

worked in pairs, which included a mother from the community. Couples were invited to some groups; only mothers to other groups. Most groups succeeded in engaging the parents' participation in child-rearing or related discussions. Judged on the basis of attendance and group process data, the participant group method seems an effective vehicle for directly delivering community clinical-psychological and educational services to low-income parents of preschool children.

If the sensitivity training (encounter) group is this century's most important social invention as Rogers (1969) has asserted, one might expect group methods to have been systematically employed in anti-poverty programs. There are surprisingly few actual reports of such efforts, either successful or unsuccessful, in spite of a recognition of the appropriateness of group approaches (Auerbach, 1968; Guerney, Stover, & Andronico, 1967; Peck, Kaplan, & Roman, 1969; Richards & Daniels, 1969). Nevertheless, in observing the development of poverty program neighborhood action committees, Zurcher (1969) noted elements of all three Tuckman-classed settings: therapy groups, human relations groups, and natural or laboratory groups. In addition, sensitivity or human relations training with low-income groups has been used occasionally with adults (Culver, Dunham, Edgerton, & Edgerton, 1969), with aggressive junior high school students (Rueveni, 1971), with juvenile delinquents (Ostrom, Steele, Rosenblood, & Mirels, 1971), and with those who serve low-income groups such as paraprofessionals and teachers (Carkhuff & Griffin, 1970) and parent educators (Gordon, 1969).

INTRODUCTION: FOCUS ON INTERDEPENDENCE

Under federal guidelines, Head Start and other early childhood programs for low-income clients must involve the parents of the preschool children in policy making (Office of Child Development, 1970), and are responsible for parent education to aid in child development (Hunt, 1971). However, direct involvement of low-income adults in an educationally oriented program in Head Start or in the public schools is an undertaking that faces formidable obstacles. People who struggle in poverty are generally alienated from middle class society, its agencies, and, especially, its schools—where many probably had negative experiences. If this is true, then adults' generalizations of their negative childhood experiences would be detrimental to their involvement in a child education program. Moreover, parents' behavior with their children is deeply entrenched and therefore is not easily susceptible to change; thus, a program designed to intervene in it would have to use relatively powerful methods.

Systematic group methods have been used to some extent with parents on school-related variables but seldom with low-income populations (see review by Wohlford, 1973). Auerbach (1968) reports a plan to engage a large number of low-income parents in small-group education. Open-ended, dynamic small groups of low-income parents of preschool children have had various orientations, including child rearing (Nechin, 1966), Eriksonian Stages of Development (Cook, 1968), and language development (Wohlford & Stern, 1968). The latter project, a pilot of which is reported here, combined informal demonstrations of ways in which parents could expand their child's cognitive world with an unstructured, process-centered, participant small-group method. It appears to be a useful technique to evaluate and, where necessary, to intervene in parent-child interactions.

The term "participant group method" refers to methods, like the T Group,[3] in which group members provide the reference group and the basic impetus for change. Because groups involve others in the same situation, group psychotherapy with low-income people seems more effective than individual therapies (Christmas, 1966). This phenomenon may be due to attitudes toward authority, social comparisons processes, following the therapist's model, and differences in the communication pattern between middle-class and low-income therapist-patient combinations (Frank, 1961). Whatever the reasons, participant group methods can exploit this source of power.

Critical for the project reported here, participant group methods enable the group members to focus on, and perhaps modify, their interpersonal behavior. As described fully by Wohlford (1973), these methods, which include task-orientation, use of trainers as role models, open communication, cooperative feedback, and democratic group process with no hidden agendas, are especially appropriate for working with low-income parents. Through participation in this type of group experience, parents should become aware of, and come to modify, their interpersonal behavior in the direction of more "ideal" relationships; and that, in turn, should create analogous relationships with their children. In sum, although few programs have succeeded in engaging low-income parents in any meaningful way, participant

---

[3]Since the inception of the Parent Project, the group movement has tremendously gained in popularity both among professionals and in the general population. As with any sudden popularization of a complex phenomenon, there have been distortions, excesses, and abuses, as recent critics have pointed out. Oversimplifications of group approaches often fail to distinguish significant differences between Sensitivity Training and Encounter Groups. With the exception of a few weeks' experiment with encounter techniques in Group 6, the only explicitly implemented small-group methods were the sensitivity training or T-Group methods.

groups offer some promise of success in intervening in key parental attitudes and behavior.

The remainder of this paper describes a field intervention research project, the Parent Project, whose primary objective was to investigate the effectiveness of participant groups in changing parents' attitudes and behaviors that would, in turn, change their children's behavior. To assess such changes, a variety of cognitive, personality, and interpersonal variables were assessed in both the parents and their children before and after the parents received participant group training (pretest—intervention—posttest design). The full context of the Parent Project, including its field intervention research rationale, systematic variation of the groups, and description of the participating parents, is presented elsewhere (Wohlford, 1972).

The Parent Project's secondary objective was to provide information about several important practical issues in conducting such groups. First, could a large proportion of a given number of low-income parents, including both fathers and mothers, be persuaded to attend group meetings regularly, and, if so, under what conditions? Would mothers without husbands attend? Would fathers as well as mothers attend? Finally, would a group's structure and content— specifically, a structured language development training group compared with an unstructured process group discussing such topics as child raising—influence its effectiveness?

This study's focus on precise effects of group intervention on low-income parent group members' and their children's behavior may render its results particularly valuable with regard to certain questions concerning basic research and field application. For instance, there are many implications for preschool programs, like the Office of Child Development's Home Start, in which the sole or primary intervention is through the parents (O'Keefe, 1973). However, the Parent Project's research design demanded using the children of nonparticipating parents as controls for the children of participating parents; thus, we could not directly involve teachers in parent groups, except where special intervention was clinically imperative. The data from the total Parent Project fall into five categories: the parents' attendance at the meetings; the group process of the eight groups; the effect on the community, as seen in the parents' postgroup attitudes and willingness to participate in future meetings; objectively measured changes in the parents; and objectively measured changes in their children. The first two issues, the parents' overall response as seen in their attendance and the group process, are represented here; the other three, elsewhere (Wohlford, 1971, 1972).

INTERVENTION STRATEGY

The underlying theory of the Parent Project's intervention strategy is presented in two ways: first, schematically in Lewinian-like diagrams; and, secondly, according to input, intraprocess, and outcome variables.

The entry of a young child from a low-income family into public school usually represents his departure from his subcultural milieu and his solitary confrontation of a rather impenetrable social class barrier as he enters that institution of the dominant middle class. The burden is clearly upon the young child; caught between two cultures, he must accommodate himself to both, but possibly at the expense of considerable conflict and internal stress. Figure 1 presents the Parent Project's intervention strategy, which reverses that burden, placing it where it should be—*back on the adults*: first, on the public school or Head Start; next, on the Parent Group Trainers; then, the neighborhood parents' group; and, finally, on the individual parents themselves. The numbers and shaded areas in Figure 1 represent the sequence of processes to prepare the preschool child for a successful entry into Head Start and public school. The ultimate goal of the intervention is to move all units—the child, his family, the neighborhood parent group, Head Start, and the school—into a more functional interdependence. In order to achieve that goal, the school must, through parent involvement in decision making, become an institution responsive to the whole community, ready to accommodate itself to the needs of its children.

The underlying theory of the Parent Project's intervention strategy can be conceptualized according to input, intraprocess, and outcome variables, as seen in Table 1. This conceptualization is based on a post-hoc analysis, so no provision for systematically investigating all the "variables" listed could have been made. Thus, it is offered here only as a way of clarifying the Project for the reader, and as possible guidance for undertaking similar projects.

METHOD

Parent Trainers

Parent Trainers are the key to the entire project, and their selection, training, and supportive supervision are therefore presented in some detail. However, as important as each of these three elements is, equally important, but more difficult to describe, are their interrelationships and their commitment to the parents, which arises as a kind of epiphenomenon when the first three elements are realized. That is, the effectiveness of the Parent Trainers seems to have been a function of all three elements; changing any element might have greatly changed the outcome.

Staff Selection. In the summer of 1969, just before the actual parent groups, eight Parent Trainers were selected for preservice training. Trainers were to work later in teams of two: a graduate student in

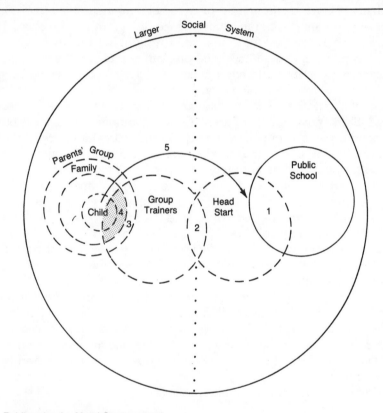

1. Public school—Head Start contract.
2. Head Start's preservice training & inservice supervision of Parent Group Trainers.
3. Parents' Group conducted by Parent Trainers.
4. Parents modify their family interaction.
5. Preschool child is better equipped for Head Start and public school.

The Parent Project's Intervention Strategy Reverses the Burden, Placing it Back on Adults. The School and Head Start Reach out into the Community for Group Trainers Who Work Directly with Parent Groups to Strengthen the Family. The Family then Modifies its Interaction with the Preschool Child.

Figure 1.

psychology or education (one black female, one black male, two white males) and a mother from the community (four black females). To emphasize the importance of the Trainer as a role model, we sought Trainers who exemplified, through their own participation in preservice training meetings, stability, responsibility, and interpersonal commitment to training the parent groups. Self-selection during the preservice training permitted us to identify the most highly motivated Trainers. The four graduate students initially selected completed preservice training and the full year of the parent meetings; however, nine individuals rotated through the other four positions, due to trial-and-error self-selection and certain unavoidable contingencies (e.g., pregnancy). Although fortunately, staff turnover occurred largely during the training phase, the unfortunate outcome was that three black female Trainers received little preservice training. After the project started in the school year, seven of the eight groups' Parent Trainer teams were stable for the duration of the group.

Staff Training. The preservice training of the Parent Trainers had six phases: First, a regular sensitivity training laboratory, which focused on personal growth, was conducted for the Parent Trainers themselves. Issues such as black/white, younger/older generation, and leadership styles were worked through. The group experience greatly facilitated the next phases, for the Trainers felt a good deal of warmth for one another, saw themselves as a group, and were enthusiastic about the project. Second, the Trainers were given the language development training, which made extensive use of a specially prepared Parent Trainers' Manual (Wohlford, 1969) for language development concepts, techniques, and materials for parents to use with their preschool children; there were teaching demonstrations, practice teaching, and the preparation of curricula for the parent meetings. Third, the Trainers considered the common objectives of the two parent group methods and the differences between them. Their intense discussions about those objectives often generated a feeling of autonomy and a sense of perspective, and the Trainers themselves then formulated a list of objectives: the ultimate objectives for the children, the second-level objectives for the parents, and the primary objectives for the Trainers themselves (see Table 2). Fourth, the assignment of Trainers to teams of two was done by self-selection as much as possible. Fifth, the Trainers met many parents through the interviews and evaluations in the pretest research phase and became acquainted with their everyday problems. Finally, just before the parent meetings, an additional brush-up and review day was devoted to each of the two methods; by this time the group experience was much more tangible, and the Trainers began to deal concretely with anticipated situations.

Table 1. The Parent Project's Intervention Strategy Conceptualized According to Input, Intraprocess, and Outcome Variables

INPUT VARIABLES	INTRAPROCESS VARIABLES	OUTCOME VARIABLES
Critical Elements Within Strategy	*Processes that Increase Likelihood of Participant Commitment to Process and Eventual Positive Outcomes*	*Goals of Parent Project[a]*

Goals of Program Sponsors

1. Learn conditions necessary for effective parent groups
2. To render a valuable group service to these parents
3. Study objective changes in parents and their children

Goals or Valued Outcomes for Participants

1. General: Help parents and their children relative to Head Start objectives
2. Slight temporary increase in money and feelings of worth that come from earning
3. Feeling of connectedness with others
4. Reinforcement that effort and participation can work (or opposite)
5. Increased competence and feelings of competence in child rearing or playing supporting role in child's education

Unintended Outcomes, Favorable and Unfavorable

See text under Results section, e.g., self-comparison of Groups 3 & 4

INTRAPROCESS VARIABLES:

1. Support from peers
2. Cohesion
3. Child reinforcement
4. Competence in group setting and in home child-parent interaction setting

INPUT VARIABLES:

1. Trainer behavior—personality, prior group experience, preservice training
2. Behavior of supervisors—preservice training and supervision
3. Concurrent research efforts—visibility, stated purpose, procedures
4. Contract—e.g., payment took risk out of it
5. Length of time
6. Composition of group—demographic, personality, interests
7. Nature of task and degree of structure used to pursue task work

[a] See also Table 2.

Staff Supervision. During the course of the parent group meetings, each of the four teams of Trainers received weekly supervision or consultation, which was facilitated by the tape recordings of all meetings.

Parent Group Meetings

Five Head Start centers in all-black areas of the center of Miami, Florida, were identified as participating centers. On the basis of the preliminary estimates, eight different participant groups were planned in the 1969-1970 school year, four in the Fall and four in the Spring. Each pair of Parent Trainers conducted two groups, a Language Development group and a Sensitivity-Discussion group. Within the general context of either Language Development or Sensitivity-Discussion, each group was free to choose its own particular direction. Each group was to comprise 12 to 15 parents, who were to meet for an hour and a half twice a week for eight weeks. All meetings were held in the evenings at the neighborhood Head Start center for maximum convenience of the parents. The schedule for the parent meetings was determined in part by the individual evaluations in the overall research design of pretest—intervention—posttest. Thus the first series of four groups began in November 1969 and ran to January 1970 with a two-week break at the Christmas holidays, rather than beginning promptly in September and continuing without interruption, as would have been ideal to gain and maintain maximum impetus. The second

---

Table 2. Objectives at Three Levels as Formulated by the Parent Trainers

Locus of Objectives	Objectives
Trainers' Objectives	1. To accept the parents by being nonjudgmental 2. To be accepted by the parents 3. To make parents feel comfortable to be open

Parents' Objectives	1. To accept the child as an important individual person
	  A. To spend time alone with the child
	2. To show the child you care
	3. To set responsible limits
	4. To explain situations to child
	5. To understand your feelings about the child and to express them constructively
	  A. For the parent
	  B. To model for the child

Children's Objectives	1. To feel himself to be an important individual person 2. To feel good as a person 3. To do things, to say things on his own, and to feel good about it 4. To express his thoughts

series of four groups, using the same pairs of Parent Trainers but with different parents, ran from February to April 1970 without interruption.

To investigate the effect of fathers' participation, fathers were invited to the parent meetings in some centers but not in others. Two principles were maintained: maximum participation in each center and equal opportunity for all parents within a center. Since many families had no father in the home, if all parents had been invited to meetings, mothers would probably have outnumbered fathers by a wide margin and fathers might not have returned to subsequent meetings. In addition, mothers without husbands probably had some unique problems that could be most usefully discussed in a group of others in the same situation. Therefore, in three of the five centers (see Table 3), there were two sets of parent groups: one group to which couples were invited whenever there was a husband in the home, and another group comprised of the rest of the mothers, i.e., those mothers without husbands. In the remaining two centers, which each had one group, all the mothers—those with or without husbands—but none of their husbands, were invited to participate in the project.

Initially, two strictly voluntary groups and six groups in which each parent would be paid five dollars per session for participation were planned. However, the less than optimal participation of the voluntary group in the first series prompted the rejection of a voluntary group in the second series. Hence, seven of the eight groups were on a paid basis, including attendance at both the parent group meetings and at parent evaluations. Baby sitting service and transportation were also provided to parents who needed it.

Every effort to fit the parent groups into the context of the neighborhood was made, with specific goals in mind:

1. To establish a solid working relationship between the parents and their center. (An additional pragmatic goal was to establish a trusting relationship that would be stable and solid enough to work with deeply entrenched behavioral patterns.)

2. To fit this program into the context of the other Head Start programs, such as the monthly parent meetings.

3. To facilitate group cohesiveness and emotional involvement by capitalizing on preexisting relationships among neighbors.

4. To foster the maintenance of such changes as did occur in the group by assuring some form of continued contact among group members after the termination of the groups.

RESULTS

The results of the Parent Project presented here—the criteria of *paren-*

tal *attendance at the parent group meetings* and a distillation of the *group process* — are distinguishable, but in a sense they are inseparable, as examples will illustrate. Parental attendance is necessarily primary: if the parents do not come to the meetings, there can be no group and no group process. However, once the parents are present at the meeting, what occurs, the group process, in part determines whether they will return to the next meeting.

Attendance at Parent Group Meetings

Table 3 summarizes the parents' attendance. The first four columns of Table 3 give the identifying information: the group and center number, the period, the method, and the parents who were invited. Six of the eight groups ran their full duration of 15 or 16 meetings; the other two groups approached that. The next three major columns give the number of parents invited, the number who attended at least one meeting, and the number who attended regularly, i.e., at least half of the scheduled meetings. Most attended regularly (70 of 119). As seen in the second column from the right, the median number of meetings attended by the mothers was nine. The final column, median attendance at meetings, indicates the degree of interest in the typical meeting. The relative cohesion of a group may be determined as the number attending regularly, divided by the number attending at least one meeting. The cohesion ranged from a high in Group 2 (13/13) to a low in Group 1 (4/12) and Group 4 (2/6).

Comparison of Mothers' and Fathers' Attendance. From a total of 155 mothers of five-year-olds at the five centers who were invited, 60 mothers (39%) attended meetings regularly, 35 mothers (23%) attended occasionally, and 60 mothers (39%) never attended. Thus, 95 mothers (61%) attended at least some of the meetings, and about two-thirds of those attended regularly.

The comparable percentage of the fathers' attendance was apparently not so great. Fathers were invited to the parent group meetings in only three of the five centers (five uninvited fathers attended a mothers' group). Invitations were sent to 61 fathers presumed to be at home. Of these, 39 (64%) never attended the meetings, 12 (30%) attended occasionally, and 10 (16%) attended regularly. Thus, the proportion of invited fathers who presumably failed to attend at least one meeting (64%) is significantly greater than the proportion of mothers who failed to attend (39%; $X^2 = 10.603$, $df = 2$, $p < .01$, 2-tailed test). However, we estimate that the number of fathers presumably in the homes may have been inflated by from 5 to 20 fathers: when registering a child in a public school, mothers tend to claim a husband. If the actual total number of fathers was 45 instead of 61, then the per-

Table 3. Parental Attendance at Parent Training Groups (read across)

Group Number	Period	Center	Method and Number of Scheduled Meetings	Parents	Number Invited			Number Attending at Least One Meeting			Number Attending Regularly[a]			Median No. of Meetings Attended[b]			Median Attendance at meetings
					Mo	Fa	Total	Mo	Fa	Total	Mo	Fa	Total	Mo	Fa	Total	Total
Fall:																	
1[c]		Center 1	Sens.-Disc. 13	All mothers	23	0	23	22	—	22	4	—	4	2	—	2 (1-10)	3 (1-7)
2		Center 2	Lang. Devel. 15	All mothers	25	0	25	13	—	13	13	—	13	12	—	12 (6-14)	11 (4-13)
3		Center 4	Lang. Devel. 15	Only father-mother pairs	26	26	52	9	9	18	8	4	12	10	6	8 (4-14)	9.5 (4-18)
4		Center 4	Sens.-Disc. 15	Mothers without husbands	12	—	12	6	—	6	2	—	2	4	—	4 (1-14)	2 (1-4)
Spring:																	
5		Center 1	Lang. Devel. 15	Only father-mother pairs	15	15	30	9	6	15	7	1	8	11	3	8 (1-14)	7 (5-10)
6		Center 5	Sens.-Disc. 15	All mothers	35	0	35	27	5	32	16	—	16	9	(1)	9 (1-14)	13 (9-20)
7		Center 3	Sens.-Disc. 12	Only father-mother pairs	20	20	40	7	7	14	5	5	10	8	8	8 (3-10)	9.5 (4-12)
8		Center 3	Lang. Devel. 16	Mothers without husbands	18[d]	—	18	10	0	10	7	—	7	13	—	13 (2-16)	7 (5-8)
Totals for groups					174	61	235	103	27	130	63	10	72	9.5	6	8	7
Totals for individuals					155	61	216	95	27	122	60	10	70				

a. Number attending regularly means attending at least half of the scheduled meetings.
b. Numbers in parentheses are the ranges of numbers of meetings attended.
c. All parents were paid five dollars per session except in Group 1 (Center 1, Fall Series), in which they participated on a completely voluntary basis.
d. Including four mothers from Center 4, three of whom attended no meetings in the Fall.

centages were: never attending, 48%; occasionally, 30%; and regularly, 22%. Furthermore, in considering those 95 mothers and 22 fathers
who attended at least one meeting, there was no significant difference
between the proportions of fathers and mothers who attended regularly ($\chi^2 = 0.016$, df=1, p is n.s., 2-tailed test). In sum, the available
overall information suggests, though with possible equivocation, that
there was no difference between fathers and mothers in frequency of
attendance.

Other Comparisons. In terms of attendance as a function of group
content, all four of the Language Development groups had good attendance, but only two of the four Sensitivity-Discussion groups had
solid success. Thus, there appeared to be a trend toward a difference
in their impact upon participants, but the difference was not significant
or conclusive.

In comparing the first and second series, all four groups in the
second series were successful, while the two least successful groups
were in the first series, and those were the same two groups which
used the Sensitivity-Discussion method. In one of those, Group 4, there
were never enough mothers present to allow full use of the
Sensitivity-Discussion method. In the other, Group 1, participation was
on a completely voluntary basis. In that group, the mothers attended
irregularly, showing some interest in participating and seemingly involved when they were there, but failing to sustain their involvement
enough to allow the group to become cohesive. Furthermore, during
the first series, the Trainers were inexperienced in conducting groups
of this kind and there was a two-week Christmas holiday interruption,
with a drop in attendance after the holidays. In the second series, the
Trainers had gained some experience and had a schedule free from
major interruptions. The experience of the first series also helped us
estimate probable attendance more accurately and enabled us to
make necessary adjustments.

In summary, six of the eight groups were unqualified successes,
according to the attendance data. The other two groups had certain
problems, but even they continued for their planned period with some
participation. Since both groups with poor attendance records were in
the first series and both used Sensitivity-Discussion, it will be of some
interest to ponder, when we turn to the Trainers' summaries of what
occurred in the group meetings, whether their inexperience, the group
content, both, or some other variable, e.g., the centers chosen, was
responsible for the unevenness in attendance.

Group Process and Content

The entire series of small-group meetings totaled over 174 hours (approximately 8 groups x 8 weeks per group x 2 sessions per week x 1½ hours per session). The sessions were tape-recorded so that objective measures of group interaction could be derived from them. However, such a process is extremely costly, and it was not done for the present report. The following narrative summary of the eight groups is based on the Trainers' reports, which were made after each meeting and discussed in weekly supervision, with additional clarification provided by the tape recordings where necessary.

Trainers AB: Groups 1 and 5. Group 1, the only voluntary group, used the Sensitivity-Discussion method with an all-mothers group. Though the median attendance of the group was only three, seven mothers attended two or more meetings, indicating some interest but little commitment. The group began with a survey of problems the mothers were having with their preschool children, including running away, eating, vomiting, nose-bleeding, and fainting; a mother also mentioned that one of her children had choked to death. The Trainers dealt with these enormous reality-based situations in a rather nondirective, or passive, fashion. Rather than deal with individual or cumulative feelings aroused in the group on hearing about these hardships, the Trainers permitted the mothers a one-by-one recitation of their problems. Not surprisingly, several of the mothers with the most serious problems failed to return after the first meeting or two.

In this case and others, the inservice supervision, occurring after-the-fact, could not do more than help the Trainers modify their future behavior and follow up on what had already occurred. Most importantly, one of the Trainers, who was also the Center's Social Service Aide, discussed the meetings thoroughly and helped mothers who did not return with their problems; e.g., a mother whose husband was recently jailed was assisted in enrolling at a neighborhood health center.

After the first few meetings, the Trainers shifted from their nondirective stance to a more active, structured, problem-solving approach. For example, the Trainers encouraged one mother, whose daughter had been vomiting and nose-bleeding without any medical reason, to spend at least some time alone with the girl every day when she was well. In a few weeks, the symptoms disappeared. In a follow-up interview six months later, this mother thanked the Parent Project for helping her daughter, who had continued to be well.

Mothers gradually introduced problems with their husbands and, midway through the series, some discussed their own personal problems, fears, and worries. One mother, who dominated the group, was very disturbed and appeared to hallucinate. The group tolerated her deviant behavior because of the small number of mothers present and the Trainers' reluctance to confront her. The Trainers' reluctance seemed to be related both to this mother's powerful role in the political structure of the center and their own personalities. In the final meeting, the three most loyal attenders expressed very positive feelings for what they had derived, and also requested meetings with teachers so they could learn what their children were doing in class.

In a follow-up critique, the Parent Trainers commented that they did not work as hard as they should have in getting their Group 1 parents to attend meetings. But it is unclear what single factor or combination of factors might have led to more interest and attendance in Group 1. What is clear is that many mothers did make occasional use of the group, but for several reasons did not sustain their involvement enough to permit the real coalescence and development of an effective group. In the first meetings, when mothers presented practical problems, the Trainers' nondirective response probably discouraged at least some mothers from placing confidence in the ability of the group to help them, and thus they did not return. Later, the one mother's domination of the group curtailed the others' sustained interest. Nevertheless, the fact that some made continued though irregular use of the group indicated that it did serve some, probably a supportive, function for them.

In the second series, Group 5, which used the Language Development approach with paid couples, was conducted by the same team of Trainers in the same center. Through repeated home visits, the Trainers made a more concentrated effort to get fuller participation in Group 5 than in Group 1. Group 5 covered the Language Development topics of colors, shapes, letters, numbers, and story-reading. The Trainers began each topic by demonstrating materials to the parents and then, in the same meeting, gave them materials to practice with themselves and also take home to their children. At the next meeting the parents would review what their children did, bringing in samples of their work, e.g., "My Own Book," which illustrated colors. Parents felt they did not have time outside the meetings to make any special materials needed, such as flash cards for letters; thus, time was spent in the meetings preparing those materials. Some commercial education spin-and-match toy materials were also circulated among the parents and were quite well received.

The parents noted that their children liked the games, lessons, and materials they brought home. In fact, there was such interest that squabbles among the children regularly ensued. The underlying issues sometimes surfaced as problems in themselves; namely, how much time does or can the mother devote to her children, and how much time can the father devote? And how is sibling rivalry handled? The Trainers recommended dealing with sibling quarrels in a practical straightforward manner, noting the developmental needs of each of the children. Parents raised relatively few individual problems concerning their children, and these were usually academic (e.g., short attention span, difficulty in learning) rather than emotional.

Group 5 ended with a party, where the parents were outspoken in their praise of the group, feeling their children had done better in school because of their activities at home with them. They said their children were sad they would not be attending more meetings. As one of the Trainers concluded:

The Group 5 parents demonstrated a marked increase of feelings of competence themselves. One could see in the group the satisfaction they obtained by becoming more familiar with the basic tools of language. The feeling of competence in and of itself, I am sure, promoted increased interactions at home.

In addition, the parents felt the program should be continued in their center in the following year.

Groups 1 and 5 were conducted at the same center in the same year with the same team of Trainers. Their very similarities make the difference in their parents' responsiveness dramatic. The two groups differed in membership, content, payment, and the experience of their Trainers; yet, of all the possible factors responsible for the differences in their effectiveness, the Trainers' lack of experience in Group 1 seems to be the most important single factor. Much like the parents they described, in the second series the Trainers seemed to feel that they were themselves more competent, found more satisfaction, and were more relaxed—and they therefore promoted increased interactions in their group.

Trainers CD and CX: Groups 2 and 6. Group 2 had the least continuity of staff from the pregroup evaluation to the group meetings, and it required two full meetings of orientation before they could begin working with Language Development. Full participation came near the end of the second meeting, in discussing the problems of rats in their homes. The Trainer asked, "How do you pull yourself and your children out of this situation?" The mothers responded, "Education." The group then settled down to the self-chosen task of writing the alphabet, having dismissed the topics of colors, shapes, and incidental teaching suggested by the Trainers. Besides writing the letters of the alphabet, Group 2's Language Development topics included size, shape, colors, expression of feelings, and much attention to storybook-reading techniques. Mothers were encouraged to bring materials on which they worked with their children. If they did not bring the materials, they were asked to talk about what they had done. Only a few mothers clearly did not work with their children at home.

At the Christmas season, the mothers helped their children make a greeting card and held a Christmas party, to which they brought all their children and much food. Group 2's meetings developed into the format of spontaneous conversation at the very beginning, then language development review and new exercises, and free discussion at the end. The free discussion evolved through such topics as the objectives of these child-oriented meetings, the mothers' own life objectives, sex education, the use of two languages, the drop-off in attendance after Christmas, the mothers' irritation that the center was closed over the holidays, and the group's termination. After the first few meetings, the mothers expressed how surprised they were at the experience of working closely with their children—how much the children knew and their feeling that they, the mothers, should have helped before. The topic of helping the children to express feelings elicited the mothers' own expression of feelings, which were frequently ones of sadness about not fulfilling their own potential.

At the group's conclusion the Trainers helped the mothers express both their positive and negative feelings about the group and its sched-uled end. For example, one mother described how she had shown her seven-year-old how to read storybooks to her five-year-old, and how beautifully the two had worked together. In sum, Group 2 was the most successful group in terms of both objective and subjective indices, includ-ing, by chance, attention to both structured language development skill and in-depth personal feelings. It might thus be considered as a model for future groups.

Group 6 had some staff turnover. When one Trainer left after five meetings, the new Trainer interviewed the group mothers, and so little disruption occurred due to staff change. Group 6, which was an all-mothers group, used the Sensitivity-Discussion method — in perhaps the best example of it. Group 6 was large and spent the first two meetings on objectives, limit-setting, and such topics as punishment of children, sex education, and husbands' irresponsibility, before the ice was broken. In the next meeting, a mother described how her husband had died, her child had been seriously injured, and how she had been cheated finan-cially both times because of lack of legal knowledge. She openly cried, and the group rallied to her support with both practical advice (Legal Aid, etc.) and emotional support. Another mother, a neighbor of the first, was surprised to learn the extent of her difficulties, which prompted explora-tion of "living with people but not knowing them."

The group next returned to the topic of the roles of the husband and wife, aided by a solitary husband who came because "his wife was sick." The group then dealt first indirectly, then directly, with the Lamar, S.C., busing incident, the court-ordered school teacher integration in Miami, and the underlying feelings about the white-black issue. In the most heated of these meetings, all three Trainers were present: a young black female, a middle-aged black female, and a young white male. The two black female Trainers, who disagreed with each other, served as excel-lent role models, and practically all the mothers present freely expressed themselves. The two languages issue was then debated, but no final agreement was reached.

In the following meeting, encounter group techniques were used because the group seemed comfortable and cohesive enough to attempt it, one of the Trainers felt prepared enough, and the group seemed at rather an impasse with "outside" issues and needed to move to the level of more personal feelings. The encounter techniques, which included non-verbal and "blind" touching and feeling exercises, worked very well with those who participated in all of the sessions, but there were problems raised by the reentry of group members after an absence. The brief encounter group experience tends to confirm our belief that it would have been hazardous, if not disastrous, to attempt with a new group. But in the ongoing group, it enabled us to arrive at a deeper (or higher) level of progress toward our objectives.

In his summary of the year's program, Trainer C gave an intriguing critique:

My overall feeling is that you can't get down on paper the smiles in the mothers' eyes and on their faces over their new-found ability to communicate with their children and neighbors. The group helped the mothers to feel good about themselves and to be able to see themselves as agents of change.

Group 6 seemed to be the most successful of the groups using the unstructured Sensitivity-Discussion approach, and it shared two characteristics of the most successful group using the structured Language Development approach: a highly competent trainer (Trainer C), who was both active and flexible; and a hybrid of training approaches, which included a combination of free discussion with Language Development in Group 2 and encounter group techniques with Sensitivity-Discussion peculiar to Group 6.

Trainers EF: Groups 3 and 7. The two Trainers were exceptionally warm and outgoing individuals, who engaged the parents with a very informal, joking manner, which put them at ease. For instance, in Group 3, which used Language Development, after some joking about how strange it was to be in front of a blackboard, fathers and mothers took turns practicing how to print the letters of the alphabet. Group 3 spent much time in role-playing various kinds of parent-child instructional interaction, e.g., incidental teaching, making "My Own Book," storybook reading, and using Sesame Street booklets and language materials from the children's classrooms. The parents themselves took a very active role in giving helpful advice and feedback to one another. As an indication of the group's cohesiveness, the parents organized and ran two Christmas parties: one at the school with the children, and another at one couple's home on a Saturday night, complete with all the trimmings for a Saturday party. The parents organized and did all the work for both parties.

Group 3 parents brought up a number of problems outside of language development, including general child-rearing issues, medical service for the children, and safety precautions at the school. The Trainers dealt with each simply and effectively, and brought in a Head Start medical team to answer the parents' questions. The parents were encouraged to make liberal use of praise or reinforcement when their children made a correct response or did something well.

In contrast to Group 3, which started briskly and maintained a high degree of interest for its duration, Group 7 began much more slowly. Group 7 also involved both mothers and fathers but used the Sensitivity-Discussion method, with less initial participation than Group 3. Only two couples appeared at the first meeting, so the Trainer had to go out and arouse more interest. This group was dominated by two fathers, and its topics were mainly on community problems and general situations, such as school integration, police relations, drug problems, delinquency, owning guns, jobs, attitudes of bus drivers, and the scalping prices of ghetto stores. At one of the last meetings, neither dominant father was present and the group moved deeper into family and personal feelings than ever before. The Trainers were rather frustrated by the group's failure to realize more family-oriented objectives, yet the nondominant parents appeared happy to participate in the community-oriented meetings. Interestingly, one of the active fathers was subsequently elected to a neighborhood political office.

Trainers GH: Groups 4 and 8. In tandem with Groups 3 and 7 of fathers and mothers, Groups 4 and 8 were held at the same centers with mothers who had no spouses.

As discussed earlier, there were only 12 mothers invited to Group 4, which used the Sensitivity-Discussion method; and since there were no more than three or four mothers at any meeting, there could be little group interaction per se. Discussion topics ranged from disciplining children to school programs, Christmas shopping, and job supervisors. Surprisingly, when considering whether to disband or continue the group, the three regular attenders steadfastly chose to continue by themselves. Follow-up interviews with eight other invited mothers indicated that they did not participate because either they were sick (when they recovered they had to work extra to make up for the loss of income), their children were sick, they had to work late, or they had to attend church revivals and meetings. Three additional mothers candidly said they would like to attend, but when they got home from their jobs and finished the work around the home, they were too tired or just didn't feel up to it. These mothers without husbands in the home appeared to be overwhelmed with day-to-day coping and just did not have the health or energy to attend the Parent Project meetings, even for pay. In conclusion, their reasons sounded for the most part very plausible.

The final group, Group 8, again composed of mothers without husbands, used Language Development, and had the second highest level of cohesion. The sequence of this group largely paralleled the other Language Development groups but followed the Parent Trainers' Manual more closely than any of the other groups, beginning with color and shape and moving on to letters. These Trainers provided Group 8 with many more tasks, and with more variation, than the other Language Development groups, including pronunciation exercises, films on communication, language puzzles and games, and singing and rhythm exercises. As an example of how effectively the Trainers involved the parents, Peter Rabbit books with cut-out characters were given to all mothers in a creativity task. One mothers' subgroup brought the books home to read to their children and encourage them to play with. The other mothers' subgroup brought home only the cut-out characters from the books and asked their children to make up stories, which the mother wrote down. The next week the two mothers' groups compared notes. On the whole, the mothers were very conscientious in carrying out assignments and bringing their children's work back to the group to be discussed. On some occasions, this group decided to bring Head Start children to the meetings. When the mothers were actually observed interacting with their children while working on language tasks, most demonstrated positive qualities, such as patience and understanding.

The Trainers concluded that the meetings helped the mothers to become much better acquainted, and they found the mothers' interactions sincere and meaningful. The parents gave one another a feeling of being worthwhile, and they continually praised one another's work when children's assignments were discussed. The meetings significantly helped the mothers work more effectively with their small children on language development—not just with their child attending Head Start but other small ones in the family also. The mothers said they looked forward to the meetings and that their children now felt that they—as well as their teachers—could do something to help them. Moreover, their children looked up to them more now, and that made the mothers feel good.

Analyses

The two sets of data, attendance and group process, tend to coincide rather closely with each other. Neither the quantitative attendance data nor qualitative group process data indicate any advantage or disadvantage to any one of the three classes (father-mother pairs, mothers without husbands, all-mothers groups) on the basis of marital status or fathers' participation. Given an equal chance to participate, fathers took advantage of this opportunity as eagerly as did the mothers. The comparison of Language Development with Sensitivity-Discussion favors the former: only one of the Sensitivity-Discussion groups attained good ratings on both attendance and group process criteria. The problems with the other three Sensitivity-Discussion groups varied: Group 4, which came the closest to failure, was the victim of poor planning, a result of inaccurate initial estimates; Groups 1 and 7 suffered from the Trainers' lack of experience and training, respectively. Therefore, there appears to be interaction between the method (including both structure and content) and trainer variables, such that less trained or less experienced Trainers fare better with the Language Development method.

Roles and Functions of Inservice Supervisors. The two inservice supervisors were limited in their roles to after-the-fact analyses. If the Trainers had performed competently and their groups had progressed smoothly, they required only positive reinforcement from the supervisors. If, however, there were problems, the supervisors' task was much more difficult. For example, one of the Trainers in Group 2, who had been highly recommended and made positive contributions during preservice training, failed to complete her pregroup interviews, attended Group 2 irregularly, and, in fact, made some disruptive comments. Repeated supervision efforts failed, but then her previously guarded personal and family crises erupted. She finally acknowledged her own need for counseling and resigned from the Project.

More generally, when the inservice supervision uncovered problems in the Trainers' performance, the supervisor's task was to use the past events as a learning device to equip the Trainers to handle future situations more effectively. The Trainers varied a great deal in their responsiveness to such guidance, which required them to generalize from past to future and always somewhat different situations.

Trainer Variables. In the final analysis, it was the Trainer selected, his personality, his previous group experiences, his preservice training, and his actual experience with the parents that most affected the success or failure of a particular group. The Trainers who were open, flexible, active, and self-reliant seemed most able to learn from training and supervision and were most effective with their groups. When the unexpected arose, those Trainers dealt with it openly, immediately, and in a professionally expert fashion, rather than remaining passive and returning to the issue at the next meeting after consulting with their supervisor. This sheds light on the difference between the two methods; for in the Language Development method, the unexpected occurred less frequently. With Language Development, all Trainers knew what to expect and were perhaps a bit more at ease, thus setting the parents more at ease. With the experience of the first series behind them, the Trainers seemed even more effective in the second series. In the successful groups, and especially the Spring groups, the enthusiasm of the parents and the Parent Trainers' excitement at the parents' responsiveness were mutually contagious; in short, morale was very high when the parent meetings came to their scheduled end.

DISCUSSION

Were parent groups effective or ineffective in arousing and sustaining these parents' interests, and why or why not? Cautioned by the pessimistic results and forecasts of most comparable undertakings, we used every reasonable technique to engage parents of Head Start children in meaningful participant group interaction. In terms of the objective index of attendance, six of the eight groups appeared clearly successful, and a seventh group (Group 1) moderately so. Despite low attendance and group cohesion, Group 1 had loyal enthusiasts who found the meetings relevant and sometimes very helpful, but who attended somewhat irregularly. From the index of group process, six of the eight groups appeared to sustain a high degree of relevant interest among the parent participants, with a seventh group (Group 7) in the marginal zone. Group 3, which had good attendance, had community-, rather than self- or family-oriented, discussions and appeared to be very dependent on a few spokesmen who presided, thereby freeing the rest of the group from the responsibility of real interaction. Only Group 4 was a failure on both criteria, and this was because of a quasi-administrative planning error in not inviting enough parents from a large enough group—a mistake attributable to our lack of experience. Therefore, five of the eight groups clearly met both the criteria of attendance and group process and two more met at least one of the criteria, accounting for seven of the eight groups. In short, according to the attendance and group process data, the Parent Project may be considered a success.

If it was a success, why was it so, in comparison with reports of other Head Start programs for parent education and consultation? First, there are no other systematic reports, and very few even anecdotal reports. Educational and mental health professionals are concerned that low-income parents of children in Head Start and day care be reached, but they often convey a feeling of inability to involve the parents meaningfully. Caldwell states, "We lowered our expectation of what we had hoped to accomplish in our parent program and have patiently followed the lead of the parents as to what they expect from us and what they will accept" (1970, p. 693). Even in reports of apparently successful Head Start parent group education, the consultants appeared to relate to individual parents, rather than to generate interaction among the parents in order to make the group a primary vehicle for change. The Parent Project demonstrated that particular group methods are at least one way of unraveling the Gordian knot posed by the need to involve low-income parents in meaningful parent education and the need (and their demand) for a democratic process that avoids professional condescension. Thus, the Office of Child Development's experimental variations of Head Start, e.g., Health Start and Home Start, should systematically test participant group methods with such variables as using the teacher as a Parent Trainer, using the Social Services worker as a Parent Trainer to confront community-level problems, or using family nutritional, health, and dental education curricula. Ironically, the use of group methods with low-income parents for nutritional and health education appeared in one of the pioneer group experiments, which attempted to change housewives' attitudes toward using more fresh milk, cod liver oil, and orange juice (Lewin, 1943).

The Parent Project intervention strategy provided trained indigenous community leaders (see Figure 1); and in this sense, its preservice training is comparable to earlier programs' use of T Groups to train low-income paraprofessionals and middle class individuals together. But many earlier programs ended just when the Parent Project's intervention began: when it used the individuals who received the initial preservice training and inservice supervisors as part of an interdependent whole in direct work with parent groups. The Trainers thereby received positive feedback from the parents, which had an upward spiraling effect, permitting them to give their fullest commitment to the parent groups. By the same token, the group experience trained the parents to be more effective with their children. Parents then received positive feedback from their children, which had an upward spiraling effect on their involvement with their group.

What role did the five-dollar per meeting payment have in gaining and maintaining the parents' initial commitment, and their commitment throughout the course of the meetings? The payment should be seen as an incentive for securing the parents' initial commitment and as a means of establishing a positive interpersonal relationship between parents and Trainers. By paying parents to participate in the meetings, we tangibly demonstrated our conviction of their importance. The most valuable function of the payment may have been to render the Project, personified by the Trainers, as more credible. As the parents whom we served trusted us, they seemed to take their roles as parents more seriously and to gain in self-esteem as individuals. If this analysis is correct, then the payment of money for attendance functioned as a rapport-building, concrete token, an interpretation supported by a comparison of pre- and postintervention attitudes about participation in group meetings (Wohlford, 1972). To establish rapport, the Trainers did many other things, including listening sympathetically to parents, praising them for actively participating, and sincerely expressing admiration for the good work they did with their children; ultimately, however, the most important kinds of feedback for the parents were from the other parents and from their own children.

Since both the Language Development and Sensitivity-Discussion groups were effective to some degree, the present data do not permit the endorsement of one approach to the exclusion of the other. However, the more structured Language Development method appeared slightly more advantageous especially for less experienced Trainers. In practice, the Trainers were relatively free to modify the approaches as they wished, and they appeared to do so according to their personal styles. Nevertheless, both the highly structured Language Development approach in Group 8 and the much more open-ended Language Development approach in Group 2 appeared to achieve very good results.

The father's role in the group structure deserves special comment, since low-income parents, especially fathers of preschool children, are often said to be impossible to involve. Like Tuck (1971), who also used non-traditional methods to involve low-income black fathers, the Parent Project began with very positive expectations concerning fathers. We regarded fathers as important members of the family and important persons in the child-rearing process, and we made every effort to encourage their participation. For convenience, the meetings were held at the Head Start center in their own neighborhoods, often within walking distance from home, and on weekday evenings when most people were free. For continued participation and the comfort of the group, we had at least one black mother from the community as a Trainer in each group, and one male (usually black) as Trainer in each fathers and mothers group. To strengthen the marital relationship and ensure that the fathers did not feel outnumbered by women, we structured the groups involving fathers to include only married couples as partners. Our strategy to involve fathers and mothers appeared to work quite well: among parents who attended at least one meeting, fathers participated as eagerly as mothers.

RECOMMENDATIONS FOR OTHER PROGRAMS

The following recommendations are offered for persons designing other programs for parents of preschool children:

1. Generally, the participant group method should be considered a potentially effective vehicle for delivering community clinical-psychological or educational services directly to low-income parents and thereby indirectly to their preschool children. That is, participant parent groups provide an arena for assessing parent and child adjustment and a potential arena for changing behavior. Group experiences involve participants in a meaningful way by providing a relevant sample of behavior and the basic impetus for change—an acceptable reference group in the form of others in similar situations.

2. In order to be successful, a parent program should be totally geared to serving parents' needs, including not only the content of the program but also convenience of meeting time and location, babysitting service, and so on.

3. If payment is not available to aid in establishing rapport with at least those parents in hard-core poverty, other fairly unusual means of developing their trust and understanding are probably necessary in order to initiate their participation in a parent program.

4. In order to involve fathers in a program for parents, meetings should have at least one male trainer, include as many fathers as mothers in the group, and should be scheduled in the evening.

5. Once the parents are there, whether or not they continue depends on the skill of the Parent Trainers. As discussed earlier, the

Trainers' effectiveness is a function of their personality and prior group experience, preservice training and inservice supervision, as well as their situation with the parents, which includes working in teams, choosing their group approach, and exercising their own individual style.

6. Whatever objectives are to be pursued with the parents should be stated in behavioral terms and embedded in highly specific experiences and concrete examples, both in using materials in Language Development groups and in discussing child rearing in Sensitivity-Discussion groups.

7. At a minimum, supervisors should have had experience in conducting regular sensitivity training groups, working with low-income groups, counseling parents, and providing clinical services to preschool children and their families. Organizational experience also helps the supervisor cope with policy and operational issues concerning the interfaces of relevant Head Start components, such as Parent Involvement, Social Services, Psychological Services, and Education.

8. Since the Parent Trainer is the key ingredient in the Parent Project, specific recommendations are offered regarding his or her role in group programs that use less than fully credentialed trainers:

Programs should anticipate that some Trainers will drop out during their preservice training and include Alternate Trainers in the preservice stage.

Trainers should be used in pairs, not only to permit the ethnic and sex distribution of Trainers for every parent group but also to facilitate their performance in the group.

The continuity of Trainers from year to year should be maximized because more experienced Trainers perform better.

9. Although the Parent Project dealt exclusively with low-income black families with preschool children, participant group methods also seem appropriate for most other programs for low-income target populations, such as adult education and community mental health.

REFERENCES

Auerbach, A. B. *Parents learn through discussion: Principles of parent group education*. New York: Wiley, 1968.

Caldwell, B. Day care for the very young. *American Journal of Public Health*, 1970, *60*, 690-697.

Carkhuff, R. R., & Griffin, A. H. The selection and training of human specialists. *Journal of Counseling Psychology*, 1970, *17*, 443-450.

Christmas, J. J. Group methods in training and practice: Nonprofessional mental health personnel in a deprived community. *American Journal of Orthopsychiatry*, 1966, *36*, 410-419.

Cook, P. E. Anticipatory guidance: An educational-group approach for parents. Paper presented at the annual meeting of the American Orthopsychiatric Association, Chicago, March 1968.

Culver, C. M., Dunham, F., Edgerton, J. W., & Edgerton, M. Community service workers and recipients: A combined middle class-lower class workshop. *Journal of Applied Behavioral Science*, 1969, *5*, 519-535.

Frank, J. D. *Persuasion and healing*. Baltimore: The Johns Hopkins Press, 1961.

Gordon I. (Ed.) *Reaching the child through parent education: The Florida approach*. Gainesville: University of Florida, 1969.

Guerney, B., Stover, L., & Andronico, M. P. On educating disadvantaged parents to motivate children for learning: A filial approach. *Community Mental Health Journal*, 1967, *3*, 66-72.

Hunt, J. McV. Parent and child centers: Their basis in the behavioral and educational sciences. *American Journal of Orthopsychiatry*, 1971, *41*, 13-38.

Lewin, K. Forces behind food habits and methods of change. *Bulletin of the National Research Council*, 1943, *108*, 35-65.

Nechin, H. First annual report of the psychological center, Department of Psychology, The City College, The City University of New York, September 1966.

Office of Child Development. *Head Start Policy Manual:* Instruction I-31, Section B 2, The Parents. Washington, D.C.: Office of Child Development, U.S. Dept. of Health, Education & Welfare, August 10, 1970.

O'Keefe, R. A. Home Start: Partnership with parents. *Children Today*, 1973, *2*, 12-16.

Ostrom, T. M., Steele, C. M., Rosenblood, L. K., & Mirels, H. L. Modification of delinquent behavior. *Journal of Applied Social Psychology*, 1971, *1*, 118-136.

Peck, H. B., Kaplan, S. R., & Roman, M. Prevention, treatment, and social action: A strategy of intervention in a disadvantaged urban area. In A. J. Bindman and A. D. Spiegel (Eds.), *Perspectives in community mental health*. Chicago: Aldine, 1969, pp. 490-502.

Richards, H., & Daniels, M. S. Sociopsychiatric rehabilitation in a black urban ghetto: Innovative treatment roles and approaches. *American Journal of Orthopsychiatry*, 1969, *39*, 662-676.

Rogers, C. R. The increasing involvement of the psychologist in social problems: Some comments, positive and negative. *Journal of Applied Behavioral Science*, 1969, *5*, 3-7.

Rueveni, U. Using sensitivity training with junior high school students. *Children*, 1971, *18*, 69-72.

Tuck, S. Working with black fathers. *American Journal of Orthopsychiatry*, 1971, *41*, 465-472.

Wohlford, P. Two participant group methods for parents of economically disadvantaged children: Parent Trainers' Manual. Unpublished paper, University of Miami, Coral Gables, Florida, 1969.

Wohlford, P. Head Start parents in participant groups: The Miami Parent Project. Paper presented at the annual meeting of the American Psychological Association, Washington, D.C., September 1971.

Wohlford, P. Final report of the Parent Project: Changing parental attitudes and behavior through participant group methods. Office of Economic Opportunity Research Grant (CAP CG-8003). University of Miami, Coral Gables, Florida, March 1972.

Wohlford, P. The use of participant group methods with low-income families. In R. M. Dunham (Ed.), *Toward a public concern for the family*. Tallahassee, Fla.: Department of Psychology, Florida State University, 1973, pp. 103-116.

Wohlford, P., & Stern, H. W. Reaching the hard-to-reach: The use of participant group methods with the mothers of economically disadvantaged preschool children. Paper presented at the annual meeting of the American Orthopsychiatric Association, Chicago, March 1968.

Zurcher, L. A. Stages of development in poverty program neighborhood action committees. *Journal of Applied Behavioral Science*, 1969, 5, 223-258.

AN UPDATE ON "HEAD START PARENTS IN PARTICIPANT GROUPS"

Paul Wohlford

When we proposed using participant groups with Head Start parents ten years ago, our rationale was based on: (a) the importance of the preschool years to a child's development; (b) the critical influence of the parents on the child's development; (c) the idea that the parent's influence can be changed; and (d) the fact that participant groups are a powerful method for inducing personal growth or change. Our project attempted to demonstrate that participant groups are an appropriate method to make parental changes that promote children's development.

In the past decade, many studies have further substantiated our arguments. Space limitations do not permit a full review of those studies, but only some highlights of the findings. Now there is a better understanding of many complexities of child development: that although the preschool years are critical, the child beyond preschool years continues to develop in many important ways; that fathers have a potent effect, even on their daughters' development; how the loss of a parent through divorce or death disrupts a child's life; etc. A variety of parent-intervention studies have demonstrated how mothers (and perhaps fathers, too) can interact more effectively with infants and preschool children in home-based programs and with older children in school-based programs. Participant-group methods have evolved rapidly into more sophisticated intervention techniques for personal growth/therapy and task-oriented endeavors. In summary, each of our four lines of inquiry has shown much activity and evolution.

However, to our knowledge there has been no replication of the major linkage that we tried to make between participant-group methods and the modification of parents' child-rearing practices for cognitive/intellectual and emotional/behavioral gains. Perhaps an exception to this will be the new Child and Family Resource Program, a spin-off of the federal Head Start and Home Start programs, the guidelines for which specify that parents should participate in groups "to reach out and share parenting experiences with others" (Child and

Family Resource Program, 1976, p. 2). However, this new program has not yet produced reports on the effectiveness of group methods for these purposes.

The closest approximations of the "Head Start Parents in Participant Groups" study can, however, teach us a great deal. In Figure 1 of the case study, we illustrated that a young child from a low-income family is caught between two cultures: his/her family's subcultural milieu and society's dominant middle-class institution, the public school. Powell (1977, p. 24), who studied child-rearing attitudes of parents and their children's day-care staff, found "fragmentation and discontinuity. For many children it appears the boundaries of the child care center and family are . . . disconnected . . . independent, detached systems." Powell contended that the presumed one-directional flow of information from the parents to the day-care staff should be expanded and improved in the other direction. He implied that staff training should be provided for purposes of communicating with and educating parents (p. 26) and that "we need new definitions of the roles and competencies of child care professionals and new designs of the scope and mode of services provided by child care programs" (p. 31). He concluded by speculating about what a child's social world might be like if his or her parents and day-care staff maintained a friendship rather than a traditional client-professional relationship or no relationship at all (p. 28).

McClelland, Rinesmith, and Kristensen (1975) also recognized that staff training and follow-up were important, although their study was in a different context. They examined the effect of power training on the staffs of anti-poverty community action agencies. The training was designed to make the staff "stronger and more effective in their jobs." The authors' recommendations were congruent with our experience: (a) training groups should be kept small—eight to eighteen participants; (b) trainers should involve participants in the workshop by whatever means necessary; and (c) follow-up visits should be a part of such social-action interventions (McClelland, Rhinesmith, & Kristensen, 1975, p. 114). Although the power training did not involve child-rearing practices, the target groups and the process recommendations were similar.

Dunn and Swierczek (1977) examined eleven hypotheses from the quite different context of organization development and found three supported by available evidence—those involving collaborative modes of intervention, participative change-agent orientations, and strategies emphasizing high levels of participation. Although the leap from middle-class organizations to low-income parent groups is great, the results of both studies are similar and should be studied carefully by groups such as the Child and Family Resource Program. The authors found that successful changes are more likely to occur if an intervention is collaborative, with goals set mutually, rather than goals set unilaterally by a higher authority, and if the change agent purposefully focuses on increased involvement in order to release the full potential of the group members. Maybe the differences between multimillion-dollar business OD groups and Head Start parent groups are not as great as they might seem.

Finally, there is a pressing need for more studies to replicate and to identify other salient interface variables between families and child-care programs, not only for low-income families, but also for middle-class families, who are increasingly involved in child-care programs.

REFERENCES

Child and Family Resource Program. *Programs for parents and their children in the prenatal-through-three age range: A child and family resource program guidance paper.* Washington, D.C.: Office of Child Development, Department of Health, Education and Welfare, April 1976.

Dunn, W. N., & Swierczek, F. W. Planned organization change: Toward grounded theory. *Journal of Applied Behavioral Science,* 1977, *13,* 135-157.

McClelland, D. C., Rhinesmith, S., & Kristensen, R. The effects of power training on community action agencies. *Journal of Applied Behavioral Science,* 1975, *11,* 92-115.

Powell, D. R. *The interface between families and child care programs.* Detroit, MI: Merrill-Palmer Institute, 1977.

A Structural Approach
to Organization Development
in a University Professional School

Lynn H. Peters

John F. McKenna

Accounts of organization development interventions typically deal with business or industrial organizations, stress the significance of an external consultant, and use group-centered educational or attitudinal change methods. This study departs from tradition in all three instances. The client system in this study was a professional school within a major western university. The primary change agent was an interim director of the school; thus, he held line authority over the business of the school as well as the nature of the change process. The intervention technique was almost entirely the manipulation of the school's structural properties. The conceptual framework for the change process stressed two primary elements: (1) the appropriateness of the Lewinian model of social-system change, and (2) the necessity to recognize the "systemness" of the intervention process. The study reviews literature in the field that is important in understanding the nature of this intervention, presents the background of the client system, discusses the specifics of the intervention methodology as well as the results of the project, and, finally, summarizes the implications of this project for the field of organization development.

INTRODUCTION

Planned Change: The Literature

Concern both in general society and within an industrial or organizational context regarding the obsolescence of organizations and the

Reprinted from *Group & Organization Studies*. "A Structural Approach to Organization Development in a University Professional School," by Lynn H. Peters and John F. McKenna, Vol. 2, No. 2, 172-185. Copyright 1977 International Authors, B. V. Published by University Associates.

human resources they draw on has led to the systematic application of planned-change techniques or organization development (OD). Although the goals of OD consultants tend to be similar (increased system effectiveness), their strategies of problem identification and treatment tend to be individualized by the uniqueness of the client system and the orientation and personal skills of the consultant. Even with this divergence, however, there do appear to be certain levels of similarity. Many noted researchers in OD maintain that in a "system" sense, several variables are critical to the process of planned organizational change (Bennis, 1969; Schein, 1969): (1) diagnostic activities are necessary in order to determine the nature and level of the problems of the organization; (2) an intervention strategy, reflecting the results of the problem analysis, is necessary; (3) the role of the consultant is critical to the effectiveness of the program; and (4) continuing assessment procedures must be built into the OD strategy in order to determine its effectiveness and to make the changes required.

If it is to be effective, planned organizational change must also reflect the individuality of the social institution in which the change is conducted. For example, projects within educational institutions often face situational problems that are not found in industrial environments. Thus, the change strategies employed may require nonindustrial values and methodologies. This paper is the result of a one-year study of a program conducted on the campus of a major western university, within the nursing school. The study was conducted during the change process and was based on extensive interviews with relevant parties to the change program and on first-hand observations of the authors.

The concept of planned change, whether for an individual, a group, or an entire organization, is concerned, in a "systematic" sense, with (1) reducing the barriers (physical or psychological) to change, (2) conducting an intervention that will facilitate movement, and (3) ensuring that the change is productive and will have long-term effects. The literature of the past twenty years has been concerned with these phases (Lewin, 1957; Likert, 1961; Schein, 1969). These authors, and others, generally recognize the necessity (in the words of Lewin) to "break loose" or "unfreeze" the existing system. Operationally, this suggests that there must be either an increase in the pressure to change or a reduction in the forces that are resisting the change. When this unfreezing has taken place, the membership of the system is much more prepared for the movement of the system. It is also assumed that once the individual members of an organization have developed favorable attitudes regarding the notion of change, much of the "natural" resistance has been dealt with, and they are more willing to support and become a part of the change process.

Another critical element of organizational change, the intervention process, requires vast amounts of planning, sensitivity, and analysis. One of the critical aspects of this process is the recognition that the system operates independently of the intervener. This implies the importance of the relationship between the consultant and the client system.

Essentially, the questions of any intervention include where to intervene and by what method to intervene. The majority of current research suggests that the most effective intervention is a "total systems" approach (Beckhard, 1969; Bennis, 1969). This means that the organizational change is not dealing with a department, unit, division, etc., but with an interrelated system in which movement in one part of the system may have consequences in other parts of the system (Seiler, 1963). The change agent must recognize and attempt to plan and control the impact of change within the client system. This awareness may lead to the development of many and diverse strategies of intervention as well as to the development of different change goals for diverse functional and vertical components of the organization (Bennis, Benne, & Chin, 1961).

Intervention strategies have taken many forms, ranging from the purely structural (Lawrence, 1958) to those dealing with client education and development (Blake & Mouton, 1967). Most planned intervention strategies combine structural, educational, developmental, and policy changes in order to achieve both appropriateness and effectiveness in the change process. The focus of some planned change may deal with such elements as the nature of the worker-work relationship (Davis, 1966); other strategies deal with the development of more effective interpersonal relationships within the work group or the organization (Bennis, 1969).

The nature of the relationship between the client system and the change agent is an important aspect of the organizational change process. This relationship is often taken for granted, with little attention directed toward it—often a mistake on the part of both parties since the roles, expectations, etc., within the client-consultant relationship may be the most critical elements of the change process.

The role of the consultant may be one of a direct change agent in the client system, or it may be an emerging consultative role—a more indirect and facilitative approach (Ferguson, 1968). The latter approach requires that the consultant and the client system join forces and work as a unit on problem identification and implementation of change strategies. The organization and the consultant share authority and responsibility for the change process. This consultative model operates on the assumption that the most effective change strategy will attempt to develop high levels of commitment and participation from the organization.

In other instances, the role of the change agent may be legally established by the organization to be one of system movement. In this case, explicit expectations regarding the behavior of the change agent should be established. Responsibilities and authority are assigned by the administration of the organization to a given individual or position, and accountability is expected.

The Organization as a System

The recognition that the organization is a system (and may be analyzed, understood, and predicted as one) has led to the application of general systems theory (GST) to the study of organizational behavior (Cleland & King, 1969).

Recent organizational literature contains a number of definitions of the nature of a system: some rely primarily on the wholeness component of a system (Johnson et al., 1964), i.e., a set of components which, if examined together, make up a unitary whole. Another perspective focuses on a network of linked units (Hull, 1962).

The systems concept provides a set of guidelines for the analysis of organizational problems and is a useful device for viewing multiphenomena behavior. It assumes that complex entities can be comprehended by dividing them into simpler, understandable units. Further, systems concepts emphasize the relationship between the parts and how these relate to the functioning of the whole (Martin, 1966). In most instances, one of the functions of the planned-change process is integrative; it must concern itself with the synthesis of organizational activities toward end products. To complicate this further, this attempt at integration is not a "one-shot" operation but, rather, an ongoing activity of the client, since the organization is an open system and must continually deal with the dynamics of its environment (Katz & Kahn, 1966). The organizational-change researcher or OD consultant deals with many of the concepts and problems of general systems theory. Such aspects of the change process as problem diagnosis, structural reorganization, developing effective unit and individual relationships, etc., are of primary concern in economics as well as in the physical and social sciences. Out of the recognition of the success of the systems concept in the natural and physical sciences, the organization development researcher has come to understand that the most effective type of organizational intervention strategy is one that impacts administrative, social, and technical systems, and recognizes how this impact affects all systems.

CASE STUDY

The Client Situation

The school of nursing on the university campus operated as a unit of a college; it consisted of approximately twenty full-time faculty, an administrator, and a small clerical staff, and it had approximately two hundred undergraduate students at the baccalaureate level. The school was functionalized into five areas of clinical specialization. Each area had a specific faculty and had responsibility for a component of the nursing curriculum. Administratively, the school had thirteen standing committees that functioned primarily in an advisory and research capacity. The decision-making and administrative processes of the school were either assumed or controlled by the school's director, who devoted almost all her time to administration and community relations. While the school of nursing had very little contact with the rest of the university, it did have strong and important relationships with the community—not only for the placing of students, but also in the utilization of local health agencies for the directed clinical training of students.

The school of nursing had experienced various organizational and educational problems almost from its inception. These problems grew to such proportions during the fall semester of 1974 that the central administration of the university, as well as the dean of the college under which the nursing school functions, could no longer deny the problems. The primary source of concern was registered in the community, while, at the same time, indications were also coming from the school itself. The president of the university and the dean decided to appoint a faculty committee to investigate the charges.

Although the data gathered by this committee did indicate that serious problems existed within the school, it was felt that the study was inconclusive, and a second and more comprehensive investigation was conducted. The results of the second investigation, which were presented to the administration of the university during the spring semester of 1975, indicated that unless quick and positive steps were taken by the university, the school of nursing would be in jeopardy of losing its national accreditation and might even be forced to close.

During the fall semester of 1975, several internal attempts were made by the dean of the college to help relieve some of the tension among the faculty. The central problems of the school had been perceived, for some time, as "relational." Because of this, the administration of the college felt that intervention strategies should focus on the development of better personal relationships between faculty, students, and administration.

The university counseling office designed a program of weekly team-building sessions that involved the entire faculty of the school of nursing as well as the administrator. Attendance at these meetings was voluntary; faculty interest in dealing with problems was high, and this led to a high level of participation. Several techniques were used that attempted to provide faculty members with a means of looking at their behavior and how it impacted the other members of the faculty as well as the goals of the school. Initially, the majority of the faculty felt that the sessions were productive in that they helped to reduce tension and lack of trust and increased commitment to the goals of the school. The meetings also provided a mechanism to help the faculty understand some of the more subtle dimensions of the problems being faced.

What the meetings did *not* produce was the motivation to deal effectively with the problems. Although the administrator of the school had been involved actively in the sessions and appeared to be most supportive of the process, she did nothing to bring the substance of the meetings back to the school setting. While faculty members seemed to "feel better" about their relationships with peers, there was no improvement in the working relationships.

The Change Project

Prior to the completion of the second investigation, the administrator of the school submitted her letter of resignation, effective at the end of the spring semester. The president of the university and the dean of the college decided that it would be productive to place the administration of the school in the hands of a committee, which would be charged with the responsibility of reorganizing the school. In the spring of 1975, an "executive committee" assumed responsibility for administering the school of nursing as well as accountability to the administration of the college for its actions. The chairman of this executive committee assumed the roles of school director and of primary change agent in the OD program.

During this semester, the second investigative committee concluded its study and presented its findings to the dean of the college. Both the president of the university and the dean of the college took a personal interest in the problems of the nursing school and demonstrated that they were willing to take any steps necessary in order to resolve them.

Problem Diagnosis

Although large amounts of data had been compiled by previous investigative committees as well as by individuals who had worked with the school, there still needed to be produced specific indications of the weak areas in the system.

There was little question that a major problem was the inadequacy of the organizational structure. The subunits of the organization, their composition, responsibilities, authority, and relations with other units were never fully understood by the membership. Since all activities of the school had been coordinated and controlled by the director, little control had been exerted by faculty members, and, for the most part, the faculty was concerned principally with transferring technical nursing competence to the students. In many instances, they were not properly informed regarding critical information, and decisions were made for them by the director. The majority of the faculty members resented their lack of authority and translated this in a very personal sense to their working relationships with each other as well as to the administrator. This had fragmented the faculty to the point where several members had retained legal counsel to represent their concerns.

Although these problems were the most obvious, and clearly generated the most concern on the part of the university administration, there were other problems that needed to be recognized. For example, the problem of identification between the faculty and the organization itself: most of the faculty members felt disenfranchised from their roles as nursing educators. Although they felt a strong tie between themselves and the professional nurse, they did not seem to feel the same type of relationship with university professors. This identity problem led to several more practical problems with their comprehension of and interest in the mission of the school; since the faculty members had not fully assumed their roles as university professors, their interface with the university community was almost nonexistent.

Because of its internal problems, the school of nursing's links with the nursing community, which were very important, had deteriorated. This caused difficulty in placing students after graduation as well as problems in providing clinics for student training. Moreover, there was some question as to whether the school was going to receive unconditional accreditation by the national accrediting agency, and the state board was under severe pressure by the "nursing education establishment" to remove accreditation from the school. Such an action would have closed the school. Neither the faculty nor the students could accept this. Finally, since the change agent, the chairman of the executive committee, was not a registered nurse, he was perceived as an interloper by the professional nurses. Thus, the intervention raised, for a short time, the environmental pressures impinging on the school of nursing.

Role of the Change Agent

One of the unique features of this organizational change program was the fact that the major change agent had to conduct several functions simultaneously within the organization. One of the most immediate tasks was the comprehension of the client system. The new director was selected from the faculty outside the college involved; although he had an extensive background in university committee and administrative activities, he had no background in the field of nursing education, and it was critical for him to develop an immediate understanding of the culture and technology of nursing education if he was to be effective in the capacities of both change agent and director of the school. Fortunately, his credentials as a manager were good and he enjoyed the full confidence of the president of the university.

The director was presented with a set of desired outcomes by the president; these related both to the organization itself and to its participation in the university. The desired organizational outcomes were (1) continued accreditation, and (2) a tolerable level of faculty conflict. These were indeed "presidential" kinds of outcomes, reflecting the discomfort of alternative outcomes. Beyond these, however, two more "academic" outcomes were stipulated that dealt with behavior of the faculty. They were (1) an overall competent level of instruction, and (2) participation in the university community.

The director was given carte blanche authority by the president; the imposition of administrative probation, in effect, deprived the faculty of its university civil liberties. This was, of course, a two-edged sword for the director, who had to proceed cautiously in order to avoid the criticism that ordinarily results from arbitrary behavior in an academic setting.

Pre-intervention Variables

Several pre-intervention situational variables allowed a smoother flow of change: (1) the resignation of the existing director; (2) the recommendation *by a faculty committee* that the program either be terminated or placed in administrative receivership until the emergency problems were alleviated (which provided legitimacy for the intervention in the eyes of the total faculty and academic senate); (3) the appointment of the executive committee to administer the school; and (4) the decision to select a new director who would begin in the spring semester of 1976. Within a matter of weeks, these situational variables placed the system in a fluid state or, as was suggested by Lewin (1939), "unfroze" the system.

The Implementation of Change

After a brief examination of all available documentation, the change agent decided on a set of system priorities, a style, and a technique. These, given the outcome expectations of the university, the incapacity of the nursing school to achieve these outcomes on its own, and the organizational beliefs of the change agent, produced a "locked-in" approach. The systematic priority was the creation of a viable structure which, in the view of the change agent, would lead to a revision of activity and, thus, to a change of instrumental behavior. The style selected was that of the "benevolent despot." Since the faculty had long operated under orders, there was little point in instituting a democratic system until some of the structural impediments had been removed. For many complex reasons, this style seemed to elicit no strong opposition. Finally, the principal technique for behavioral change was to structure the reward system so that those who were willing to contribute toward the external outcome expectations were rewarded in all the ways the university could provide. The faculty was overwhelmingly in support of these expectations and had been for some time. It was simply a matter of not knowing how to achieve them.

Following the development of the expected outcomes and the implementation style and technique of the change agent, an interim outcome set was developed. This set consisted of organizational (structural) outcomes and personal outcomes. The first of these outcomes was the decentralization of decision making and the free flow of information. The responsibilities of each of the component parts of the new structure were then developed and approved by the faculty themselves; i.e., the faculty generated an organizational constitution that provided some protection against administrative encroachment when the situation was again normalized, as well as the ability to extract accountability from each other. Of primary concern was an opportunity for professional growth on the part of the faculty. The travel budget, which had been a secret, was made public, and all faculty members were invited to submit proposals for seminar and workshop attendance. Schedules were reworked so that faculty members might pursue advanced degrees; leaves were granted for the same purpose. The interactions of the faculty were, as far as possible, based on professional roles rather than on personal relationships. Recommendations for reappointment, tenure, and promotion were opened to all tenured faculty, and the rationale for recommendations was publicly scrutinized. Finally, faculty members were assigned to class duties on the basis of their competence for the particular task rather than on the basis of personal favoritism, as had previously been the case.

The fundamental building block of the structural change process was the development of the operations committee, which consisted of representatives of all the functional areas within the school as well as the chairpersons of all the standing committees. This committee was given not only an advisory but also a decision-making capacity for specific operational matters. Only when a decision could not be reached was the matter brought before the director (chairman of the executive committee).

The second major aspect of reorganization was the redesign of the school's committee structure. Although the committees of the school of nursing were the logical units in which to place responsibility for important student, policy, and personnel decisions, it was imperative that these committees realize the importance of their operations and conduct them in a responsible manner. Previous conditions had included overlapping of committees, multiple memberships of faculty, and innumerable reports of each committee. The committees were reduced from thirteen to six, including the operations committee.

By this time, faculty members of the school of nursing had begun to understand the necessity for them to be specific in the allocation of duties, authority, and responsibility to fellow faculty members, school committees, and the administrator of the school. In keeping with this level of concern, the faculty had spent a great deal of time and effort developing a comprehensive "governance document," which spelled out in detail how the administration of the school of nursing should be conducted. Subsequent to this, it became the responsibility of the committees to develop similar documents that set down the purpose and procedures for operation of each of the committees. The faculty members also felt that it would be appropriate, and perhaps necessary, to describe the responsibility and authority of the director of the school. In the past, the allocation of many of the administrative responsibilities of the school had been left unstated; it was assumed that such roles would be specified by the structure of the school. Now the majority of the faculty felt that positional-responsibility decisions must be made and that policy should explicitly state the results of these decisions.

The third major area of concern, the school's reward system (primarily grant money and assigned time), had operated on a political, rather than a merit basis. Under the new structure, organizational rewards were given to individuals based on their contributions to the operation of the school. In most instances, these were individuals on whom the school would have to rely for its growth and development in the future.

A principal assumption behind the structural change process within the school of nursing was that the members of the system were capable of dealing with the relational problems that had developed over the years. The only ingredient needed to be provided by the internal consultant was the development of an equitable, responsible, and clear organizational framework. Since the faculty was employed to design the system, *the members felt ownership of the changes in the system* rather than reliance on the expertise and recommendations of the consultant.

The consultant viewed himself as a structural architect who, in order to be effective in meeting the needs of the client, needed to familiarize himself fully with the organization's structure, culture, relevant environments, and problems, in order to make decisions and recommendations for the effective movement of the organization.

Finally, he started the intervention with three assumptions regarding the renovation of a badly deteriorated organizational system, in part based on the application of GST:

1. The requirement of a change in the output of a system will, in itself, force a change in the input and thru-put components of the system.

2. One of the major factors facilitating change in the thru-put process is the construction of an organizational structure that provides for proper information flow and allows for the development of psychological conditions for effective membership performance.

3. There is a need to "unfreeze" all the components of the system at the same time to ensure that the system's natural resistance to change will have no focal point from which to grow.

Consequences of the Intervention

Although it was not possible to directly extract performance or effectiveness criteria from the nursing organization, it was obvious to these researchers—through lengthy discussions with the faculty—that several distinct and notable changes had taken place. One was the recognition by the members of the nursing faculty of their role as university professors rather than simply as professional nurses. This had several implications for both the operation of the school and the behavior of the faculty: (1) it produced a much more "external" view of the university by faculty members, resulting in greater involvement in university activities; (2) the nursing school was now recognized by the university as an integral educational unit; and (3) although the master's degree is typically the highest one sought in the nursing-education field (nursing faculty are seldom afforded the academic training and socialization process of the doctoral degree), more of the faculty members seemed to be concerned with pursuing advanced degrees.

Both by initiation of the change agent and by the spontaneous actions of the faculty, there had been a radical and amazingly smooth shift in power from a select few senior faculty members and the administrator to a group of competent and aware junior members of the faculty. This was the result of their willingness to perform the hard work necessary to reorganize the program. Although the shift was subtle, it suddenly became apparent to all members of the faculty. To some extent, this placed most of the faculty members in an uncomfortable position; while many of the junior faculty members felt uncomfortable in assuming formal authority and responsibility for the school, many of the senior members recognized their loss of control and felt threatened. However, through this power shift emerged the necessary skills and orientations that enabled the business of the school to be conducted in an efficient and professional manner.

In interviews held as the change was almost completed, it was observed by several faculty members that there was much keener interest in problem identification. Rather than labeling the school's problems as "personality problems," the faculty began to have a clearer understanding of what the real issues were and was more willing to make an effort toward problem resolution. In many instances (some of which were crisis situations), faculty members clearly demonstrated a high level of professional maturity in identifying problems, in allocating resources for coping with the problems, and, ultimately, in providing solutions.

They also demonstrated a stronger sense of the concept and value of an organization. At the beginning of the organizational change process, the faculty seemed naive about what was required in order for diverse (and sometimes antagonistic) activities to comprise a functioning system of nursing education. Halfway through the OD program, a significant portion of the faculty understood the necessity for an organizational structure that would allow such a system.

It appeared to these researchers that several of the areas of critical concern to the school of nursing were, by the end of the fall semester of 1975, well on their way to being resolved. One year after the OD program was initiated, the placement of nursing graduates in the local community had improved, and many of the local agencies that had been reluctant to sign training contracts during previous semesters were now willing to allow the training of student nurses in their facilities.

Student grievances regarding faculty members, curriculum, and other areas had increased for the previous several years and had reached open rebellion in several instances. Through the reconstitution of an official student committee, the majority of student problems were dealt with before they became crises. It was also obvious to the students that, even when no action could be taken, their grievances were being heard and that the administrator and faculty of the school were concerned.

After the creation of the new organizational structure, the termination or resignation of several faculty members, and the resignation of the original director, the faculty's relational problems became almost nonexistent. Faculty members became willing to discuss and resolve organizational and educational problems professionally, on a nonpersonal basis. This significantly reduced the conflict and tension that had existed within the faculty.

SOME IMPLICATIONS FOR OD

The following two elements, although not central to this process, did seem to have important implications for its success.

1. The significance of a "common enemy" (Bakke, 1950). In this study, the enemy was the state board of registered nursing. This agency posed such a powerful threat to the school of nursing, as well as to the university, that the administration did not hesitate to grant a high level of support to the change agent in order to ensure the survival of the school. If the board had withdrawn its accreditation, the school of nursing would have been closed and the faculty members would have lost their positions.

2. The consequences of a limited-term administration. All recognized, as a result of the university president's decree in the spring of 1975, that the change project would take no more than two years. If the situation was not radically improved by then, the school would be closed. Given these alternatives, the question was whether the faculty members would support an unknown director who would be leaving the following spring and who would have no further effect on their careers.

The statements made and the conclusions drawn in this study are the results of judgments made by the researchers and are not the consequences of empirical evidence. The lack of original empirical data remains an inherent problem in the field of organization development. Therefore, the implications of this project focus on some of the knowledge that has been gained by the authors with regard to change processes in organizations and not on the testing of hypotheses of change.

Many approaches to planned change in organizations fail to isolate the independent variable in the study, while others avoid the issue by utilizing "package approaches" to organizational change (Blake & Mouton, 1969; Blake, Mouton, et al., 1964). In either case, the effect is to confound the comprehension of which elements of the treatment actually contributed in producing the observed effects. In the school of nursing, the independent variable (structured change), its sub-elements, and even some of the synergistic characteristics of the intervention may be spelled out.

A second element of this study is that the dependent variable (behavioral change) may well be that of the total organization and not limited to the improved effectiveness of a few individuals or organizational units. In many instances, the research reported in OD consists of accounts of incidents that may have affected only a limited number of members or units. This study demonstrates the impact of the change process on the entire organization; thus it is safer to generalize the results to similar organizations faced with similar problems.

A final, yet significant, issue raised by this study deals with the unnatural separation of organizational structure and process. While process variables have received the greatest degree of treatment in the OD field (Argyris, 1970; Beckhard, 1969; Blake & Mouton, 1967), other authors (Katz & Kahn, 1966) have recognized that the ability of an organization to meet its objectives is the result of sets of independent events that must effectively link organizational elements, behaviors, and attitudes in a complex fashion. To intervene in this process of activities in order to make the recurring behaviors of the participants more effective would suggest, by definition, the manipulation of both structural and process elements. The approach detailed in this paper clearly attempted to exercise a high degree of control over both of these sets of variables; while the primary treatment was structural, there was a high degree of monitoring of changes in the recurring behaviors of the members of the organization.

REFERENCES

Argyris, C. *Intervention theory and methods: A behavioral science view*. Reading, Mass.: Addison-Wesley, 1970.

Bakke, W. *Bonds of organizations: An appraisal of corporate human relations*. New York: Harper & Row, 1950.

Beckhard, R. *Organizational development: Strategies and models*. Reading, Mass.: Addison-Wesley, 1969.

Bennis, W. G. *Organization development: Its natural origins and prospects*. Reading, Mass.: Addison-Wesley, 1969.

Bennis, W. G., Benne, K. B., & Chin, R. *The planning of change*. New York: Holt, Rinehart and Winston, 1961.

Blake, R. R., & Mouton, J. S. *The managerial grid*. Houston, Tex.: Gulf, 1967.

Blake, R. R., & Mouton, J. S. *Building a dynamic corporation through GRID organization development*. Reading, Mass.: Addison-Wesley, 1969.

Blake, R. R., Mouton, J. S., Barns, L. B., & Grinner, L. E. Breakthrough in organizational development. *Harvard Business Review*, 1964, *42*(6).

Cleland, D. I., & King, W. R. *Systems analysis and project management*. New York: McGraw-Hill, 1969.

Davis, L. E. The design of jobs. *Industrial Relations*, 1966, 6(1).

Ferguson, C. K. Concerning the nature of human systems and the consultant's role. *Journal of Applied Behavioral Science*, 1968, 4(2).

Hall, C. L. *Systems analysis*. New York: McGraw-Hill, 1962.

Johnson, R. A., Kast, F. E., & Rosenzweig, J. E. Systems theory and management. *Management Science*, January 1964, *10*.

Katz, D., & Kahn, R. L. *The social psychology of organizations*. New York: John Wiley, 1966.

Lawrence, P. *The changing of organizational behavior patterns*. Boston, Mass.: Division of Research, Harvard Business School, 1958.

Lewin, K. *Field theory in social sciences*. New York: Harper & Row, 1957.

Lewin, K. Patterns of aggressive behavior in experimentally created social climates. *Journal of Social Psychology*, 1939.

Likert, R. *New patterns in management*. New York: McGraw-Hill, 1961.

Martin, J. A. The systems concept. *Business Horizons*, Spring, 1966.

Schein, E. H. *Process consultation: Its role in organization development*. Reading, Mass.: Addison-Wesley, 1969.

Seiler, J. A. Diagnosing interdepartmental conflict. *Harvard Business Review*, September-October, 1963, *41*(5).

AN UPDATE ON "A STRUCTURAL APPROACH TO ORGANIZATION DEVELOPMENT IN A UNIVERSITY PROFESSIONAL SCHOOL"

Lynn H. Peters and John F. McKenna

We are pleased to have this opportunity to share our further thoughts on the intervention, with an emphasis not on what happened and how it happened but on the possible longer term consequences. Reflection has convinced us that the central issue in this change was the philosophy of governance—the shift from autocratic-hierarchical to collegial-participative. Although the consequences for the faculty were articulated at the time, what we did not pursue then were the potential consequences for students and, through them, for the health-care profession. We would like to speculate on those matters now, bearing in mind that our conclusions depend on the following assumptions: (a) continued emphasis on baccalaureate education for nurses and (b) generalized introduction of the collegial model of governance into university schools of nursing.

The nursing program we described is now in comparatively good health; the changeover to a more traditional administrator was accomplished smoothly. The faculty members have accepted, in varying degrees, the idea that they should subscribe to and accept university professional standards in all matters, e.g., reappointment, tenure, and promotion criteria.

The typical university administration purports to have a norm of collegiality or shared governance. What these terms mean and the degree to which they exist in a particular institution vary widely. However, one common denominator is that the chief executive officer of the unit operates under some formal internal constraints on the unilateral exercise of authority, and the faculty members are perceived not only as employees but as professionals, part of whose responsibility is providing the terms and conditions of governance. This style, collegial or participative, is in contrast to the far more autocratic and hierarchical apparatus generally found in health-care institutions, particularly hospitals. The autocratic mode is especially felt by the nursing profession, whose members only occasionally are part of the governance mechanism in hospitals.

In our study, although the faculty had been in rebellion against the director, they had seen themselves primarily as nurses, and the cause of the conflict had not been the use of the health-care model of administration but the arbitrary and capricious manner in which it had been applied.

When the change agent introduced the collegial model, both structural and personal modifications began to occur in the faculty. However, in the article we did not discuss the effects of this general shift in philosophy on the students in the program, so we would like to address the issue here.

In professional higher education how the professor feels about the system is usually transmitted in some manner to students. In this case at first there were mixed signals because of the confusion of the faculty between the two roles or role sites of professor and nurse or university and hospital. As the university role of professor began to predominate over the hospital role of nurse, the transmission of faculty attitudes also changed and was clarified. Earlier, the faculty had emphasized the new role of nurses, assertiveness, and the democratic process, but the talk did not ring true because they had no such independence in the hospital setting themselves.

During the intervention, as the nursing faculty began to see themselves as participants in the system of the university, that attitude was transmitted to the students. The students had a continued role conflict. As students, they were part of the generation that had demanded a piece of the decision-making action when the nursing-school faculty had been reluctant to make such demands. As nursing students, however, their "place" in the hospital, as contrasted to that in the university, had remained essentially unchanged—low on the totem pole.

The faculty in the nursing school had always been perceived by the students as role models for behavior as nurses, as indeed the faculty members had seen themselves. When faculty behavior changed as a result of a shift in perception of primary role affiliation, the students still viewed faculty as role models and thought they were seeing the "new style" nurse they had read and been told about. What they were seeing was a change from nurse-professor to professor-nurse. In large part, the student resolution of role conflict was based on a false assumption, and what they observed was a fundamental revision of their role models as faculty, but not necessarily as nurses. The change was critical for the faculty as professors but misleading to students about to enter the health-care profession.

POSTLUDE

Whether or not the faculty will carry their new attitudes into their relationships with health-care facilities remains to be seen. Some of them had been new style nurses all along but had not been able to translate that attitude into the university setting.

More critical, however, is the matter of student attitudes and behaviors as they move into the nursing profession. The contradiction between roles as university student and student nurse had been in large part resolved in favor of the collegial model of the university student, but no one can say whether this behavior can be maintained in the realities of the health-care administration setting. It would be premature, and not logically defensible, to say that independence will collapse or will prevail. What is almost certain, however, is that as the education of nurses shifts to the university setting, nursing students will have or will want to have a say in the upcoming conflict over the style of health-care administration.

Contributors

Alfred Alschuler
Professor
Department of Education
456 Hills South
University of Massachusetts
Amherst, MA 01003

Vernon R. Averch
Nagob Woods, MA 07718

Dr. Michael Beer
Graduate School of
  Business Administration
Harvard University
Soldiers Field
Boston, MA 02163

Dr. David E. Berlew
Situation Management Systems, Inc.
Box 260
West Brooksville, ME 04617

Peter Block
Senior Vice President
Block Petrella Associates
1009 Park Avenue
North Plainfield, NJ 07060

John C. Croft
Professor
Department of Administration
  and Supervision
College of Education
University of Houston
Houston, TX 77004

Dr. Samuel A. Culbert
Professor of Human Development Systems
Graduate School of Management
University of California
405 Hilgard Avenue
Los Angeles, CA 90024

Jack M. Davey
Regional Grocery Merchandizer
First National Supermarkets
500 North Street
Windsor Locks, CT 06096

Dr. William G. Dyer
Professor
Department of Organizational
  Behavior
Brigham Young University
Provo, UT 84601

Edgar F. Huse
Chairman
Organization Studies Department
School of Management
Boston College
Chestnut Hill, MA 02167

William E. LeClere
Director
Institute for Planned Change
6524 Wiscosset Road
Bethesda, MD 20016

Robert A. Luke, Jr.
Assistant Visiting Professor
Department of Education
George Washington University
Washington, DC 20052

Dr. Robert F. Maddocks
Staff Vice President
Organization Development
  and Compensation Planning
Room 5215
RCA Corporation
30 Rockefeller Plaza
New York, NY 10020

Dr. John F. McKenna
Assistant Professor of Management
School of Business
California State University
Chico, CA 95926

Dr. J. Weldon Moffitt
Professor
Department of Organizational Behavior
302 JKB
Brigham Young University
Provo, UT 84602

Dr. Lynn H. Peters
Professor of Management
School of Business Administration
San Diego State University
San Diego, CA 92182

Victor Pinedo, Jr.
President
Fundashon Humanas
Lundhuis Groot Kwartier
P.O. Box 398
Willemsstad, Curacao
Netherlands Antilles

Dr. William J. Underwood
Director
Engineering Professional Programs
RCA Corporation
Route 38 & Haddonfield Road
Cherry Hill, NJ 08101

Dr. Paul Wohlford
10206 Frederick Avenue
Kensington, MD 20795